3 AUG 2019

D0539520

Stabl

Gemma Hogg is currently assistant trainer at Micky Hammond Racing, which is based in Middleham in North Yorkshire, having got a job there straight out of the Northern Racing College in 1998. As well as operating as Micky's right-hand woman when it comes to training horses, Gemma mentors new staff and is also passionate about rehoming retired racehorses. In 2016 she was named Employee of the Year at the prestigious Godolphin Stud and Stable Staff Awards, where she also triumphed in the Leadership category. In 2018 she celebrated her twentieth anniversary of working for Micky, who has long since been her mentor.

WITHDRAWN FROM
BROMLEY LIBRARIES

Bromley Libraries

30128 80391 728 8

GEMMA HOGG

Stable Lass

Tales from a Yorkshire
Racing Yard

PAN BOOKS

First published 2018 by Sidgwick & Jackson

First published in paperback 2018 by Sidgwick & Jackson

This edition first published 2019 by Pan Books
an imprint of Pan Macmillan
20 New Wharf Road, London N1 9RR
Associated companies throughout the world
www.panmacmillan.com

ISBN 978-1-5098-4765-5

Copyright © Gemma Hogg and James Hogg 2018

The right of Gemma Hogg and James Hogg to be identified as the
authors of this work has been asserted by them in accordance
with the Copyright, Designs and Patents Act 1988.

All photographs courtesy of the author, except for page 1 top © Conrad Elias / Alamy
Stock Photo and page 5 top right © Allstar Picture Library / Alamy Stock Photo

All rights reserved. No part of this publication may be reproduced,
stored in a retrieval system, or transmitted, in any form, or by any means
(electronic, mechanical, photocopying, recording or otherwise)
without the prior written permission of the publisher.

Pan Macmillan does not have any control over, or any responsibility for,
any author or third-party websites referred to in or on this book.

1 3 5 7 9 8 6 4 2

A CIP catalogue record for this book is available from the British Library.

Typeset by Palimpsest Book Production Ltd, Falkirk, Stirlingshire
Printed and bound by CPI Group (UK) Ltd, Croydon, CR0 4YY

This book is sold subject to the condition that it shall not, by way of
trade or otherwise, be lent, hired out, or otherwise circulated without
the publisher's prior consent in any form of binding or cover other than
that in which it is published and without a similar condition including
this condition being imposed on the subsequent purchaser.

Visit **www.panmacmillan.com** to read more about all our books
and to buy them. You will also find features, author interviews and
news of any author events, and you can sign up for e-newsletters
so that you're always first to hear about our new releases.

For Mum and Dad

Contents

Prologue

It was a crisp March Monday morning and I was on the High Moor gallops at Middleham. It was the first time it'd been light going into work since last October. Consequently, it was the first day since then that I hadn't had any problems getting out of bed. It hadn't been like that a month ago. The York-shire Dales turns into Finland during February and on some days, we seem to have about two hours of daylight. That's why I used to use three alarm clocks; all set at five-minute intervals and all positioned in different parts of the room.

Dawn was only just beginning to break when my first alarm went at 5.15 a.m., but there was enough light shining through the curtains to assure me that spring had finally arrived. Well, that and the fact that I wasn't freezing my bum off and fighting my boyfriend for the duvet!

Monday mornings usually put a cloud over everything, but not that day. We'd had three winners on Saturday; two at Hexham and one at Sedgefield. That had definitely helped us to celebrate the arrival of springtime. There'd also been an incident in town involving a member of our staff which had put a smile on everyone's face. A stable lad called Kenny had got hammered and he'd ended up getting smacked in the face by a lass from another yard. Apparently, he'd drunkenly suggested that women were inferior riders to men and got a fat lip for his trouble. He looked like Mick Jagger when he walked through the yard gates! He also had a massive hangover, bless him, and a reputation that was temporarily in tatters. He was on the far side of the gallop on a horse called Salute the General that had won last time out, and I could tell that everyone was ribbing the hell out of him.

I was on a seven-year-old bay gelding called High Country and the following day I was due to ride him in the 1.50 at Wolverhampton. It was to be my first ever race as a jockey and I don't mind admitting that I was absolutely petrified. I'd already had three or four people ask me if anything was wrong that day.

The 'what ifs' had been incessant and new ones had been appearing daily. What if I fall? What if he won't come out of the stalls? What if I come last?

The reason my boss, Micky, had put me on High Country was because he was a seasoned pro. What's more, he absolutely loved going racing. To this day he's the only horse I've ever known who spins around in his stable when the horsebox arrives. He used to get so excited. This morning had been no exception and when a horsebox pulled into the yard just after breakfast he'd gone bananas. I was putting his tack on at the time and if I hadn't had him tied up

I'd have been in trouble. When I eventually led him out, the horsebox door was open and he'd tried to walk straight in! He was gutted when he realized it wasn't for him and had sulked all the way to the gallops.

Because he was running the following day, High Country was taking it easy that morning and once Kenny and his tormentors had cleared the gallop we prepared for a seven-furlong canter. He'd stopped sulking by then but as we approached the entrance I got the feeling he was going to be tricky. He was already pulling a bit, so keeping him to a canter was going to be tough.

As we lined up alongside the two other horses and riders, I gave the signal to set off. The moment I did I knew I was in trouble. There's a point when you realize that a horse has taken back control of its actions, and this was it. His body had stiffened up and my commands, both physical and verbal, were being ignored. As the other two riders set off as ordered I tried wrestling back control, but it was no use. This was obviously revenge for not getting in the horsebox and going racing. The question was, what punishment was he going to dish out?

Just as I was trying to reason with him by stroking him behind the ear he suddenly took a few steps back. *Oh no*, I thought. *Please don't go backwards!* This had happened to me before, but never on the gallops.

'You listen to me,' I shouted. 'Don't you dare start going backwards. I mean it! If you start going backwards there'll be no racing tomorrow!'

Why can't horses understand English?!

I knew there were horses waiting to start behind me.

'Clear the gallop!' I screamed. 'I've lost him!'

Fortunately, he only got up to a backwards slow trot so everyone managed to get off in time. He wasn't stopping though, the little sod. I just had to sit there and wait till he'd had his fun. You get a very different perspective going backwards on a horse. Normally I love the scenery on the high moor, the multitude of green fields that stretch from Wensleydale across the Vale of York to the North Yorks Moors. It's less appealing when it's moving away from you instead of towards you. Funnily enough, you also get a very different reaction. Everybody on the gallop was laughing. Even the horses, I think.

When High Country finally came to a halt I was treated to a nice round of applause and a few cheers.

'Well done, Gem!' somebody shouted. 'That bodes well for tomorrow.'

Many a true word said in jest. What if he did go back-wards at Wolverhampton? I hadn't thought of that! Why did I ever open my big mouth? I'd been dreaming about riding as a jockey ever since I was a little girl and I'd been hassling Micky about it for years. What is it they say though, be careful what you wish for?

1

Dropped in the Dales

'Isn't our Gemma brave becoming a stable lass?' is what Mum and Dad had said to absolutely everyone they'd come into contact with over the past six months. Had they known what the job really entailed, they'd have locked me in my room and wouldn't have let me out again until I was aged at least forty. Now, sitting on the back seat of my dad's old Ford Sierra on the way to Middleham and my new life, I felt petrified. Not only was my safety net (Mum and Dad) about to be taken away from me, but I was also about to embark on a career in one of the most dangerous and physically demanding professions there is. What on earth was I doing? I wondered to myself.

As we drove out of Horsforth in Leeds, which to me at the age of sixteen represented the world, civilization and everything, I felt no bigger than a pin. Until then I'd always been Little Miss Confident, striding around home, schools and assorted shops, leisure centres and friends' houses like a mouth on a stick. Yet now I was silent (thankfully, Mum would say).

Apart from spending a few weeks at racing college, I'd never even been out of Leeds without my parents before; as soon as we'd made our way through the market town of Wetherby and on to the A1, I blurted out, 'Mum, I don't feel too well.'

'Are you feeling car sick again?' Mum turned to look at me in the back seat. 'I'm surprised you made it as far as the A1,' she said wryly. 'Norman, pass me a carrier bag, would you? There's a Morrison's one in the bottom of your door.'

I was always car sick, and Mum was right: I could never usually make it to the end of our road without asking for a bag. This was different, though, as normally I couldn't give you a reason why I felt sick. Now I could have given you a thousand.

The reason for me wanting to swap my cosy, cosseted life in suburban Leeds for a potentially perilous new adventure was an all-consuming – some might say obsessive – interest in horses. Ever since I'd first sat on a pony at the tender age of seven, I had thought about nothing else (no pop stars or hunky soap actors on my bedroom walls, thank you very much), and this was the result of my passion. Up until then my new career had always been described by my proud family as me going off and 'living the dream', but now it was actually happening I had this awful feeling that that was exactly what it should have remained – a dream. As well as worrying about whether I'd be up to the work and whether anyone would talk to me on my first day, I had the deeper concerns of someone still in their teens who had always lived at home. Who was going to make my meals and wash my clothes?

We arrived in Middleham, which was to be my base for the duration of my adventure, at exactly 2 p.m. on 21 October 1998.

'Where are your digs, Gem?' Dad asked me, looking round curiously.

'Up here on the left,' I said. 'Opposite the shop.'

These were the first words I had spoken since announcing to Mum that I felt sick; since then I had answered all her enquiries as to how I was feeling with just a nod.

Middleham is a 'chocolate-box' market town on the edge of the Yorkshire Dales. It is simply brimming with character and history, and I'd visited it before when I'd done a bit of weekend work in Micky Hammond's yard. But as I stepped out of the car, my usual excitement – even gratitude – at being in such a stunning location had been replaced by an overwhelming feeling of absolute dread. Once again, I wondered, what on earth was I doing?

'Come on, then,' said Mum, beaming at me from the other side of the car. 'Let's go and find your room.'

I thought Mum and Dad were behaving like a couple of large, excited school kids, while all I wanted to do was burst into tears and scream, '*Please, take me home!*'

'All right, Gem,' said Dad, taking control while I just stood there silently. 'I've got all your bags. Let's go and have a look.'

Castle House, which has nine bedrooms, was certainly

not a castle, and, in the true sense of the word, it wasn't even a house. In fact, as far as I know, before it was invaded by stable lads and lasses, it had been a very popular restaurant and a regular haunt of the cast of *All Creatures Great and Small*. Though that was well before my time!

When Dad opened the door to my bedroom, which was on the first floor, my heart sank. It was awful – like something out of a really bad 1970s sitcom. The wallpaper, which had a gap of about two centimetres between each strip, was a sickly yellow colour, and the carpet, which looked like a ginormous scouring pad, was dark green. The curtains – sorry, curtain – only covered one half of the window and looked more like a see-through nightie. If I wasn't careful, the shopkeeper and his wife would be getting a right eyeful at bedtime.

'Oooh, this is quite nice,' said Mum.

I didn't have the heart to complain. She and Dad had moved heaven and earth putting me through college, and they were the ones who were going to be paying for my digs until my trial period was over. It had been really hard for them, although they hadn't said as much, and as I sat down on my bed (the mattress was so old my bum almost touched the floor), I looked up and smiled at her.

'That's better,' she said. 'You see, everything's going to be fine.'

It was going to have to be.

Dad, who was an electrician at the time, had to get back home so he could pack for a job he was starting down south, and so after around twenty minutes, he uttered the words I'd forgotten were coming but had been dreading.

'We've got to leave you, I'm afraid, Gem. You're on your own now, love.'

His words hit me like a flying horseshoe, and the urge I felt to run around the bed, slam the door shut and then lock it before swallowing the key was the most powerful compulsion I'd ever experienced.

'Are you all right, love?' asked Mum, putting an arm around me. 'You look a bit scared.'

'Of course she's scared!' said Dad. 'She's not going to have you running around after her, is she? You spoil that girl, Moira.'

'Be quiet, Norman! What is it, love? What's wrong?'

'I'm just a bit nervous, I suppose,' I admitted quietly.

'What's there to be nervous about? You've had twelve weeks at racing college. And you've had some work experience at the yard. They don't teach you all that stuff for nothing, you know. You watch. In a few weeks' time you'll have forgotten about us and you'll be riding winners here, there and everywhere.'

'I still don't know if I want to be a jockey, Mum!'

'I think you might have to be if you're ever going to earn any bloody money,' said Dad, giving me a wink. 'And make sure you send me a few tips. I want to get some of my investment back.'

'Norman!' Mum scolded him. Then she turned back to

me. 'Right love, we'd best be off. Take care of yourself and remember to ring me tomorrow after work.'

'OK, Mum.'

As my parents left Castle House and got back into the Sierra, a wave of homesickness washed over me. Tears wouldn't come for some reason, and I'm glad they didn't because, once the car was out of sight, I suddenly resolved to pull myself together.

Apart from the nine bedrooms, Castle House had just two bathrooms (which meant it could get quite interesting first thing in the morning), a kitchen, which I just ignored, and a large, damp-smelling sitting room. This was without doubt the most eye-catching room in the house, as on top of the sickly mint-green carpet sat a turquoise leather-look sofa, one beige geriatric armchair, in that it was at least sixty-five years old and had a high back to it, and an old black-and-white television that took almost as long to warm up as I did on a cold January morning. It even had some decorative horse brasses on the wall. Bizarrely enough, this would become my favourite room and, despite the damp smell and the 'interesting' decor, it always felt very cosy.

To avoid just hanging around aimlessly for the rest of the day, I went for a wander around Middleham. Sitting on the north-facing side of the stunning open valley of Wensleydale – well known for its crumbly cheese – and on the outskirts of the Yorkshire Dales National Park, it has a population of about 900. I wandered the winding streets, stopping to stare at the old school house at the top of the town with its bell tower and tall arched windows, and at Jasmine House, a beautiful Georgian townhouse in the marketplace. This large cobbled square is flanked by houses that mainly date from the seventeenth and eighteenth centuries, and is home to the vast majority of the town's commercial establishments. I counted four pubs, a fish and chip shop, a minuscule restaurant which was basically a converted cottage, a fruit and veg shop and a few B&Bs. Just a few yards north of the marketplace, on the road leading out to Coverdale, sat the town's only shop, Central Stores, and opposite that was Castle House.

I managed to do a full tour of the town in just a couple of hours, but the only building I dared venture into was the church. I wasn't looking for guidance (yet!), but because it was open and seemingly deserted I decided to have a look.

According to a history of the church which was displayed on one of the walls, St Alkelda's Church had been built in the thirteenth century, and as I looked around the beautifully preserved medieval building, I noticed it had the most striking stained-glass windows I'd ever seen, the colours deep and bright. St Alkelda was an Anglo-Saxon princess who had been murdered by two Danish women in AD 800, and whose bones were apparently buried somewhere underneath the church. Later on, as I was having a look around, I noticed a depiction of her murder within one of the stained-glass windows. *That's nice*, I thought.

Also featuring in the long history of St Alkelda's Church was the Duke of Gloucester (later Richard III). I knew he'd spent his childhood at Middleham Castle, which stands proudly on the edge of town. Built early in the twelfth century, it has the largest castle keep in the north of England. Realizing that Richard III had been a worshipper in this very church as a boy was strange and quite poignant. After all, he wasn't the only one who'd give his kingdom for a horse! Indeed, Middleham is often referred to as the racing capital of the north. When I arrived there were thirteen racing yards, many of which were in the town, hidden behind houses and cottages. There were nearly as many racehorses in Middleham as there were people, plus about 250 stable staff, almost all of whom lived within a couple of miles of the town.

When I got back to Castle House I noticed one or two people shuffling around. To be honest, I didn't feel up to meeting new people so, after buying myself a sandwich and some crisps from the shop across the road, I scurried off to my room, locked the door and read for a while.

The last thing I did before getting into bed was to open the wardrobe and put my empty suitcases in the bottom of it. As I was closing the door, I accidentally caught a quick glimpse of myself in the mirror that was attached to its back, and the shock of what greeted me almost made me jump out of my skin. I don't often wear make-up, and because I'm not especially vain I rarely have cause to look at myself in the mirror. In the past, I suppose I'd always looked – and felt – like a little girl. But that wasn't who was staring back at me. I wasn't yet a fully grown woman, but I was certainly no longer a child, and after the initial surprise had faded away I somehow felt able to cope with whatever was about to befall me. By the way, just so you can picture the person falling off the assorted racehorses, I was 5 feet 2 inches small, about a size 10 (I originally put 8 but remembered there are going to be photos), and had shoulder-length brown hair.

2

First Day at the Yard

Funnily enough, I slept quite well on my first night in Middleham, and it was all down to that springless mattress. I know it wasn't good for my back, but after slowly sinking into the middle of it I actually felt very safe and secure. It was like being cocooned.

I think the best way of describing me on my first day in the racing yard is 'all the gear, some idea.' I know the popular phrase is 'all the gear, no idea', but after twelve weeks at the Northern Racing College, where I got my NVQ Level 1 in Racehorse Care, I could muck out, tack up, ride out, feed, water and brush down horses just as well as the next terrified, inept novice. These tasks are basically what make up a stable lass's working day. So what's the problem? The problem is that at racing college you do everything at your own pace. There's never any pressure.

'Shall I muck out now?'

'Yes. Take your time, though. There's no rush.'

At college we didn't even lift a yard brush until 8 a.m., whereas in a racing yard everyone has to start feeding by

6 a.m. at the latest. I know it's only two hours, but to some it's the difference between night and day – or, if it's a Monday morning, between life and death!

In race terms, life at college and in a yard could be compared with two well-known flat races. College would have to be the Queen Alexandra Stakes: two miles, five furlongs and – until the last few – it's just steady away. Whereas life in a racing yard would have to be the Derby: one mile and four; you go like the wind, and if you fall off or make a mistake, you're screwed.

On my first day it was, as we say in Yorkshire, siling it down. That didn't matter though. Some places don't lend themselves to bad weather, but that could never be said of the Yorkshire Dales. And, besides, I was wearing a brand-new waterproof puffa coat, not to mention new jodhpurs and a nice new pair of riding boots. These had cost my Dad £95, which in Yorkshire money is about £500.

I'd actually been to the yard before. The woman who taught me to ride, Georgie Pullein, had worked at the yard in the past and, before I went to racing college, I used to help her out on the odd weekend. That was more akin to a child helping out on a busy farm really, and I hadn't noticed anything much apart from the horses. Aside from Georgie, nobody had really acknowledged me and, because I wasn't allowed to ride out, I'd spent the majority of the weekends mucking out, feeding and trying to keep out of the way.

This time I would be getting paid but it would remain to be seen if anybody was bothered about me being there. I'd heard all kinds of horror stories about new people either being bullied or frozen out at stables or in racing yards, and I knew one girl who'd ended up thumping somebody on her first day. You don't get too many shrinking violets in racing and, back then, if you encountered any trouble, you were expected to fight your corner as opposed to telling your boss. It's different now, thank goodness.

Somebody in Micky's office had arranged for a girl who worked in the next yard to give me a lift from my digs each day and, as I shut the door of her car and walked up the road, I kept having to remind myself over and over again that you only ever hear about the bad experiences. What about all the good ones? That must be the majority, right?

Strangely enough, what scared me the most as I walked towards those yard gates was seeing the sign hanging outside. *Micky Hammond Racing*, it read, and it had a logo next to it. I remember thinking, *Bloody hell. I don't remember seeing that before. He's even got his own logo.* It all looked so professional.

Micky's yard was situated on a large country estate off the Coverdale Road, called Tupgill Park. Built on a hill about three miles west of Middleham, it covered about twenty acres and consisted of a large manor house, a big pond and a succession of racing stables. I thought back to the very first time I'd set eyes on the yard, when I'd worked there before I went to college. My initial reaction had been that it looked like a town from the Wild West – a very well-lit road, flanked on both sides by hundreds and hundreds of boxes. In truth, there were only forty – twenty on each side – but at that moment it had seemed never-ending, like some kind of stairway to an equine heaven. Above the right-hand block of stables was the office, and the tack room and the feed room were on the bottom right-hand side at the far end of the yard.

Now I was working here in an official capacity, though, and – once I'd finished freaking myself out – I looked at my watch and saw it was already five past six. I was late on my first day! I picked my feet up, put my head down and walked as fast as I could through the yard gates, only to realize that all the muffled conversations and sounds that had been emanating from the yard had stopped.

Oh no! I thought. *They're all looking at me.*

This made me slow down, for some ridiculous reason, after which a mixture of curiosity and stupidity made me look up. At first, I didn't see any humans, although I definitely heard them. In the absence of any voices bidding me to 'step into the light', I took it upon myself to continue walking along that celestial stairway and, as I made my way past the first few boxes, I began to notice my audience. They were attentive, I'll give them that, but they were also smiling and giggling. I knew I was late, and obviously I was also a new recruit. But why the amusement?

'I say!' one of them called out. 'Nice puffa!' Then another shouted, 'Shall I saddle one up for you, Your Majesty?'

It was the clobber! As my eyes finally acclimatized to the lighting, I took the opportunity to get a better look at my public. They, of course, were all sporting a mixture of jeans, tracksuit bottoms, fleeces and old coats. I, on the other hand, looked as though I had stepped straight out of a shop window, and must have resembled a shorter, poorer and less well-connected version of Zara Phillips.

Those one hundred yards from the gates to Micky Hammond's office felt like a thousand and, as I passed the last of my twenty or so colleagues, I was left in no doubt whatsoever that they thought I was just a helmet, a hairnet and a riding crop away from appearing on the Horse of the Year Show.

'Good morning, ma'am,' said the last of them. 'Aren't we looking splendid this morning?'

That one got a big laugh, which was fair enough.

By the time I got to the yard office, I'd gone from a walk, and then a trot, to something approaching a gallop, but instead of knocking and waiting like any polite stable lass should, I barged through the door, slammed it shut and, without even thinking said, 'Thank god for that!'

'Good afternoon, Gemma,' said a voice.

'Jesus!' I yelped. 'You scared the living daylights out of me.'

Micky's office was a kind of L-shape and so his desk wasn't visible from the door.

'No, I'm not Jesus,' he said, walking into view. 'But as far as this yard is concerned I am God, and God says that we're here and ready to feed by six a.m.'

I think my jaw dropped when I caught sight of Micky. I'd

obviously met him before but he seemed very different from the way I remembered him. First of all, he was a bit older. There was something amiss height-wise, too. Micky is about 5 feet 6 inches tall (if you met him he'd insist he was 5 feet 8 inches), but I remembered him towering over me. I also thought he had fair hair, and a good head of hair at that, when in fact it was quite clearly brown and was short on the top and shaved round the sides. Had I actually met George Michael that day instead? Lastly there were the clothes. He'd been quite smart at my interview, as later that day he'd been going to the races, yet now he looked like a tramp. He's going to kill me when he reads this.

Micky was thirty-four at that time (ancient!) and had already been training for the best part of ten years. Before becoming a successful racehorse trainer he had a long career as a jockey, riding a total of 232 winners. In fact, had it not been for two concurrent leg injuries, Micky would have run the great Peter Scudamore very close to becoming Champion Jockey in the 1987/88 season.

'Yes, I'm so sorry,' I said, trying to hide my shock. 'I was looking at your logo.'

'I'm not even going to go there,' said Micky. 'Anyway, you're here now. Let's get you mucking out. I'm starting you off with four boxes and we need them all done by seven a.m.'

All of a sudden, my mood shifted from extreme shame and embarrassment to blind panic.

'But it's already quarter past six,' I cried. 'How am I sup-posed to muck out four horses in forty-five minutes?'

'How long did you have at college?' asked Micky.

'About half an hour.'

'For how many?'

'Per box. Maybe two boxes, if I got a wiggle on.'

Micky's eyes almost popped out. 'Maybe two if I got a wiggle on?' he said disbelievingly. 'You'd better shift your arse then.'

I'm not sure if this was all part of some kind of cruel ini-tiation ceremony (I bet it was), but as we left Micky's office he handed me a pitchfork, a spade and a yard brush.

'Follow me,' he said. 'Time's ticking!'

When it comes to tidiness, not to mention personal hygiene, horses can be as pernickety, or indeed as slovenly, as any human being. What's more they adhere to many of our human stereotypes: fillies (young females), for instance, are usually quite tidy and well organized. They always poo and pee in the same area, keep their straw where it should be, and you'll rarely find food on the floor. I'm not sure if horses can suffer from things like OCD, but I remember one filly we used to have who was absolutely terrified of poo and wee; even her own. Her number ones and number twos were always left at one side of the box, as close to the wall as possible, and she was never happy until I'd mucked her out in the morning. She used to look over to me while I worked as if to say, 'Don't you dare miss any,' and if I ever did she'd let me know about it.

Geldings are basically four-legged eunuchs. Like fillies, they often keep quite a tidy box and their behaviour indoors is usually mirrored once they've been tacked up. They're the ones you always want to ride out, by the way. Fillies are OK, but at the end of the day they're female. Would you like to ride out the horsey equivalent of a premenstrual woman whose other half had come in drunk the night before? Geldings, once the vet's been, have it neither on them, nor in them, as the saying goes.

And then you have colts.

Colts, two-year-old males, are basically an equine version of fourteen- or fifteen-year-old boys, and are about as well-behaved and hygienic as . . . well, fourteen- or fifteen-year-old boys. They can both defecate and urinate at will, and, what's more, they don't care where it goes. In fact, the further it travels, the happier they seem to be. When it comes to their straw, their food and their water, exactly the same rule applies. So when you open up the box first thing in the morning, not only are you faced with a bad-tempered, hormonal adolescent who's itching to kick, bite or mount something – usually you – but you're also faced with what looks like the aftermath of a particularly wild and disgusting stag party.

Two of the four boxes I was charged with mucking out on that first morning were, not surprisingly, housing the colts; the only ones we had in the yard.

'OK then,' Micky said after pointing out the boxes.

'You've got everything you need. Get your head down and I'll see you back in the office just before seven, OK?'

It was going to have to be.

As I peered over the door of the first box, there, standing in front of me, was a gorgeous-looking bay colt named Golden Tyke. He never made the grade as a racehorse and was sold into eventing as a three-year-old, but he looked fabulous, like a young Red Rum. I kicked the bottom of the box door to let him know I was there and, as he looked round to where I was standing, he curled up his top lip, which is what horses do when they detect an unfamiliar smell. And then he snorted, which is what they do when they're pissed off. The perfect start.

While I was deciding what to do next, I began to sense there were people standing behind me. Sure enough, when I took a quick glance back, I saw a crowd of about six or seven of my new colleagues.

'He's a bit of a misogynist, this one,' said one of the lads, smirking. He was tall and skinny and had a very sharp face, like an illustration from a Roald Dahl book. Jason was his name. 'Hates women, he does, especially ones with brand-new puffa jackets.'

'Thanks for that,' I replied, desperately trying to give off an air of good-spirited nonchalance.

'Are you not going in, then?' said another new fan, who was like a smaller version of me. 'He won't bite you.'

'Yes, he bloody well will,' protested Tommy, a short, redheaded apprentice jockey, who was a member of the yard's very large Irish contingent. 'He tore a feckin' chunk outta me last Wednesday and I ended up at Leyburn Surgery.'

Now I needed the loo.

'Don't let him see you're scared,' said Jason again, now trying to appear authoritative and knowledgeable.

'I'm not,' I lied.

'Yes, you are. You're shaking.'

He was right on both counts.

Finally, I was saved by Micky's forty-year-old head lad. Well, sort of. He was called Andy Crook – or Crooky, to his friends and colleagues – and he had a ruddy face, short dark hair and was about 5 feet 2 inches in heels. For now, let's just say he was a bit of a character.

'Get on with your jobs, you lot,' he yelled, 'otherwise you'll be out on your arses. Gemma, get a head collar on that colt now and get him tied to the back of that box and mucked out, otherwise I'll put you on a bus back to Leeds and you can get yourself a job in Tesco.'

Crooky, like many people I've met in racing, did a quality line in tough love. He was great when you got it right, and moved heaven and earth to help you achieve what you wanted to achieve; mess him about, though, and he'd come down on you like a box of heavily pregnant mares.

The ying to Crooky's shouty but well-meaning yang came in the form of a fellow stable girl called Rachel. She was quite tall for a stable girl, about 5 feet 7 inches, and had long dark hair and ruddy cheeks, like a gardener. She'd left racing college a year or two before I had and so, by the time I entered the industry, she was already an experienced and extremely capable horsewoman. More importantly, she was a very warm and welcoming human being.

'You're not going to get all these done by seven a.m., are you?' she said to me as I was attempting to shift what felt like a ton of colt dung and wet straw out of Golden Tyke's box. 'I've almost finished mine, so why don't I give you a hand?'

I promise you, I almost cried with relief.

'Thanks,' I gushed.

'Always get in close when you're mucking out colts,' Rachel said to me. 'And if you have to go around them, always go via the head – not the arse.'

The closer you are to a volatile horse, the less of a kick they can take, but it's difficult advice to follow when your natural instincts are telling you to get away from an animal that could harm you. In this instance I managed to take Rachel's advice and, although I can be a slow learner some-times, I'm pleased to say it stuck.

Jason was right when he said not to let Golden Tyke see that I was scared, but that's all down to confidence, and that only comes with experience. Watching Rachel was like being given a master class on how to handle difficult ani-mals; even though Golden Tyke wasn't her horse, she had an air about her that seemed to act almost like a sedative, and from the moment she entered the box he was as good as gold.

For me, one of the most important aspects of the job is the relationship that exists between a horse and its carer. Not the jockey, the owner, or the trainer, but the carer: the stable lass or stable lad who tends to it. And why? Because it's unique. From our point of view – the lasses, that is, not the lads – we see the horse as part pet, part friend, part colleague and even part confidant. Communication with your horse when riding out is deliberately restricted to words of command and encouragement, but during mucking out and feeding you can have a good chat. The first thing I do when I'm feeding a horse is to ask them how they are and how they slept. Then, once I start mucking them out, I get onto the nitty-gritty. 'That new lad's a bit of a prat,' or, 'If I see that boyfriend of mine I'm going to kill him.' The only pattern being that it's almost always a gripe about men. And, providing you look after them, horses can be great listeners. It genuinely does seem as if they're listening to you intently, which I suppose is one of the reasons we feel we can talk to them so freely. Perhaps they are? The point being that the relationship is made up of the same ingredients as the majority of human relationships: love, understanding, kindness, compromise, and, most importantly of all, an almost indescribable amount of trust.

Once I'd finished feeding and mucking out, it was time for breakfast, which we had in Micky's kitchen. Depending on the state of your boxes and the strength of your stomach, it can be anything from a bacon or sausage sandwich to just a cup of tea or coffee. It was going to take more than a dirty horsebox to put me off my food, and I ended up having two bacon sandwiches! I think you'll find that most stable staff are the same. We're like gannets. Unless you're a jockey with a weight to reach, which I definitely wasn't, this is advisable, as I probably used more calories in that first morning than most people would in two days. Shifting and shovelling horse poo, even at my relatively slow post-college pace, was extraordinarily hard work. Some people don't listen, though, and over the years I must have seen dozens of stable staff come off simply because they're out of fuel.

Before I move on to tacking up and riding out, which are probably two of the main reasons why people (girls especially) want to get involved in horse racing, I just want to touch briefly on the early mornings, which, conversely, is one of the main reasons they want to leave.

It's relevant now because on that first day of mine, during breakfast, one of my fellow stable lasses came up to me, but instead of introducing herself and saying 'Hi', she simply told me that I should never speak to her before 10 a.m.

'I'm being serious,' she said, stony-faced and bleary-eyed. 'Don't talk to me before ten, OK? I hate mornings.'

'Sure, no problem!'

I remember thinking: *I'd be happy to extend the no-talking rule till 10 p.m., if you prefer.*

Three days later she handed in her notice and, once she'd gone, there was a definite sense of relief around the yard.

'Thank god for that, Gemma,' Micky said the day after she left. 'We don't all have to be swinging from the chandeliers every morning, but she was the limit.'

By the time I finished my breakfast, I'd almost forgotten that in just a few minutes' time I'd be tacking up and riding out a racehorse in its prime for the very first time.

'You're going out with the second lot,' Micky said when I walked back into the yard. 'I promise you it's not a colt, though. You are OK riding out, aren't you?'

'Yes, of course I am!'

This I said with complete confidence, a confidence born from riding show ponies and long-retired racehorses at a canter and in a controlled environment. At that point I had never ridden a thoroughbred at the peak of its fitness over gallops at 40 mph, but in my naivety it hadn't clicked that there might be a difference. As Micky walked me towards the box of my mount, I had the air of somebody who could have ridden Desert Orchid side-saddle around Aintree.

'You ready to go?' Micky asked me.

'Can't wait,' I replied, nonchalantly.

'How did you get on with the mucking out, by the way?'

'A bit of a slow start, but Rachel helped me.'

'She's a good girl, is Rachel. Keep in with her.'

'I intend to.'

'Come on then.'

Tacking up a horse – or saddling up, as it's sometimes

known – is begun in the same way that mucking out is: by putting the bridle on the horse's head and then tying it to the back of the box. Once that's done, you then brush the horse's mane and tail, swing your tack on, which is your saddle, your stirrups and your bridle, choose your cover sheet depending on the weather, and then lead them out into the yard. The last thing you do before you mount a horse is to make sure your tack is buckled on properly, and then you check its hooves. One of the oldest sayings in racing is 'No foot, no horse'; in other words, unless you check your horse's feet with a hoof pick, both before and after you ride out, you could easily end up with a lame animal. It's a job most of us hate, for some reason, but it's so important. I know lots of people, stable lads mainly, who haven't bothered and they've ended up in really big trouble. Some have even been sacked. There's no hiding place, you see. No excuses. That horse is your responsibility, so the buck stops with you.

The horse Micky had assigned to me was a very small but incredibly beautiful chestnut gelding named Polo Venture. As well as being the first horse I ever rode out, he also became the first I looked after full time.

That morning I was joining a string of about eighteen horses and riders, and when I mounted Polo Venture for the first time, I actually felt every inch a stable lass. Though I was not yet the horsewoman I thought I was, sitting astride Polo Venture on that wet October morning I no longer felt self-conscious about anything. What's more, all the fear and trepidation that I'd been carrying around with me since I had arrived that morning had completely disappeared. It would come back, though, big time – and very much sooner than I'd expected.

3

Middleham Gallops

Sitting directly in between Middleham and Tupgill Park is Middleham gallops, a world-famous training facility that's spread across High Moor and Low Moor and has been used for training thoroughbreds since the mid-eighteenth century. The Low Moor, where we were heading, is the larger of the two moors, with a long stretch of grassland. As well as being used for dog walking it has three different gallops – a seven-furlong all-weather gallop, a three-furlong all-weather gallop and another grass gallop. They're all unusually bouncy, because the land was used by the army during the war to practise manoeuvres; after the gallops started to sink, they put wooden sleepers down and then covered them with turf. This turned out to be a blessing in disguise as the gallops drain brilliantly. All are in use six days a week and, for anybody who has a love of both horses and beautiful countryside, there's no better place on earth.

Ever since I knew I'd got the job at Micky's, this much-talked-about rural amenity had been giving me dreams and nightmares in equal measure. As Polo Venture and I followed the rest of the group out of the yard and up towards the moor, two worst-case scenarios were racing through my mind: *what if I fall off*, and, worse still, *what if they put me at the front?*

I'd only ever ridden alongside people before, two or three abreast at most, but in a group of eighteen that was never going to be the case. If they put me at the front of the group they'd all see something I wouldn't wish on my worst enemy – my bum.

The logic behind this fear might be a bit hard to follow at first. After all, I was about to take a racehorse worth perhaps tens of thousands of pounds out for a dash at about twenty-five miles an hour (you don't gallop first time out), so you'd think I might have other concerns on my mind. However, regardless of how well things went, I still knew full well that the moment I changed from a trot into a canter (which is when the sun rises, so to speak), there were going to be seventeen pairs of eyes all staring at my backside, and roughly the same number of people making comments about it.

'Jesus Christ, she's blocking out the light!'

'Look, she's got a VPL!'

Although it felt like the end of the world, I tried to ignore the prophet of nether-regional doom that was riding pillion with me and to concentrate instead on the job in hand. After all, we were still about a mile from the gallops and, according to Rachel, it could be tricky getting there sometimes. The problem was, she didn't say why.

As we rode, all the chatter and bravado I'd had to face during my first morning at Micky Hammond Racing died down suddenly.

'Why's everyone gone quiet?' I asked Rachel anxiously.

'It's the calm before the storm,' Rachel told me. 'These horses have been in the yard since Saturday lunchtime and so everyone's a bit nervous.'

As I said, Tupgill Park is well off the beaten track and the only way you could get racehorses from the yards to the gallops, without having to negotiate a very narrow but well-used B-road, was to make your way over the rougher side of the moor. This, for me, posed a multitude of issues.

First you had to ride your horse up a steep, narrow bridleway, part of which is flanked by hedgerows and the occasional tree. This shouldn't have been a problem, really, save for one very beautiful but unpredictable member of the bird family. Namely the pheasant. The bridleway was only about two metres across, which meant that if you did happen to disturb a slumbering fowl or two, all hell was momentarily let loose.

Polo and I were the penultimate members of the string, but of the eighteen horses and riders that passed along the bridleway, only one of us turned into an avian alarm clock when a pheasant suddenly exploded into life just to the left of us. My chestnut mount took it all in his stride. I, on the other hand, dropped the reins, leant forward, grabbed his mane for dear life and let out a scream that would have shattered a diamond.

I can say with a fair amount of confidence that never before had that bridleway seen so much laughter; as Polo Venture nodded merrily away with me still clinging on to his mane, our entire convoy just erupted.

'Once we get onto the Cross Banks, which is the rough stretch between the bridleway and the gallop, the horses start getting frisky and want to run,' Rachel told me. 'Try and keep him to a hack if you can, though, and for god's sake watch out for hares!'

'Hares as well as pheasants?' I cried. 'Oh my god. They're like giant rabbits, aren't they?'

A lot of people are surprised when I tell them that the vast majority of stable people actually hail from urban areas. So, as ridiculous as it may sound, this sixteen-year-old rookie stable girl from Leeds had never seen a hare before. I knew that they were quite large and that they were definitely bunny-shaped, but that was all.

'That's right,' said Rachel, giggling. 'Watch out for the giant rabbits! There might be a few sheep, too, so make sure you keep your eyes peeled.'

'Sheep as well?'

'Believe me, they're a lot easier to negotiate than the hares.'

Because it's common land, Middleham Moor, which is where the gallops are situated, used to have a lot of farm animals grazing on it, but in recent years the farmers and trainers have come to an agreement, thank goodness, so there are fewer animals up there now.

As we made our way through what's called the top gate

and on to the edge of Cross Banks, I could feel Polo starting to pull.

'Remember, Gemma,' Rachel shouted, 'just keep him to a hack if you can. Cross Banks is plain moorland, so it can get a bit rough in places.' A hack is a cross between a trot and a canter, so it seemed sensible advice.

'OK, thanks!'

It seemed like fortune was favouring Polo and me when Rachel set off with some of the group and flushed out the majority of the giant rabbits: one less thing for me to worry about.

By the time all the others had set off along Cross Banks, Polo was literally champing at the bit and so, to prevent him from taking the lead, I sat up, tightened my rein slightly, delivered a light kick with my right boot and shouted, 'Gee up!'

This should have been the greatest moment in my burgeoning equestrian career but, instead of hacking smoothly over Cross Banks, dodging hares, jumping sheep and punching the air triumphantly, my tack started slipping after about ten strides. Before you could say, 'And they're off,' I was on my arse staring at Polo Venture as he ran unhindered towards the gallops.

You stupid cow! I said to myself. Talk about a schoolgirl error. *The* schoolgirl error, in fact. The last thing Rachel had said to me before we set out was: 'Now, are you sure you've checked your tack?' I'd been so wrapped up in the moment and so desperate to get out that I had just nodded.

'Yes, yes. All done,' I'd replied.

Stee, the assistant head lad, was the first person to spot my predicament and, after very generously calling everyone back for a bit of a look and a laugh, he asked Rachel to go and collect me. He is about 5 feet 10 inches tall, and at the time had a nice mop of short brown hair – but not now. He was the yard's sergeant major, but as well as being similar to Crooky in the tough-love stakes he actually had – or has – an encyclopedic knowledge of racehorses, and in particular breeding. In addition to that he also has the filthiest sense of humour and the most extensive vocabulary of swear words I have ever known. Rightly or wrongly, swearing – or 'effing and jeffing', as my granddad used to call it – is rife within racing; I figure it must be the fault of all the falls, bites and other mishaps that assail us every day. Over my time at the yard, Micky, Crooky and Stee all added considerably to my list of profanities.

Now Stee was ordering: 'Sort her out, will you, Rach? I'll get Polo.'

Despite no longer having a rider, Polo had come to a halt about five hundred yards from where I'd fallen and was soon delivered back to me.

'You're not the first and you won't be the last to look like a twat on your first day,' he said, caringly. 'You dropped like a sack of shit, though, according to Jason over there. You're lucky he was the only one who saw you because if I had I'd have crucified you. Great fall, though, apparently.'

I *so* wanted to die.

Rachel was next.

'Have you learned your lesson, then?' she said, managing to temper the shame I was feeling with a warm maternal smile.

'Oh yes. That will never happen again,' I assured her.

'You'll fall again,' she said. 'There's nothing so sure. But by checking your tack before you go out, you'll eliminate one of the causes.'

I love Rachel.

This may sound ridiculous, but in hindsight I'm actually glad I came a cropper, because once I got to the gallops I was approached by about ten of my fellow riders.

'How's your arse?' was the main line of enquiry, but as they all left my side after I told them I was OK, every single one gave me either a pat on the shoulder or a smile. They didn't have to do that, and in some stable yards I dare say I'd have been ripped to shreds. I was no pushover, but to be shown so much consideration at such a pivotal moment in my career was quite special. It galvanized me, I suppose; so much so that when Stee told me to move to the front of the group so he and Rachel could keep an eye on me, I did so without any feelings of self-consciousness. I had an arse. So what?

'Remember, everyone,' Stee bellowed. 'No galloping. Just a canter. Right, away we go.'

There's one very big advantage in being a hang-up-free rookie at the front end of a riding group: you have nobody else in front of you. When you're taking a thoroughbred out onto the gallops for the very first time, that can be a tremendously liberating experience, and as Polo Venture began to canter my entire body was filled with pure elation. All of a sudden I wanted to scream, and so that's exactly what I did. God only knows what the group behind me thought, but I honestly couldn't have cared less. I was a virgin at the time, but I was sure this must be better than sex.

What made the experience even better was the knowledge that if something awful happened and I fell, there'd be one or two people behind me who would stop and help. They'd take the piss out of me mercilessly afterwards, of course, but feeling like one of the crowd, even for a short while, meant that the only thing I had to worry about was staying on and enjoying it. That's racing, though. It can be such a cruel business sometimes, yet it can also gift you some incredible highs.

When Stee called for the session to end, I had to stop myself from saying, 'Aww, do we have to?' This had been a genuinely life-changing experience.

Providing the excitement doesn't kill you, which it almost did me, once you're safely back in the yard again, you tie your horse up in its box, check its feet for stones and then remove your tack. I'd done this hundreds of times at college and it was the one thing I was confident of doing without messing up or having the piss taken out of me. Fortunately, Polo behaved perfectly, which was a relief, and after carrying his tack back to the tack room (tack weighs an absolute ton, by the way), I washed away the sweat patches where the girth and the bridle had been and then set about finding him a rug. In the winter you have to hose your horses down, as their legs will be caked in mud. That job alone can take fifteen or twenty minutes per horse, particularly if there's a queue at the hosepipe.

As it was my first morning, Micky had only allowed me to go out once, and so after the next lot had gone out I set about boring Micky with tales of how Polo Venture and I had bravely made our way across the wilds of Tupgill Park and Cross Banks onto Middleham gallops and then back again. The way I went on, you'd have thought I was the first person who'd ever sat on a horse but, to Micky's credit, he humoured me generously and made all the right noises.

'A pheasant? Well, I never.'

'No? He didn't, did he? Bloody hell, you did well to stay on.'

Although the replies he gave were probably well rehearsed, they were still very much appreciated. Micky was obviously used to receiving these barrages of youthful enthusiasm but, even today, now I'm the one responsible for 'breaking in' the newbies and feigning amazement, he'll still come in and listen. We love it.

Whenever a newbie returns to the yard, especially after a maiden gallop, I always put the kettle on, call Micky in, and then we'll wait expectantly for them to rush into the office. It's one of the best parts of the job.

'Gemma, Micky, you'll never guess what happened?'

'Really? That must have been terrifying!'

The more they talk, the more we want to listen.

At about 1 p.m., once the horses were done and we had finished cleaning the tack, the lads and lasses disappeared for some lunch, either at home or in the pub. It's effectively a split shift, as at 4 p.m. we had to come back to the yard and finish off for the day. I was no workaholic, but I rarely chose to take the full three hours' break as – if I did – by 4 p.m. I would find it almost impossible to get back up again. I discovered that about an hour and a half usually saw me right, and when I arrived back at the yard, the first thing I would do would be to brush my horses down and then muck them out all over again. I often used this time to have another chat; at this time of day the mood and the dialogue are generally more relaxed and optimistic.

Once we had finished boring our horses half to death, we would check their boxes for bedding to make sure they had enough, have a quick look at their feet and then feed them.

The final task of the day, which was always performed by Micky and Crooky, could often be quite nerve-wracking but it encouraged conscientiousness. Basically, they would go around and check every horse for injuries and then check our work. Woe betide anyone who hadn't done their job properly. If you hadn't, you'd get both barrels!

On my first day, apart from going to the gallops or popping to the shops, I didn't leave the yard for a minute and when Micky and Crooky had finished their inspection they had to literally push me out of the gates.

The last thing Micky said to me as he and his lieutenants evicted me was, 'I'll see you tomorrow at about nine, OK?'

At the time I thought nothing of it, really; my only concern being the number of hours I'd have to wait until they let me back in. But at roughly four o'clock the following morning, Micky's cryptic parting shot began making sense, because as I woke up and tried to move I realized that my entire body was in absolute agony: my neck, shoulders, arms, wrists, fingers, stomach, bum and legs. Even my ankles and feet were killing me. Without any word of a lie, it took me over three-quarters of an hour just to go to the loo, and by the time I made it into work, it was, wouldn't you know it, just approaching 9 a.m.

When I opened the door to Micky's office, he and Stee were already killing themselves laughing.

'You look like shit,' said Stee.

'I feel like it!'

'Nine o'clock, on the dot!' said Micky triumphantly. 'Here,' he said, throwing me a large tube of Deep Heat. 'Rub some of that on yourself and then think about getting your arse in gear.'

That was a long day. From a physical point of view, I was still feeling the effects of that first day well over a week later. I'd done most of the work before, of course, just to a lesser degree. And I think it was the intensity that took my body by surprise. Thank god for Deep Heat!

What happened that first day is as vivid now as it was when I tried dragging myself out of bed. And, although I didn't know it then, it was a microcosm of what was to come: the highs, the lows, the doubt, the pain, the shame, the language, the wisecracks, the weather, the characters, the camaraderie and, of course, the horses. It was all there really, except for a good romance and a death. Those I could wait for.

4

A Load of Old Pony

Stable work seems to be one of the last true vocations and, once someone is locked in, it's often very hard to leave. If a stable hand stays the distance and either retires normally or gives up when they are knackered, the chances are they'll leave the profession with at least one of the following: dodgy hips, dodgy knees, dodgy elbows or a dodgy back. Micky once said that if he had a pound for every time he'd asked a stable lad over a certain age how he was, and got the answer, 'Fucked,' he would be able to buy himself a plastic hip to have as a spare. But, on the plus side, if you do stay in the business for a number of years, you'll end up hobbling away from it with a memory bank full of experiences that will stay with you for the rest of your days – and you just can't put a price on something like that.

If most members of the public were ever to see a job advert for stable staff, they would probably not give it a second glance.

Hours: 40 hours a week over six days
Pay: Starts at £157 a week, rising to £288 a week for the
over-25s
Risk of injury: High
Early mornings: Infinite!
Weekends off: Not many
Out in all weathers: Yes
Miserable Boss: Definitely – apart from Micky Hammond
Career prospects: Minimal

Nope, it doesn't grab me much either.

Why do we do it, then? Well, when I first went into racing a lot of the girls were there because they loved horses, plain and simple. Some aspired to become jockeys, but the driving factor was definitely an almost overwhelming yearning to be around horses. With the lads it was the other way around. They all loved horses, of course, but their ultimate ambition wasn't to look after them and ride them on the gallops six mornings a week; it was to win races on them. That almost always wears off after a while, because to make it as a jockey you have to be cut from a very special cloth. But they nearly always stay on as stable lads. These days it's different, and more and more girls are entering the profession with a similar burning ambition to the lads. Jockeys like Hayley Turner, Michelle Payne, Josephine Gordon and Lizzie Kelly have been at the vanguard of new opportunities for us girls. I too tried my hand at it for a while. But for now, let's go back to the olden days, shall we? Nineteen ninety-three, to be exact.

My dad used to coach the second team at what is now Leeds Rhinos rugby league club, and one day he got chatting to a family who were big, big fans of the club. Derek and Tracey Pullein were their names and, unbeknownst to Dad, they were just about to open a riding school. I'd been badgering him to let me have some riding lessons for ages, but he hadn't got around to it. I'd never actually seen a pony close up, and I certainly hadn't sat on one, but I liked the look of them from afar.

About a week later, Derek and Tracey invited Mum and Dad to a local cricket match.

'We'd love to come but we don't have a babysitter,' they said.

'Well, bring them up to ours,' said Tracey. 'Our Georgie will look after them.'

Georgie, who is about seven years older than I am, is Derek and Tracey's daughter, and she had recently qualified as a riding instructor. I vividly remember getting into Dad's car with Mum and my little sister Becky and being driven to the farm, bursting with excitement at the prospect of seeing something horse-shaped at long last.

'How far is it now, Dad?' I asked, more than once.

Eventually, after what seemed like an hour, Dad gave me the news I'd been waiting for.

'There it is, up there on the right. Greenacres Farm. Blimey, Moira, that was the longest twenty-five minutes of my life. Right, come on girls. And don't forget your packed lunches!'

Once the grown-ups had disappeared to the cricket match, Georgie, who had a friend with her called Kirsty, started showing Becky and me around the stables. Georgie was a little bit taller than me (who isn't?) and had a slim build, big boobs and long fair hair. I already wanted to be her!

One of the first boxes we came to belonged to a dun pony, cream-coloured with black legs, named Candy.

'She's gorgeous,' I said to Georgie. 'Can I give her a sugar lump?'

Georgie had given Becky and me a handful of sugar lumps each, and, through a basic fear of the unknown, I hadn't yet dared hand one out.

'I'll tell you what,' said Georgie. 'Why don't you take her for a ride first? Then you can give her a sugar lump.'

I was too overwhelmed to reply – Georgie had to make do with wide eyes and an open mouth.

'I take it that's a yes,' she eventually said with a smile. 'Kirsty, would you mind putting a saddle on her and grabbing a helmet?'

Apart from trying to give one or two nervous pats on the nose, I still hadn't actually made contact with a pony yet, and so it still didn't seem real somehow. That started to change when Kirsty put the helmet on my head and Georgie put her hands out to lift me.

'Come on then,' said Georgie. 'Let's get you up and on.'

It was only when I was suspended over Candy that I

realized I'd have to part my legs, and when I did so Georgie began lowering me down. When my bum finally made contact with the saddle, and my feet the stirrups, I felt completely at home.

'Come on then, let's go for a little ride.'

What felt like a trek through the hills of Wensleydale was actually a short walk from the stables to Georgie's patio and back – about a hundred and fifty yards, all told – and, despite me having hold of the reins, or at least part of them, Georgie was most definitely in charge.

'How was that then?' she asked as she lifted me down. 'Did you enjoy it?'

Apart from, 'Yes, thank you,' I don't think I said very much at all after the ride. I was just too moved. Can seven-year-olds have epiphanies? I think they can. In fact, I'm living proof.

Just before we left that day, Georgie said something that, looking back, changed my life forever. As we walked towards the car she said, 'By the way, Gemma. You can come and help out here whenever you want.'

The ride on Candy had obviously been astonishing, but this was something else; like hiring a posh car for the weekend and then being told you can keep it. If I'd pestered Dad on the way *to* Georgie's, I plagued him mercilessly on the way back. The poor man didn't stand a chance, I'm afraid, and in the weeks following that visit, if I wasn't repeating stories about my experiences at Greenacres, I was begging him to let me have a pony.

'You don't understand, Dad,' I'd plead. 'I actually *need* a pony. I do!'

Dad had a really good business at the time, and I suppose you could say Becky and I were, not spoiled exactly, but indulged. At the end of the day, though, what father doesn't want to treat his daughters occasionally if he's able? The reason I wouldn't call us spoiled is because Mum and Dad always taught us the value of things and, as well as being grateful for what they did for us, we never expected anything. We could be persistent, like most kids, but if Mum or Dad said no to something and we'd thrown a tantrum, we would have been for the high jump.

What smoothed the wheels for Becky and me, with regards to horses and ponies, was that Dad was a racing fanatic; it was about that time that he started taking us to Wetherby races. Mum, bless her, had no interest in racing whatsoever, but she always came along and made the best of it. Her favourite part was trying to guess which horse would win best turned-out, and before Becky and I became hooked on horse racing, we were in the same camp.

'We're not here to look at a plaited mane, Moira!' Dad would say indignantly, before shaking out his copy of the *Racing Post* and turning his attentions to the 3.10 at Fontwell.

As well as helping out at Greenacres as often as was humanly possible, I also started having riding lessons there every week and, because I was getting so much pony time, I completely forgot about having one of my own.

Helping out was just an absolute joy, and after feeding, mucking out and leading the kids who were taking lessons there all day, I was finally rewarded with a thirty-minute ride.

The day before my eleventh birthday, Dad gave me a lift up to Greenacres as usual. For some reason Becky and Mum came with us, but I didn't think anything of it.

'We're just going to say hello to Derek and Tracey before we go,' said Dad as we pulled into the yard. 'You go and find Georgie.'

When I did find Georgie, she was grinning like a Cheshire cat.

'Could you start mucking out, please, Gemma,' she said. 'You can start with that box over there. It's a new arrival.'

Georgie pointed to a box on the far side of the yard. By the time I reached it, I could hear footsteps. I looked around, and there walking towards me were Mum, Dad, Derek, Tracey, Georgie, Becky and Georgie's brother, Richard.

Oh god, I thought. *What have I done?*

'Am I in trouble?' I said. I don't know why, but large groups of adults seemed to spell trouble to me.

'Of course you're not,' said Dad. 'We've just come out for a walk.'

'Have you had a look at that new pony yet?' Georgie asked.

'No, I was just about to.'

I opened the stable door and stepped inside. There before

me was a gorgeous liver-chestnut pony that stood about twelve hands high.

'He's called Firefly,' said Georgie.

'He's all right, isn't he Gem?' said Dad.

'Yeah!' I replied, enthusiastically. 'How old is he?'

'He's about four years older than you,' Derek told me.

'Can I take him out after work?' I asked Georgie.

'That's up to you, isn't it, Norman?'

You obviously know what's coming, but I'm afraid I still hadn't twigged. In fact, I was just getting more confused.

'How do you mean?' I asked.

'Gemma, he's yours!' Dad said finally. 'Happy birthday, love.'

If there's ever a global award for being particularly slow on the uptake, I would like to be considered for it, because to this day I seem to operate on a five-minute delay. Surprises and practical jokes always work on me.

After the penny finally dropped and I realized what was happening, I gave everyone a massive hug and then spent the entire day riding Firefly and generally making a fuss of him. He had a nice temperament, except when he was being fed. Then he was an absolute sod and would kick and bite like a good 'n. Or a bad 'n, in his case. He was a fantastic ride though and, as well as being an obedient little thing, he would jump anything you put in front of him. In fact, the only thing Firefly liked more than a succession of obstacles were broad open spaces, and therein lay a bit of a problem. Open fields would fill my new friend with an irresistible urge to gallop – and without any warning what-soever. He'd be off like a rocket and there was no stopping him. The first time it happened I was petrified. I remember screaming my little bum off as he sped around one of the fields at Greenacres at about twenty miles an hour, but my god it was fun. Better than any rollercoaster. The second time it happened I was less terrified but even more excited, and by the third or fourth I had developed a full-on addic-tion to speed. Firefly taught me how to control animals in a hurry, and that's something you can only learn from experience.

A few weeks later, thanks to Georgie, I had the oppor-tunity of competing at my very first show; within a few months it had turned into a bona fide family obsession. Dad, who had been playing or coaching rugby league for most of his life, even decided to give all that up just so we could start attending these shows as a family. He bought a horsebox after a couple of years, which Becky and I loved, and pretty soon he was buying and selling ponies with the best of them. He even became a member of the local Show Pony Society. I honestly couldn't believe it. My tough, working-class grafter of a dad had swapped rugby league for show ponies!

For the benefit of those of you who have never sampled the delights of competing with ponies, there are three kinds of shows: local shows, which are mainly for kids; local affiliated shows, which are the qualifiers for the Show Pony

Championships; and then county shows, such as the Royal International and the Horse of the Year Show.

As I said, we started competing with show ponies first, which are the 'supermodels' of the equestrian world. In order to impress the judges, you have to complete a routine in a ring that involves walking, trotting, cantering, galloping and standing perfectly still. It's actually a lot more difficult than it sounds, and the pony also has to be elegant, well turned out, and to have impeccable manners and behaviour. Unfortunately, while the ponies generally managed to meet the last two requirements, it couldn't always be said about the children riding them; if I had a pound for every time I'd seen a spoilt little brat start shouting at their parents because they hadn't won, I'd be able to buy Frankel's tail.

Dad used to glare at these little idiots, and every time we saw it happen he'd call us over to him. 'If I ever see either of you two behaving like that, I'll pull the plug. Do you understand?'

'Yes, Dad.' We weren't daft.

The closest either of us ever came to showing any kind of dissent was when Becky came third at a show one day. I forget which class or category it was in, but afterwards Derek Pullein told her that she'd been robbed and Becky, being Becky, decided to take it up with Dad. I remember seeing her stomping across the ring like some angry pixie.

'Dad!' she roared in a broad Leeds accent. 'Av bin robbed! Derek sez av bin robbed!'

Dad, who was wearing a flat cap, just pulled it down over his face and walked off.

After entering show ponies for a while, we eventually switched to the working hunter category. This combines elegance and good behaviour with an ability to jump, and the fences are always plain as opposed to coloured. This is to reflect the fact that it's supposed to resemble a fox hunt, and the judges are looking for a clear round – obviously – coupled with good conformation, manners and turnout.

One of the reasons Dad went off the whole show pony scene was because the judging, although based on a set of rules, often basically comes down to personal opinion, and at some of the shows – although I won't say which – he and many other entrants had a sneaking suspicion that it was as much about the owners as it was the ponies. So there was just a little bit too much schmoozing going on for his liking. 'Moira,' he used to say, 'I wouldn't trust that lot as far as I could throw them. It's time we moved on.'

The working hunter pony scene was a little less snooty, and that suited us down to the ground.

Meanwhile, Becky and I were also becoming obsessed with the world of horse racing. As much as we loved showing ponies, it was nowhere near as exhilarating as being at the races. Everything was bigger – the animals, the crowds, the stands, the jumps – and everything was obviously faster. A lot faster! We followed jockeys, horses and even trainers. We used to think we were the only girls on earth who followed racing in this way, so it felt like being a member of a very exclusive club. My friends were into pop stars, film stars or soap actors. None of which interested me in the slightest. I did experience similar emotions, I think, but my objects of desire were horse-shaped and my heroes were either 5 feet 2 inches tall and about seven stone, or wore trilby hats, sheepskin coats and had cigarettes hanging out of their mouths.

I think I must have been about eleven or twelve when I started compiling scrapbooks. Poor old Dad used to spend a small fortune on papers and magazines. The *Horse & Hound* and the *Racing Post Weekender* were always my favourites, and the moment they arrived the glue and the scissors would come out and I'd start cutting them to pieces.

My favourite jockey was the great Richard Dunwoody. I thought he was amazing; not just because of the way he rode, but because of the way he conducted himself on TV. He was the complete package, really: erudite, confident and extremely good on a horse. I'm not sure if I fancied him. Maybe a bit. He's not a bad-looking bloke, I suppose, but I think it was more appreciation than adoration. Sorry, Richard. You must be gutted.

It was while reading the first few pages of one of his books that I got the jockey bug. He was talking about how he had first got into racing, and the story just enraptured me. I think he was riding a pony one day and, after falling off, he said to his panicking father, 'Look Daddy, I rolled like a jockey!' At the time I remember thinking that was just the best story ever, and from that day I was desperate to give it a go.

She'll probably kill me for telling you this, but Becky's favourite jockey at the time was Frankie Dettori. She used to keep a little photo of him in a 'Friends Forever' frame.

If I'd had transport at the time I would probably have been a bit of a jockey-stalker, but as I only had a bicycle I had to wait until we went to the races. One of my first victims was a man called Conor O'Dwyer. He's now a trainer over in County Kildare, but on 7 April 1997 he was a successful jump jockey who was about to ride in the Grand National. Unfortunately for Conor, I was his biggest fan, and what sealed his fate was that I was at Aintree too that day together with Mum, Dad and Becky.

About half an hour before the big race, I saw Conor coming out of the weighing room. Despite him looking quite shy and sheepish, I was convinced that he needed a big kiss. 'Back in a tick,' I said to Mum and Dad, and before they could stop me I gave chase. I forget whose colours he was wearing that day, but they were distinct enough to enable me to follow him quite easily, and after barging past dozens of intoxicated racegoers, I finally reached my prey. Without even thinking about the consequences, I grabbed poor Conor, kissed him on the cheek and said in a very loud voice, 'Good luck, Conor!' The look on the poor man's face was a picture. Pure, unadulterated fear! There are few things in this world scarier than scaling the fences at Aintree, but that's probably one of them. He finished eleventh, by the way.

One of my favourite horses back then was called Bimsey. Trained by Martin Pipe, he was a beautiful plain bay gelding, and although he only ever won five or six races he had a kind eye and was such a genuine horse. I just loved him. He was the first horse I fell in love with, I think.

The first horse I ever followed, as opposed to went all soppy over, was the great One Man. Trained by the late Gordon Richards, he was a grey gelding and had a total of eleven major wins including the King George VI Chase (twice), the Ascot Chase and the Queen Mother Champion Chase. Because he was small, Gordon Richards used to call him the little bouncing ball, and a certain jockey called Richard Dunwoody rode him on both his King George wins.

The only time I ever bunked off school was when the Cheltenham Festival was on. It was only once a year and, because I was so well behaved for the other three hundred and sixty-one days, I used to get away with it. I'd sign in at lunchtime and then, instead of going to my lessons, I'd sneak off home, without the knowledge of my parents. In the week leading up to the festival I could hardly contain myself, and even though I watched every single second of every single meeting live, I'd record the TV coverage of it all as well, and then watch that back when I got home. Flat racing was never quite as exciting to me, and it didn't matter where we went on holiday or what I got for Christmas, nothing could compare to the excitement of the Cheltenham

Festival. Nothing's really changed, by the way. They're still my favourite four days of the year.

That only leaves racehorse trainers. My first ever favourite was Philip Hobbs, who, surprise, surprise, is a bit of a Cheltenham specialist. Although he's one of the top trainers in the country, I originally took to Philip – and his wife, actually – because they were so personable and the way they spoke about their horses was different to other trainers. Without wanting to sound too emotional, they seemed to really care about their horses, and when they spoke about what they did for a living, it always seemed to me that they viewed it as much more than just a business. That struck a big chord with me, and I've always tried to emulate their attitude.

Not long after pouncing on Conor O'Dwyer, I decided that I wanted to work in racing. That was a genuine watershed moment for me and, from the second the notion materialized in my young mind, I swear to you that I never thought of anything else until I'd formally been accepted into racing college. Tunnel vision, a one-track mind – call it what you will. I knew what I wanted to do, and the realization that it might be possible filled me with elation. It was the best feeling ever.

I was fourteen when Georgie Pullein left Greenacres Riding School and got a job working for Micky Hammond. In hindsight it must have been fate, but at the time Becky and I thought it was the end of the world. Once she'd settled in at Micky's, Georgie began inviting me up at weekends to help out, and that properly sealed the deal. I soaked up that atmosphere like a sponge and, although I was obviously on the fringes of the operation, I received just enough recognition to feel as though I was a part of it. Both the racing industry and the profession that I hoped was waiting for me were now tantalizingly within reach, and it was definitely a case of 'when' I would start my career in racing, as opposed to 'if'.

After I'd taken up most of Georgie's weekends for about a year, I started turning my attentions to racing college. Or rather, Dad did. He saw an advert for an open day at the Northern Racing College in Doncaster, and so Dad, Mum, Georgie and I all went along. My poor sister Becky was left at my aunt's house. As we pulled into the car park, I don't think I had ever been as excited in my life. Although working at Micky's had been fun, I was obviously not a paid employee. Nor would I be, until I'd spent at least twelve weeks here. This place was my gateway to a life that I'd spent every waking hour thinking about for at least a year – it sounds a little fanciful, but I can assure you it's the truth. As far as I was concerned, this was what I had been born to do, and the Northern Racing College was my portal to paradise.

For some reason, we'd arrived at the college just over an hour early and, when I asked Dad why this was, he had muttered something vague about early birds catching worms. Mum shook her head and the two of them bickered for a minute or so while I looked out of the window at the huge red-brick building that to me looked like a stately home. The first thing I did as I got out of the car was to vomit onto the gravel. It had all become a bit too much.

'Are you all right, sweetheart?' Dad asked me as Mum tried wiping my mouth with a tissue.

'Get off, Mum,' I said, pushing her away but taking the tissue. 'I'm fine, really. I was just a bit nervous.' Though that wasn't entirely honest: I was incredibly apprehensive about the open day, but extremely excited as well.

One of the people running the event, a man called Malcolm Bycroft, very kindly offered to give us a quick tour before everyone else arrived. Malcolm had spent most of his career working for a trainer in Thirsk called Jack Ramsden, but had obviously now decided to do something different. The college was open at the time and, as Malcolm began pointing out some of the horses they had (the majority of which were retired racehorses), I in turn began telling Malcolm who'd trained them, who'd ridden them and where, if anywhere, they'd won. This impressed him no end, and by the time he'd finished showing us around we were on first-name terms and were happily talking shop.

Some people who attend racing college have never been near a racehorse, let alone ridden one. That's obviously not their fault, nor is it necessarily a disadvantage. After all, we all have to start somewhere. What my experience gave me, however, was a foot on the ladder, and when Dad suggested that I apply to do my work experience at the college while I was still at school, I jumped at the chance. I was accepted straight away.

Although daunting (terrifying, actually), the experience was quite character-building, as I was basically put in a B&B for a couple of weeks, thirty miles from home, and had to catch a bus to the college every day. Strangely enough, that was the first time I'd ever been on a bus and I quite liked it. Fortunately, I became friendly with a couple of girls on the course, and so for the time I was there they took me under their wing. They ended up working in Middleham a few years later, and it was great to see them again. It's hard to imagine a schoolgirl being allowed to live away from home these days. I loved it, though, and when the two weeks were up I *so* did not want to go home. I knew I would be back, though, and after that I'd be after a job.

When I told my dad that I wanted to go into racing, I felt so passionately about it I said I'd do it for nothing. Dad was drinking a cup of tea at the time and he almost choked when I told him.

'You bloody well will not, young lady!' he spluttered. 'Once you start having to pay your own way, you'll realize that there's more to life than just horses.'

Not surprisingly, I took absolutely no notice of him whatsoever.

I left school aged sixteen and went straight to the Northern Racing College, this time boarding there. Everything was done for us apart from our laundry; in all other ways, it was just like living at home. That said, it did take me about a week and a half to learn how to use the washing machine. I remember one lad from the north-east who'd had quite a hard upbringing saying, 'It's like a bloody holiday camp, this place. I've never, ever been so well looked after.' That was a bit sad really, but nice all the same.

The majority of students attending the college were – and still are – either sixteen or seventeen, and you get absolutely all sorts there; from city-dwelling delinquents who've spent their entire lives in care, to the sons and daughters of wealthy farmers or landowners. The thing is, it doesn't matter how many surnames you have, how cosseted you've been, or how many times you've been arrested; once you're through those gates you'll find there's a lot more that binds you than separates you, and that's another thing that makes the whole experience so unique. It's an equestrian melting pot, I suppose. And it obviously works.

Day-to-day life at racing college is designed to be like life in a yard. You have morning and evening stables, too, as you would in a yard, so on the face of it you might be forgiven for thinking it was like a dress rehearsal, from which the students would move seamlessly into opening night and the full performance. But, as I've already mentioned, that is definitely not the case. Everything we did at college was carried out at our own pace, give or take, as we obviously had to become proficient in all the duties, and that could take time. I suppose they could have tried to force us to muck out four or five boxes in an hour, as I would later have to do, but the level of work wouldn't have been up to much – and neither would the level of enthusiasm. Because the average age of the students was so young, most of us had very little experience in terms of working hard and full time, so the shock to the system of going flat out would probably have put too many people off. As it was, it seemed bad enough: starting work at 8 a.m. was purgatory, and the fact that somebody had had the audacity to ask us to muck out two horses in an hour was bordering on outrageous. You should have heard the whingeing that went on – you'd have thought we'd been asked to do morning stables in an eighty-box yard single-handedly.

After morning stables we would have lunch, where we'd whinge a bit more, and then we'd have lessons before setting off for evening stables. In terms of hours worked, it was actually quite a long day – 8 a.m. until 5.30 p.m. – and for the first five or six weeks I was completely exhausted. If I could have changed anything about the course, it would have been to have a little more warning about the shock that awaited me – though, looking back, it was actually a bit of a charmed life. These days students are properly forewarned and, in addition to the Foundation Course, which is what I first did, the college also offers an Apprenticeship, which is a Level 2 Diploma, and an Advanced Apprenticeship, which is a Level 3 Diploma. I've done all three now, and the Northern Racing College and the British Racing School, which is in Newmarket, are two of the best stable staff and jockey training facilities in the world.

5

Horseplay

Over the years I must have looked after, or helped to look after, hundreds of thoroughbreds. I honestly couldn't tell you how many we've had through the yard. Thousands, probably. One thing I can tell you is that there is as much variation in character within the equine population as there is among us humans. In fact, I'd go so far as to say that generally their characteristics and eccentricities are even more pronounced than ours.

One of the strongest characters in the yard when I first joined, humans included, was a ten-year-old bay gelding named Valiant Warrior. I know several people who still wince when they hear his name. He used to be kept in a barn right at the back of the yard, and in that barn were three large stables. Valiant Warrior lived in the middle one and you only ventured near his box if it was absolutely necessary. Some horses hate human beings, plain and simple, but Valiant Warrior's loathing was far more wide-ranging. He didn't just hate people. He hated *everything*. People, horses, dogs, cats, birds. If it moved, he hated it.

I was introduced to Valiant Warrior on my first day. It was a momentous occasion in that it was the first time I'd ever heard a horse growl. They do, I promise you, although it's not like a doggy growl. It's more of a snorting growl really, and they do it for all kinds of different reasons. Some horses growl because of respiratory ailments, and some growl when they're in pain. Some growl because they simply like the sound and others because they're vexed. Valiant Warrior's growl was quite easy to categorize because it also came with an evil stare. He did it because he wanted to scare you and to let you know who was boss.

Shortly after lunch that day, Stee took me around the yard and introduced me to all the horses. He wouldn't normally do that, but I'd been badgering him to do so ever since the first lot came in from the gallops. He just wanted to shut me up. There's nothing like a bit of persistence.

Once we'd done the boxes on the left-hand side of the yard, we eventually came to the barn. The left and right boxes were vacant at the time and, as I peered over Valiant Warrior's door, he was standing in profile. When he saw he had visitors, he froze.

'Aww, he's cute,' I said, before reaching over the box door and beckoning him to come and say hello.

'Put your hand away!' Stee said quickly. 'He's cute all right. Do you remember that commotion earlier on when one of the lads got thrown?'

'Just before the third lot went out?'

'Aye, that's it. Well, here's your culprit. He's called Valiant Warrior, but we all call him Weasel.'

Earlier that morning, one of the lads had been trying to take Valiant Warrior out. Even before they'd got as far as the gates, he'd already been thrown three times.

'Is he really that bad?' I asked.

'Worse,' replied Stee.

Just then, Valiant Warrior shifted his head sideways and looked straight at me.

'GRRRRRRRRRRRRRRRRRRR.'

'Oh my god,' I said, taking a step back. 'Did he just growl at us?'

'Not at us,' said Stee. 'He growled at you. I bet you've never seen or heard anything like that before.'

He was right, I hadn't. I was captivated, but at the same time slightly terrified.

'Maybe he doesn't like being talked about?' I suggested.

'Aye, maybe,' said Stee. 'Or maybe he's just a miserable old fart.'

Right on cue, Valiant Warrior growled again.

'Well,' I said defiantly, 'I don't care what he does or what you lot call him. I think he's cute.'

Stee gave me an exasperated look, the kind a parent gives a child when they're showing off.

'You'll learn,' he said, shaking his head and walking away.

Before I followed Stee to the next box, I looked back at Valiant Warrior and gave him a big smile. He growled again and then kicked out his hind legs. Not far, but enough to make me jump.

'You don't like me, do you?' I said, trying to sound hurt. This time he just turned his back.

Maybe Stee was right.

A few days later, we had a lot of staff away at the races, which meant those who were left had to muck in with the mucking out, so to speak. As luck would have it, Valiant Warrior was on my list, and when I went to ask Stee for some advice, he already had a few notes prepared. He'd offered to do it for me, which was nice, but in some respects that had been the story of my life. As daunting as it undoubtedly was, I was determined to do it myself.

'Well, if you're sure,' said Stee.

'I am,' I reassured him. Although not myself.

'For a start, don't try and bully him. OK? Like for like doesn't work with this one. It'll only make him worse. Whatever you ask him to do, he'll do it. But only if he thinks he's in charge.'

'OK, thanks.'

My fork and sack, which are tools of that particular trade, had been left by the muck heap and, after picking them up, I walked slowly towards the barn. The condemned stable lass takes her final steps . . .

'Get a bloody move on,' Stee called after me. 'You look like you're going to come to a halt.'

'Sorry,' I yelled before breaking into a trot.

A few seconds later, the only thing separating me from

the scourge of Tupgill Park was the bottom half of a stable door. 'Morning,' I said, trying to appear confident and in control. Who was I kidding?

To be honest I didn't really feel threatened by my new friend, although there was no doubt who was in charge. A lot of people think that horses can sense fear, and that's probably correct. But it's how they react to it that matters, and on this particular morning Valiant Warrior was obviously feeling merciful. Lucky me.

Stee was right. Everything I asked him to do, he did, but on a delay, and only when I'd started doing something else. That made it seem like it was his idea, if you see what I mean, and although it took a bit longer than usual, it went a lot better than I'd expected. I even offered to do him again. Some people will argue that horses could never be that calculated, but I'd disagree. Horses are incredibly intelligent and insightful creatures and, although they have a herd mentality, which is often present but not necessarily prevalent, they are definitely independent of mind, body and spirit.

The next two horses Stee introduced me to on that rainy afternoon were Invest Wisely, who was a chestnut gelding with a really long back, and Wise Advice, a big bay gelding. 'These two are known as the Kray twins,' said Stee.

Not knowing who on earth the Kray twins were, I started making lots of 'Awwww' noises. 'You don't look like twins to me,' I said, in that really annoying voice people use when they're addressing either dogs or babies.

'The Kray twins were gangsters,' said Stee, once again sounding exasperated. 'They were killers. Don't you know anything?'

This time I just ignored him and went to stroke Wise Advice.

'The reason they're called the Kray twins is because they're as thick as thieves and a couple of sods,' continued Stee.

'How do you mean?'

'Well, stand back and watch for a minute.'

As I joined Stee between the two boxes, I started noticing the interplay between the two horses. It was like watching a couple of old women chattering over a garden fence. There was lots of nodding and lots of neighing. It seemed like a conversation.

'It looks like they're talking to each other,' I said.

'I think they probably are,' replied Stee. 'God knows what they're saying though. Make sure you throw that new girl, probably.'

'Thanks!' I said. 'What do you mean when you say they're a couple of sods?'

'Well, Wise Advice tends to pull really hard on the gallops. You've got to be quite strong and experienced to take him out.'

'And what about Invest Wisely?'

'Well, he's the opposite on the gallops. In fact, he's nigh on perfect.'

'What's the problem then?'

'The problem is that the moment you get him off the gallops, he'll try and throw you.'

'Aaah, I see.'

Although I wasn't allowed to ride him out at first, I used to brush Invest Wisely all the time. Some horses hate being brushed and will start twitching and nipping you the moment you start. Others, like Invest Wisely, just live for it. He used to stand there and almost purr when I brushed him; after about ten minutes or so, his back would start to sink, his tongue would loll out and his eyes would glaze over. None of this made the slightest bit of difference when I eventually rode him out. Although Invest Wisely had been allocated to me, it was a good two weeks before I could go with him. When it came to handling difficult horses, I was an unknown quantity, and Micky and Crooky had to be satisfied I could cope. Not on the gallops, which was the usual and more obvious requirement, but off them.

The day before, I must have spent about an hour brushing him down, and I was praying that would hold me in good stead. Stee was sceptical.

'You can brush him all you like. He won't do you any favours.'

According to Stee and Micky, the reason Invest Wisely used to act up when he came off the gallops was because his adrenalin levels took longer to come down. Everything in front of him was either an obstacle, as in something to jump over, or an issue, as in something to be scared of. The second time I rode him out I remember him losing it over a puddle.

It was quite a big one, to be fair, but in his mind we were obviously approaching a lake on the scale of Malham Tarn and he didn't like it one little bit. Instead of either going around the puddle or through it, like any normal horse would have done, he reared up a couple of times, trotted on the spot, and then just stood there like a lemon. I couldn't move him for love nor money, and in the end I had to literally drag him around the puddle. It took about half an hour. God only knows what he thought was going to happen to him.

Because he was quite long-backed, Invest Wisely had a flat withers (the space between the shoulder blades), which meant I didn't have a lot of room in front of me when I rode him. In some instances this made me feel more as if I was aboard a rodeo bull than a horse, especially when he started fooling around after the gallops. Occasionally – and completely without warning – he would drop his shoulder; the shortness of his wither made it terrifying. There's no doubt he did this on purpose, by the way. It was just sport to him.

Another horse who had a similar penchant for unexpected mischief was Minster York, a gorgeous chestnut gelding who arrived at the yard shortly after I did. Rachel and I used to ride him out a lot and generally he was fine. He used to savage you outside his box, mind you, and the first time my parents came to visit me at the yard, he took a chunk out of my dad's hair! On the way back from the gallops, if he felt that I was ignoring him, he'd flick his bum out just to remind me he was there. That used to scare the living daylights out of me but it certainly worked. Once I'd been suitably chastised, he'd then nod a few times in approval. *Remember me? Less chit-chat, if you please.* He'd never try and get you off, by the way. All he wanted was a little bit of attention.

Shoulder-drops and Malham Tarn-sized puddles notwithstanding, the only time Invest Wisely came close to getting me off in those early days was while we were on our way *to* the gallops. Something must have spooked him and, after rearing up once or twice, he then sped off with me clinging on for dear life. Fortunately this caused a chain reaction and another horse that had been spooked by the commotion ran straight across his path. This brought Invest Wisely to an immediate halt and, before he could cause any more trouble, I rode him to the gallops. That was definitely one of those times when I thought that somebody up there must like me.

Wise Advice was actually OK to ride if you were a girl. He might try it on occasionally and pull a bit, but he always kept himself in check. It was as if he could gauge the strength of his rider, and if he didn't think you could put up much of a fight, he'd relax and go easy on you. Things are a bit more even now with regards to how strong the sexes are, which is why there are so many good female jockeys. But back then the difference was more noticeable, and if a lad ever had to ride Wise Advice on a Monday morning after he'd been confined to the yard for a day and a half, the chances were he'd have a real job on his hands. You could always tell if Wise Advice had a lad on his back because the language would be appalling.

'Give over you shithouse! For god's sake, will you just give over!'

Incidentally, for some reason grey horses seem to have a reputation for being troublesome, but in my experience that's not the case. Greys can obviously be problematic, but then so can any horse. The ones who actually deserve the mantle of being difficult so-and-sos are chestnut mares. In fact, they even have their own proverb, which is, chestnut mare – beware! These alpha mares, as they're known, are generally stroppy, fickle, arrogant and manipulative. Like an equine Elizabeth I, in fact. An article in the magazine *Horse & Hound* once advised, 'To get the best out of your chestnut mare, it helps if you have mind-reading skills, a Machiavellian ability to manipulate, and a grim determination to get your own way. Because that's exactly what she has.'

I couldn't have put it better myself.

The only box Stee didn't take me to that afternoon belonged to a horse called Broadwater Boy.

'I think we'll give him a miss,' he said.

The look on his face stopped me from asking why, but naturally it created an immediate fascination.

Surely he can't be as grumpy as Valiant Warrior, I thought to myself.

Although we didn't really need to, the last box we visited on my first day was Polo Venture's. No introductions were necessary, of course, but Stee knew I was smitten and so, before he went off on his afternoon break, we went to say hello.

Polo Venture lived in what's called the Derby Box, which was in the top left-hand corner of the yard. It had once been home to a very famous horse called Pretender, who in 1869 had won the Epsom Derby for a trainer called Tom Dawson. A plaque had been erected above the door commemorating Pretender's achievement, and I remember already feeling proud that Polo was living in such a historically important abode. It seemed right, somehow. The box, which is made of stone, is absolutely huge, and because Polo was so small he almost got lost in there.

'Everybody loves this horse,' said Stee as we both peered in. 'You're lucky to have him.'

'I know,' I said, smiling. 'I love him to bits.'

Stee looked over towards the barn. 'It's funny, isn't it?' he pondered. 'That horse over there would quite happily attack anything that drew breath, whereas this little thing wouldn't hurt a flea.'

He was right. One was a lover and the other a fighter – or rather, a potential murderer!

Polo Venture was bright chestnut; as well as having perfect white socks he had what looked like a white star on the front of his head. God, he was adorable! As I said, he was small, and so we made the perfect couple. Have you ever watched *The Moomins*? Well, Polo had a nose just like a Moomin. Kissable and just gorgeous. Some people reading this will probably feel sick at this point, but there'll be others who'll be nodding their heads frantically.

In those first few weeks Polo was my rock, and I don't just mean emotionally. While I was finding my feet and making all the usual mistakes, I needed something to restore my confidence, and working with him did just that. He never gave me any problems and, because he had such an amazing temperament, he allowed me to practise my craft using him as my guinea pig, as it were. It's actually difficult to emphasize the importance of that. As if I needed any more reasons to love him!

A few days after I arrived at the yard, I found out exactly why Stee had kept me away from Broadwater Boy.

By the time the fourth lot of riders came in from the gallops, he still hadn't been out, so I asked Stee what was wrong.

'Hang around for half an hour or so and you'll see why,' he said. 'Make sure you keep out of the way, though.'

I was still none the wiser.

Just over half an hour later, when the majority of people had disappeared, I heard a commotion outside in the yard. I was in the tack room at the time, having a cup of tea, and as I poked my head around the door I could see Crooky, Stee and Micky all standing outside Broadwater Boy's box. All three of them looked terrified, like they were about to wrestle a wild animal, and the noise coming from inside the box suggested that might just be the case. I'd heard horses make a racket before, but this was just extreme, like something out of *Jurassic Park*.

Just then Micky caught sight of me peering around the door.

'What the hell are you doing here, Gemma?' he said, in a kind of loud, nervous whisper.

'I told her to stay on,' said Stee.

'You did what?'

'Come on. You've got to admit, it's pretty exciting.'

With that, Micky walked over to the tack-room door.

'Broadwater Boy, in case you hadn't noticed, makes Weasel look like Polo's maiden aunt.'

'I know, he's terrifying!'

'In order to get him onto the gallops, we have to take him out when the yard's quiet. It's the only way. You were here all day yesterday, weren't you? I'm surprised you didn't hear it.'

'Rachel gave me a lift to the shops after the fourth lot came back, so I must have missed it.'

'Well, suffice to say, Broadwater Boy is an extremely dangerous animal, so tomorrow, make yourself scarce.'

Listening to the lad trying to tack him up in his box was genuinely frightening, but not nearly as frightening as watching him emerge. It was like watching the police trying to move a dangerous criminal, and when the stable lad finally mounted him, he immediately began rearing up. Had there been a bookmaker to hand, I'd have bet everything I had on them not getting him out of the yard, let alone onto the gallops. The fact that his lad was willing to ride him out left me wondering whether he was quite sane.

Despite the hullabaloo, that was the only way they could exercise Broadwater Boy without him causing absolute chaos, but needs must. In human terms he was like a Category A prisoner, and how they'd ever got him to a racecourse I have absolutely no idea. They had, though, and he'd already run twelve times.

'One win, one second, four thirds and twenty-five counts of assault and battery,' was how Crooky described his record.

The last time Broadwater Boy had run was in May, a good five months ago. Ever since then, Micky and the boys had been trying to tame him, but unfortunately he'd got worse. A few months later they retired him and, as far as I know, he's still alive. God knows what he's doing, though. Maybe the French Foreign Legion have got him?

The day after witnessing all this, Crooky told me a story that surpassed anything I'd ever seen or heard with regards to equine savagery, and even now it makes me shiver just thinking about it.

Not long after starting at Micky's, I'd noticed that part of Crooky's left ring finger was missing. Despite him being approachable, I still hadn't plucked up the courage to ask him how he'd lost it and, as it was, I didn't have to.

'You see this,' he said, holding up his left hand and wiggling what was left of the ring finger.

'Yes,' I said tentatively.

'The rest of that finger was bitten off and eaten by a horse I used to look after called Ubedizzy.'

I had to sit down at this point, as I was in danger of fainting. I was also unable to speak, so Crooky carried on.

'Have you heard of a trainer called Steve Nesbitt?' he asked.

'I think I've heard my dad mention him,' I replied. 'Wasn't he at Kingsley House?'

'That's right,' said Crooky. 'He trained in Dingle first and then Newby Hall in Ripon.'

Kingsley House is a large white-painted building that lies just below St Alkelda's Church. It mainly dates to 1752, though parts of the house are medieval and seventeenth-century; it was originally the rectory. Charles Kingsley was appointed canon of St Alkelda's in 1845, and legend has it that he wrote *The Water Babies* in the house. In the late 1960s, stables were built in the grounds, and ever since then it's been a racing yard. Steve Nesbitt trained there from the early 1970s through to his death in 1982.

'Ubedizzy was without question the most dangerous horse in Britain at the time,' said Crooky, staring at his bitten finger. 'I wasn't there, but one day at Newmarket, in 1975, he grabbed a racegoer who was leaning over the rails of the parade ring and attacked him so savagely that the television cameras had to be turned away.'

'A horse actually ate part of your finger?' I asked, staring at his hand in disbelief.

Sensing my revulsion, Crooky pushed the nub of his severed finger towards my face and began waving.

'For god's sake, Crooky,' I screamed, lurching backwards.

It would take a lot more than severed fingers to dampen this man's sense of humour. More's the pity.

'Come on,' I pleaded. 'Tell me what happened.'

Crooky loved nothing more than having an attentive and enthusiastic audience and, now he had one, he continued.

'I was taking his tack off in his box one morning and the little sod just went for my left hand. He'd gone for me hundreds of times before in this situation but I'd always been too quick. Not today though! When I pulled my hand away I noticed one of my fingers was missing. Well, the top third of one. All I could see was bone.'

I almost heaved at this point!

'We never found anything,' continued Crooky, 'so I suppose he must have eaten it. If I was offered a thousand pounds a day to do him now, I wouldn't. The times I used to come out of his box with a leg missing off my trousers, or my shirt torn to bits . . .'

I was properly speechless.

Ubedizzy, by the way, was a fantastic sprinter, who in 1975 had won the William Hill Trophy at York. His speciality had been biting any horse that challenged him in the final furlong and he would even go for a jockey's legs. He was later forced to wear a muzzle, but he made up for being unable to bite by barging into every horse and jockey in sight.

'Do you know what first made us decide to put a muzzle on him?' Crooky asked darkly. He knew I was scared!

'No,' I replied.

'Well, we were galloping him down at Ripon Races one day. Me and a lad called Gary Dowthwaite. When we arrived at the course Gary stuck his head in the back of the box and Ubedizzy grabbed him and pulled him in. Fortunately, I got Gary out before he could get stuck into him, but the screams Gary made were blood-curdling. He thought he was going to die.'

Yet again, I'm afraid I'd lost the power of speech.

'That Hannibal Lecter bloke had absolutely nothing on this animal,' said Crooky. 'I'm not joking. There was something wrong with him.'

'Were you actually scared of him?' I asked.

'No, not really,' said Crooky. 'I knew what he was like, and even though he got me once or twice, it never stopped me going in with him. That's why I started looking after him in the end, and riding him. None of the other lads would do it, and there wasn't a jockey in the world who wanted to ride him more than once. Actually, there was one occasion when I started to sweat a bit.'

This was going to be good!

'We were at Newby Hall at the time and me and some of the lads had been to the pub for a few pints. When we got back one of the lads who'd stayed put came running out.

"There's a loose one!" he shouted. After we all ran over to the yard, I told this lad to go and turn the lights on. We could hear hooves, but we still couldn't see which horse it was. When the lights came on, there was Ubedizzy standing right in the middle of the yard. He'd kicked his door in. The other lads all ran off the moment they saw him, but I didn't. *Oh, bloody hell*, I thought. *This is all I need!* I'll tell you one thing, it's a good job I'd had a few pints.'

'What happened next?' I asked.

'I just walked up to him and led him into an empty box. I'm not saying I wasn't nervous, but I wasn't going to run. No chance! It was just fun to him. A bit of sport.'

'What was he like in a race?'

'Oh my god! He was a flaming nightmare. He used to amble for the first two or three furlongs and then make ground during the fourth. Most of his results were a photo finish. He was best over six furlongs, but also good over five.'

'And what was he like beforehand?'

'Again, he was a nightmare!'

Poor Crooky.

'What was his best season?' I asked.

'Oh, that was 1977,' said Crooky, swapping his grimace for a grin. 'He held the record that year for being the heaviest handicapped horse. He carried sixteen pounds extra and then came in at 33 to 1.'

I'd never heard anything like it.

'The following year,' continued Crooky, 'he was running

in the Abernant Stakes at Newmarket. He came second to a horse called Boldboy ridden by Willie Carson, but it was close. When his groom, a lad called Martin Taylor, took him to the unsaddling enclosure after the race, all hell broke loose. Ubedizzy had an angleberry – which is a wart-like growth – in his armpit, which was obviously quite painful. His jockey, Edward Hide, undid one of his two girths while Martin undid the other and unfortunately he let it hang. What Martin should have done was whip the whole thing away quickly, but the hanging girth obviously knocked Ubedizzy's armpit and it sent him ballistic.'

'What did he do to him?' I asked, fearing the worst.

'He knocked him down, knelt on him, and started trying to eat him.'

'Oh my god!' I cried. 'The Hannibal Lecter comparison wasn't a joke then.'

Crooky just shook his head.

'It gets worse, I'm afraid,' he said. 'A lot worse. After that, Ubedizzy was banned by the Jockey Club from every racecourse in the country, and so he was sold and went to Sweden. He became a champion sprinter there, but about two years later he ended up killing his trainer's son. He kicked him, apparently.'

Any humour there might have been in the story had started to evaporate long ago, but now there was nothing left. It was one of my few serious conversations with Crooky.

Incidentally, in 2016 the racing journalist and presenter Alastair Down wrote a piece for the *Racing Post* about rogue racehorses, and Ubedizzy was deemed to be the most dangerous there had ever been in British racing. Before Crooky started riding him, a total of eighteen different jockeys had ridden Ubedizzy, including Lester Piggott, Willie Carson, Pat Eddery, Geoff Lewis and Greville Starkey. Crooky, though, was the only jockey who was prepared to ride him more than once.

These days the approach to troublesome horses is completely different. As opposed to taking a horse out at different times to the others, we will try and get inside its head and find out what's making it behave like it is. Papering over the cracks is all well and good, but if you can get to the nub of the problem you'll stand a much better chance of solving it. Equine psychology is big business now and, as well as there being dozens of books on the subject, there are even courses you can take and quite a few practising equine psychologists. They must have a big couch.

Some people decry animal psychology, but to me it's an obvious way forward. After all, every animal has a brain and all of them work differently. Because we're not trained in the subject, a lot of what we do is trial and error based on past experiences, and because the horses can't speak it can often be quite time-consuming working out what the problem is and how to fix it. I think it's important that animals are treated as individuals.

We have a gorgeous bay gelding at the moment called Le Deluge, and for a time he refused to go onto the gallops. For the life of us we couldn't work out why, as there were no symptoms, so to speak – he would simply come to a halt once he reached the Low Moor.

The first thing we did was try to find out if he was in any pain. We checked his teeth and his back first, which were fine, and then we jabbed his joints with steroids. We even put some anti-inflammatories in his food, just to make sure, but everything seemed to be OK. After that we thought it might have been the wind, and so for the following two weeks we only took him out when it was calm. No change. Shortly after that we tried leading him up the road to the gallop instead of riding him, and that actually worked – for a time. After a few days he reverted to type, though, so this time we tried moving him to another yard and riding him through the fields to the gallop as opposed to using the road. You know what they say: a change is as good as a rest. Once again, this actually worked, this time for over a week. As soon as it became the norm, however, Le Deluge started refusing, and from roughly the same distance as he had before. The conclusion we eventually came to with Le Deluge, apart from that he was an absolute fruit loop, was that he seemed to despise any kind of order, routine or repetition. And, after arriving at this eureka moment, we acted accordingly. Everything we do with him now is random, apart from the basics such as feeding and mucking out. We take him out on different days, move him around a bit, and generally change his approach to the gallop as often as is humanly possible. Whether that's going to work long-term,

I honestly don't know. It all depends if he cottons on, I suppose!

Le Deluge had won for us, by the way, and won well, so we knew he had a good engine. He's a nightmare at the races, though. The first time he won was at Redcar, and Rowan Scott, his jockey, had to do a full lap of the course before he could pull him up. One mile four furlongs, to be exact. How's that for a lap of honour? The last time he ran, or was supposed to run, was at Pontefract, and instead of trotting down to the start, he flew off with Rowan and ended up doing two laps! That's over four miles. We only wanted him to run ten furlongs – and preferably in the actual race. I went onto the track to try and stop him at one point and, as he came towards me, I started waving my arms. At first, he showed signs of slowing down slightly, but when he was about fifty yards away I realized that he had no intention of stopping, and so I rapidly decided to give way. 'Keep trying,' I shouted unhelpfully to Rowan. He was powerless, bless him.

So Micky and I have scratched our heads long and hard over this horse, and the fact that we've got this far is actually a bit of a miracle. Anyway, if you ever see a bay-coloured racehorse cantering through the streets carrying a desperate-looking jockey answering to the name of Rowan Scott, you'll know exactly who it is.

6

Broken In

Luckily for me, there were two couples living in Castle House when I moved in and one of the two girls took pity on me after seeing how inept I was at looking after myself.

'Can you honestly not cook a thing?' she asked me a couple of days after I moved in.

'Nothing,' I replied. 'I can't even boil an egg.'

'What about ironing?'

'No idea. I can use a vacuum cleaner though, a bit. And I can dust.'

I remember her looking at me with a mixture of pity and disbelief.

'Are you being serious?' she asked. 'Is that really all you can do?'

'Nobody ever taught me, I'm afraid,' I said, shrugging my shoulders. 'Mum's a bit of a fusspot so we always left her to it.'

There was no use pretending otherwise. I was useless! Well, let's just say I was a work in progress. The thing is, I didn't really want to learn how to make a curry or iron a blouse, nor did I have any interest in things like interior design or soft furnishings. I just wanted to ride and look after horses. As long as I had somewhere to sleep and a bathroom, I didn't really care what it looked like or what kind of state it was in. It had been the same at home. Once Becky and I had ponies of our own they were our responsibility, and we'd taken that very seriously indeed. In fact, you could say I'd been in training to become a stable lass since the age of about eleven or twelve.

When I'd called Mum at the end of my first day, she'd asked me if I was feeling homesick, and without even thinking about the question I just said, 'Nope, not one bit. I'm worn out though. But I'm not homesick.'

'Oh, OK then,' she said a bit flatly. 'So long as you're OK.'

If I had my time again I would probably let her down a little more gently, but that was the truth. I'd been working towards being in this position for so long, and now I was here it was the only place in the world I wanted to be.

It was only after being in Middleham for a few days that I started to realize how cosseted my life had been, and the sense of freedom I felt was exhilarating. By far the best part of my first few months was getting to know the staff. I loved working with the horses, obviously, but what I hadn't had much experience of at the time was people – especially older people – and so that was all new and interesting. Talk about a baptism of fire, though. Not only was I the youngest person in the yard, but I was by far the most naive, and because there were no allowances made for my innocence I had to grow up very quickly indeed. For a start, the language there was just mind-boggling, and for somebody who hadn't been exposed to that much swearing it was like learning a different language.

I remember asking Stee what a bell-end was one day, and without even flinching he just pointed at Crooky.

'He's a bell-end,' he said.

Crooky, who was berating somebody for not sweeping out a box properly, began to laugh. Andy Crook has the dirtiest, most mischievous laugh on earth and, as well as being infectious, it often spelt trouble.

'That's right,' he said chuckling away. 'I'm a bell-end and Stee's a knob-head. What are we?'

'You're a bell-end and Stee's a knob-head,' I said obediently, not knowing what on earth I was saying.

'Ten out of ten. Now go and get on with some work.'

Luckily for me, Crooky was also from Leeds – Morley, to be exact – and together with Rachel and another lad called Ashley Hopkins, he took me under his wing. Although Ashley's a couple of years older than I am, he'd done his training at the same time as me, except he'd attended the British Racing School in Newmarket. As well as being quite tall he had short brown hair and, because he'd only been at the yard a couple of weeks, we were kind of in the same boat. I quickly found out that Ashley, who is one of the most laid-back people I've ever met in my entire life, only cared about two things: horses and Lincoln City Football Club. The less said about the latter, the better.

Crooky might have been the head lad, which is basically a member of the management team who is in charge of all the stable staff, but instead of spending his time in the office with Micky like he probably should have, he always preferred being in the tack room with the hoi polloi. The tack room is also the staff room, by the way, and as well as being the place where everyone gets changed, it's also where I did the majority of my growing up. They all differ slightly from yard to yard, but ours was basically an old feed house with some seats scattered around and a lot of tack hanging about the place. They're invariably quite messy places and, unless the yard happens to be full of teenage girls who change their clothes three times a day and spray perfume everywhere, they stink to high heaven. Ooh, that alluring mixture of horse manure and human sweat!

Being a people person who liked a joke but had no sense of smell, that was where Crooky was always happiest, and he managed to achieve a balance between being a boss and being a buddy. People in positions of power or authority rarely manage to get that delicate equation right, and most don't even want to. In Crooky's case it was both natural and sincere, and his relationship with me, and with everyone else in the yard, was testament to that. As somebody who was young, new and nervous, I often found it difficult asking for help, but he made it easy and would always take the time to explain things or help me out. He'd tease me mercilessly while he was doing it, of course, but that was a small price to pay – and it was nearly always funny.

'Crooky, one of my horses lost a shoe on the gallop. What should I do?'

'Take him to the shops and buy it another one, you big fanny! He's a size seven. Wide fitting.'

Pause while I looked at him stupidly.

'Failing that, you could always ask me to call the smithy for you . . .'

'Thanks, Crooky.'

'No problem, soft arse. Now bugger off and do some work.'

Stee, who was Crooky's assistant, was equally as happy to help but was slightly less approachable, and I don't mind admitting that at the beginning he used to terrify me. I remember the first time I was ever late for work. Actually, the second time – I'd forgotten about the first day.

I'd been sick for some reason and had missed my lift. This meant I had to run the full three miles up to Tupgill, and by the time I got there I was as white as a sheet.

'I'm so sorry I'm late, Stee,' I said, gasping for breath as I ran through the gates. 'I was sick earlier on and I missed my lift.'

'Oh aye,' he said cynically. 'Pull the other one, it's got bells on.'

I was horrified! I remember thinking, *But why would I lie?*

The beautiful Middleham Castle.

A bright Middleham morning out on the gallops with
Wensleydale in the background.

I loved spending my weekends at Georgie Pullein's farm.

My first pony, Firefly.

Riding Primula, one of our ponies, at one of the shows we competed in.

My little sister Becky ready to compete!

My first Grand National in 1997. Coincidentally, Valiant Warrior is actually the horse with the red and yellow silks just over the jump.

My favourite jockey, Richard Dunwoody, and the great One Man.

A normal day at racing college!

With close friends Louise and Emma.

The site of Micky's first yard at Tupgill Park. Today it's a restaurant called the Saddle Rooms.

Micky in 1994, during his jockey years.

Making our way back to the yard.

My first digs,
Castle House.
It's the one with
the red door!

Having fun with
Rachel – she really
took me under
her wing in the
early days.

Riding towards the gallops, keeping a close eye out for pheasants
and giant rabbits!

Mum and I with the gorgeous Polo Venture.

Cantering across the High Moor on a brisk morning.

The ever-grumpy Valiant Warrior in action.

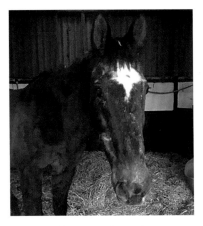

Valiant Warrior today.

Becky having a cuddle with Shake It Up.

The Low Moor gallops covered in snow – just another one of those freezing mornings!

'No, I *was* sick,' I pleaded. 'I promise I was. It must have been something I ate.'

It didn't matter what I said, Stee simply would not believe me, and in the end I just skulked off and got on with my job. I think that's when I first started using some of the new words I'd picked up in the tack room and, instead of talking to the horses like I usually did as I mucked them out, I just mumbled away to myself.

'You even get told off for telling the bloody truth in this bloody place. What a complete load of arse!'

I wasn't quite Sweary Mary, but it was a start.

To be fair to Stee, he was used to people trying to pull the wool over his eyes, and from then on I was never late again. Well, not for a while.

Because they were so different, Stee and Crooky complemented each other perfectly and had a kind of good-cop, bad-cop partnership. Stee was, as I said earlier, very knowledgeable, and if a horse was ever injured he'd call me over and explain how and why it had happened. To somebody who wanted to spend the rest of their life caring for horses, that was invaluable.

About a year after I started, my sister Becky came up to help us one weekend, just as I had done in the past with Georgie Pullein, and she too was terrified of Stee. Becky was only about thirteen years old at the time, but I remember him taking the cork out of a bottle of wine one night and then taking a swig before handing the bottle to Becky. Very nervously she took a sip, just to impress Stee, and when she handed the bottle back to him he winked at her and said, 'Same taste in wine, eh? You'll do for me, kid.' Becky was over the moon!

When you start in a yard, one of the first things the head lass or lad will ask you is what your aspirations are, and in my case – as with the majority of stable staff – it was to become a jockey. Stee happened to be the person who asked me the question, and when I told him he said, 'OK, we'll do our best to make it happen for you.' Apart from my family, Georgie, and one or two friends, I hadn't mentioned this ambition to anyone, and so for somebody within the industry to almost bring it to life and say that they'd try and make it happen felt extraordinary.

When it came to the tack room, Mondays were always the most 'enlightening', shall we say, as throughout the morning everyone would discuss what they'd been up to over the weekend. It's no different these days, of course, except that I'm slightly less easily shocked. Back then it was the easiest thing in the world to make me squirm; in addition to going crimson every time I heard a story relating to sex, I'd become nervous and would start fidgeting. Whenever Crooky saw this happening, he'd say, 'Come on Gemma, love, don't get all embarrassed. The hungry have to be fed.' I had no idea what he meant at first, but I do now!

As with every other aspect of life in the yard, I was completely unprepared for all this; the first time I ever heard one of these racy conversations I almost ran screaming from the yard. Some of it went over my head, thank god, especially some of the phrases and the sexual innuendo, but a lot of it didn't, and one morning just a few weeks after I joined, I got the shock of my life. It was a Monday and, after riding my last horse out, I was in the tack room having a cup of tea. Suddenly, two stable lads came in and started chatting about a mate from another yard.

'Did you hear about Richard?'

'No, what happened?'

'He got caught shagging Kevin's wife again in the back of his car on the moor. Kev gave him a right kicking, he did. Knocked out two of his front teeth, apparently.'

'Serves him right. The dirty little bugger. What did you get up to?'

'I got pissed at the Black Bull on Friday, same again on Saturday, and then last night I ended up shagging that lass I'm seeing from Mark Johnston's. She wouldn't let me go to sleep!'

'Aw, you lucky git. I'd shag her any day of the week.'

I suppose that might sound quite tame to some people, but to a sixteen-year-old school leaver who'd had a pretty sheltered upbringing, it was tantamount to pornography. I don't think I said a word to anyone for the rest of that day – I was in a state of shock.

My husband Tim, who has also worked with horses since he was sixteen and is now an assistant trainer too, is in charge of ten young women all aged between sixteen and twenty-two. There are no stable lads in the tack room; it's just him and ten females. Ten sexually active women who have no problem talking about what they got up to the night before. Because Tim's at least twice the age of any of the girls, they consider him to be a bit of an old dodderer and tend to talk to him like he's a virgin, or way past doing anything anyway. Not surprisingly, this infuriates racing's very own Hugh Hefner, and his standard response is always, 'You lot didn't invent sex, you know. I was doing it before you were even born.' I still don't think they believe him.

The sexual exploits of Richard, Kevin's wife, and the rest of them faded into insignificance a day or two later. Once again, I was in the tack room having a cuppa. Stee and Rachel (who was his girlfriend, I'd just discovered) had come into the room. While Rachel put the kettle on she called over to Stee.

'Have you heard from Titchy?' she said.

'Naa. Fuck knows where he is. Prison, probably. One thing's for sure, though, he'll have a couple of pairs of old knickers in his pocket.'

I was intrigued.

'Who's Titchy?' I asked.

'Who's Titchy?' repeated Stee, feigning disbelief. 'Tell her, Rach.'

'Bloody hell,' said Rachel, frowning. 'Where do I start?'

'Just tell her what he's like,' said Stee. 'Then I'll tell her what he did in his spare time.'

Now I was very intrigued – and a bit scared.

After sitting down next to me, Rachel took a sip of tea, thought for a moment and then began.

'Titchy arrived here about a year ago,' she said. 'I think he said he was from a council estate in Manchester originally and had been chucked out of his home. Don't ask me why he was thrown out but, as well as weighing no more than about five or six stone, he couldn't read or write.'

'You mean he's illegitimate,' I said proudly.

'That too,' said Rachel, laughing. 'He can't be more than five feet tall and he's got really scruffy brown hair. He looks like a little goblin.'

'How old is he?' I asked.

'About Stee's age, I suppose. Mid-thirties?'

'Fuck off! Yes, he is about my age, and I'm twenty-five. Cheeky cow.'

'What's his real name?'

'You'd have to ask Micky that,' said Stee. 'But I doubt even he knows.'

Listening to Stee, I thought Titchy seemed to be quite a sad character and I began to feel sorry for him. That soon evaporated, though, as it seemed as though his personality more than made up for his lack of size and education.

'I've never known anybody with as much confidence in my entire life,' said Stee. 'Certainly, when it comes to his gob. Whenever he wanted to attract my attention he'd say, "'Ere, Hoggy, yer twat." He's got a very nasal voice and sounds absolutely hilarious. The first time he said it to me I couldn't believe it. "Who the hell are you calling a twat?" I said. I was about to tear him a new arsehole. Then he started laughing. "You, yer twat," he said, and then flicked the Vs. I just pissed myself.'

'What happened to him?' I asked. 'He can't have been gone long.'

'About two or three months now,' said Rachel. 'He just wasn't strong enough. He could barely lift a full water bucket, let alone control a racehorse.'

'If Micky told us to do a swinging canter,' said Stee (a swinging canter is faster than a canter but not quite a gallop), 'the horse would just run away with him. He couldn't exercise that kind of control.'

I felt sorry for him again.

'Did you sack him?' I asked.

'No,' said Stee. 'We knocked him on the head and put him in a bucket.'

For a split second I actually thought he was being serious!

'For his own safety we had to let him go,' said Stee.

'Poor Titchy,' I said sadly.

'Don't feel sorry for that dirty little knob-head,' he said. 'With a gob like his, he'll be all right. As long as he's got some used knickers to sniff.'

I remembered this from the start of the conversation.

'What do you mean, knickers to sniff?' I enquired slightly uncomfortably.

Latching on to my awkwardness, Stee continued, 'You mean you've never heard of the Demon Knicker-Sniffer of old Middleham town,' he said theatrically. 'We only found out just before he left. He's not the only one, though. Knicker-sniffing is rife in Middleham. It's famous for it.'

As my imagination started doing cartwheels, Rachel continued: 'Titchy used to break into girls' bedrooms and pinch their dirty knickers,' she said. 'He always used to carry a couple of pairs with him, apparently, and would sniff them all day long. At first, we all thought they were handkerchiefs, but after a while we realized he was sniffing in, as opposed to blowing out.'

I was horrified.

'Did anybody catch him?' I asked.

'Just once,' said Stee. 'It was at a party in Castle House. Titchy said he was going to the bog and ten minutes later one of the girls caught him with his head inside her wash basket.'

'Oh my god! That's dreadful.'

'Not really,' continued Stee. 'Everyone liked Titchy, so apparently she gave him a couple of pairs. I've known funnier fuckers than him.'

'When he left they found about fifty pairs in his room,' said Rachel. 'Nobody wanted them back, though.'

'I'm not surprised!'

Just then Stee leant forward. 'As I said, though, he's not the only one. I know at least ten lads in Middleham who are knicker-sniffers. It's like glue to them.'

Rachel nodded in agreement. 'There's at least three in Castle House. It's been a problem there for a while now. I'm surprised you haven't had any trouble.'

'I hope you've got a lock on your wash basket,' said Stee.

Normally I'd have realized I was being wound up, but because Rachel was involved I took it as gospel.

'No, nothing's happened to me,' I said, wide-eyed.

'You mean you *think* nothing's happened to you,' said Stee mysteriously.

'How do you mean, I *think* nothing's happened?' I looked from Stee to Rachel and back again.

'It'll be sniff and run,' said Stee. 'What do you think, Rach?'

At this point Rachel made a funny noise, covered her mouth and then got up and left. Stee also had one of his hands covering his face, and I should have realized then what was going on.

'What's sniff and run?' I asked anxiously.

'It's when they run into your room, have a quick sniff of your dirty drawers, and then run off again.'

'Oh my god! Really?'

Fortunately, my tormentor could take it no more and, as he removed his hand from in front of his face, I could see that he was on the verge of hysteria.

'No, not really!' he said, finally coming up for air between gales of laughter. 'Christ almighty. You're easy to wind up, you are.'

I couldn't get angry. I felt too embarrassed.

'It's true about Titchy, though,' said Stee. 'He loved to sniff a pair of knickers after a hard morning on the gallops. Nothing nicer!'

'You're disgusting,' I said to him, trying not to laugh.

It's no word of a lie that I received all my sex education from the tack room at Micky's. The theoretical aspects, I hasten to add, not the practical! Shrinking violets don't last five minutes in racing, so you either learn from it and let it flow over your head, or you go and join a nunnery.

It's funny, but all the little cliques that are formed in places like the tack room tend to find each other whatever the situation, and it's fascinating to watch. I was with an owner the other day on the moor and, as a string of about fifteen horses and their riders started making their way back to the yard, I told the owner to watch them carefully. Slowly but surely they all began either holding back or moving forward, and within about two or three minutes they were all safely ensconced in their little groups. It seems to happen almost automatically and I love watching it.

That journey from the yard to the gallops and back is also the time when any airing of differences – either between colleagues, people from different yards, or even trainers – takes place. I'd say the majority of disagreements between colleagues are sorted out in the yard, but occasionally they do carry on outside, and when that happens you can pretty much guarantee that whoever's responsible will be in for a proper tongue-lashing when they get back. It rarely turns into fisticuffs, but they don't half give their tonsils an airing sometimes. The majority of these conversations tend to be about some kind of infidelity, but it could also be an argument over a horse, some tack, or just a clash of personalities.

Either way, it's always best to sort it out before you head for the gallops.

'It doesn't matter whether you're in the pub, at the races, or on your way to the moor,' Stee said in my first week. 'You are always representing the yard.'

Every trainer in the country works by the same rule, and the vast majority of stable staff behave impeccably. The same can obviously be said for the trainers, mostly, but there was one famous clash between two strong personalities, both now deceased: the great Captain Neville Crump, who won the Grand National three times, and Dicky Peacock, whose father Matthew had been the last northern trainer to win the Derby. Dicky had done well since taking over from his father, and in 1958 he not only had the country's top-rated two-year-old filly, but the country's top-rated two-year-old colt too.

I think it's fair to say that Captain Crump and Dicky Peacock were two very different people, and perhaps that's why they never saw eye to eye. For a start, Captain Crump was always very hands-on as a trainer and so, instead of taking a car onto the gallops like most trainers would, he would always ride up on his old black horse. Dicky, on the other hand, was slightly more laid back in his approach, and would sometimes stay in bed until well after his horses had returned to the yard.

I don't know if it was done either out of spite, a sense of mischief, or a belief that if he himself was out of bed then everyone else should be, but as Captain Crump used to pass

Dicky's house, which is on the west of the town on the way to the gallops, he would suddenly let out a tirade of abuse.

'GET YOURSELF OUT OF BED, PEACOCK! IT'S SEVEN O'CLOCK IN THE F****** MORNING! COME ON YOU LAZY BASTARD, F****** GET UP!'

Captain Crump's diatribe only ever lasted the time it took him to pass Dicky's house, and the moment he was past it he would fall silent again. I've no idea whether or not Dicky managed to sleep through the din, but if he didn't he must have been absolutely furious. After all, this used to happen six mornings a week without fail.

My guess is that he did manage to sleep through the alarm, as if he hadn't Dicky would surely have released Atty, his kamikaze-like and permanently enraged black French poodle. Although long since dead, Atty is still a legend in the West End of Middleham and, according to Stee, whose original family home is just a few yards up from Dicky's, he would attack every single vehicle that passed his master's home. Size and speed were unimportant to Atty, who would chase whatever you were driving and try and bite your tyres. Legend has it that he was once run over by a horsebox driven by a man called George Wilkinson, but when George stopped the box, fearing the worst, Atty simply got up, barked at George, bit one of his tyres, which was probably twice his size, and trotted triumphantly off.

When it came to bad behaviour, we always tried to keep ours within the confines of the yard. More often than not the instigator was Crooky.

There used to be a travelling tack salesman who visited the yard every few weeks. One day, after he'd gone, Crooky came into the tack room and sat down on one of the benches, rubbing his hands together and chuckling to himself. Stee recognized the signs of mischief.

'What have you done?' he asked him suspiciously.

'Nothing!' said Crooky, pretending to be offended.

'Come on,' persisted Stee. 'You only laugh like that when you've either heard something, said something, or done something.'

By now Crooky was giggling away like a demented pixie and, after getting up and closing the tack-room door, he slowly produced a brand-new bit from under his coat.

'Where the hell did you get that?' asked Stee, putting one hand on his forehead.

'Well, while you were talking to the tack man, I was having a look in the back of his van, and this bit just jumped into my hands.'

While everyone else fell about laughing, I just stood there in shock. My sense of humour was just developing, whereas my sense of shock was fully matured.

'Oh my god,' I said. 'That's *theft*. You could go to jail!'

This just made everyone worse.

'Don't worry,' said Crooky, standing up and ruffling my hair. 'Bugger me, you're like an old woman!'

Old woman or not, I was outraged.

'But what if you get caught?' I said.

'Look, Miss Marple, if I get caught I'll be out in a couple of years. You can come and visit me.'

I'd never seen anybody break the law before, and I never wanted to again.

From then on, every time the tack man came to the yard, Crooky tried to create a diversion so that he could get to the van and pilfer something small and shiny. He was like a magpie.

'Micky's after some new reins,' he'd say to the salesman. 'Just pop up to the office and have a word with him, would you? I'll look after your van . . . Hee hee hee hee.'

I found out later he was leaving money on the front seat, but he loved outwitting the tack man.

After I'd been at the yard a few months, Micky decided we needed to brighten the place up a bit. As well as a bit of a paint job, he suggested us getting a few hanging baskets.

'Just you leave that to me,' said Crooky.

'Here we go again,' said Stee. 'What are you going to do, mug Alan Titchmarsh?'

'Don't worry,' said Crooky. 'They'll all come from a legitimate source.'

'Legitimate my arse,' replied Stee.

When we turned up the next day, the entire yard was festooned with about fifteen beautiful hanging baskets.

'Bloody hell,' said Micky. 'That's exactly what I wanted. Where did you get them from, Crooky?'

Crooky was in the tack room at the time and all we could hear was, 'Hee, hee, hee, hee.'

'There's your answer,' said Stee.

At first, I'd been as impressed as everyone by the new floral additions, but as soon as I twigged that they might not have come from a garden centre, at least during opening hours, I felt sick. I'd lived such a sheltered life – to me this kind of behaviour was unheard of.

'He's robbed B&Q!' I said to Ashley, though even I had to admit the result was great.

'Have I heck robbed B&Q,' said Crooky. 'It was Homebase.'

As it turned out, Crooky had got the hanging baskets from a friend of his who worked at a garden centre – it had all been legit – but he wasn't going to tell us that in a hurry. He was happier us thinking he'd raided Homebase.

As a head lad, Crooky was top notch. As well as being a brilliant horseman, he knew how to get the best out of his staff. Not just have a laugh with them, as I've already mentioned, but make them want to work for him.

Some head lads or lasses only have one setting, but Crooky was like a chameleon and would adjust his behaviour to suit your character or personality. That's a very special talent, and together with Micky, Stee and Jedd O'Keeffe, who was the travelling head lad, they created a brilliant working atmosphere. They had firm rules and working practices, though, and certainly didn't tolerate idiots; the few people who refused to conform to their way of thinking did not last long. That was a rarity, though, and it was no coincidence that the turnover of staff at Micky's yard was one of the lowest in the area, if not the industry.

Jedd was Stee's best mate, but because he used to travel to the races a lot I didn't see a great deal of him. He was a bit shorter than Stee, with short brown hair and a ruddy face and, like his partner in crime, seemed to know everything about horses and the industry.

One of my favourite pastimes in those very early days was listening to stories told by Micky and Crooky. As a young racing fanatic, I was already aware of their illustrious pasts and was always a willing and attentive audience. I've already mentioned Micky's pedigree, but Crooky too had been a very decent jockey in his day and used to work for the four-time Champion Trainer, trainer to the Queen, and sixteen-time British Classic winner, Major Dick Hern. Like Micky, Crooky had been through one of the old-fashioned apprenticeship schemes and, although he liked a laugh and a joke, everything in your boxes had to be absolutely immaculate. That's the way he'd been taught by Major Hern. According to Crooky, you got praised when you pleased him and disciplined when you didn't. During my first few weeks at the yard, Crooky would keep reeling off the list of jobs I had to complete. Day after day after day he did this. 'Have you checked the horse's girth? Have you washed out the manger? Have you washed out your buckets? Have you washed the horse's arse?' The list was obviously a long one and, until Crooky was satisfied that it had all become second nature, he just carried on harassing me. In the end, the only way to make him stop was to get it right.

Many of Crooky's favourite memories of that period involved three very special horses: Sallust, a chestnut colt, who, in 1972, won no fewer than five group races, Sun Prince, who won the St James's Palace Stakes at Ascot in the same year, and the great Brigadier Gerard, who was once rated the best British-trained racehorse of the twentieth century.

Although Sallust and Sun Prince were both trained by Major Hern, the pleasure of riding them usually went to people like Joe Mercer, who, as well as being Crooky's favourite jockey, was also a fellow Yorkshireman, and to Major Hern's assistant, Brian Proctor, who was also one of the country's best stable jockeys.

One Saturday Crooky had taken a horse called Irish Song for a racecourse gallop at Newbury. He was due to ride Irish Song in a race at Leicester the following Monday and the two other horses galloping alongside them that day were Sallust, who was being ridden by Joe Mercer, and Sun Prince, who was being ridden by Brian Proctor. Despite it not being a race, and despite him being told by Major Hern to take it easy once he was on the straight, Crooky was keen to put in a good show among such esteemed company, and he and Irish Song got off to a flyer. About three furlongs before the straight Crooky took a quick look back to see how the famous four were faring. Nowhere! *Brilliant*, thought Crooky. *I'll be in the lead once I ease off.* It would be a small victory, but a victory all the same.

A few seconds later, while he and Irish Song were still

going full pelt, Crooky suddenly heard the unwelcome sound of a horse approaching at speed – *thubalup, thubalup, thubalup, thubalup*. Two seconds later, whoosh! Sallust and Sun Prince passed him and Irish Song as if they were standing still, even though – according to the intrepid Crooky – Mercer and Proctor barely had them out of first gear. It might not seem like much of a story to some, but every time he told it Crooky used to well up. 'You have no idea what it's like riding with or against horses of that calibre,' he'd say. 'Irish Song was no slouch, but those two were just incredible.' Incidentally, Crooky ended up winning at Leicester on Irish Song. That was his first win as a jockey.

The story regarding Brigadier Gerard was shorter and more comical, and it used to have us all in stitches. Once again, this was probably amplified by the effect it had on Crooky and you could tell that when he told the story he was picturing it in his mind.

Brigadier Gerard's first race as a two-year-old was at Newbury in a race called the Berkshire Stakes. With odds of about 33/1 he obviously wasn't fancied, but with only five runners there was always a chance. Major Hern's wife Sheilah didn't think so, however, and when she went to place a bet to predict all seven winners on that afternoon's race card she overlooked her husband's horse in favour of the odds-on favourite, a horse called Young & Foolish. I bet you know what's coming next. Despite being well behind for the first three furlongs, Brigadier Gerard created a gap of eight lengths in the final two and, after easing down before the finish line, he ended up winning by a good five. Crooky, who was there on the day, said that he'd never seen anything like it, either before or since. Poor Mrs Hern was absolutely demoralized as she ended up predicting the winner of every other race. Heaven knows what she would have won, but with Brigadier Gerard alone being 33/1 you can bet it would have been a few quid.

The incident Micky always enjoyed recalling was of an entirely different type; in fact, it once featured on *A Question of Sport* in the 'What Happened Next?' round. It was November 1989 and Micky had a ride at Sedgefield in what was literally a two-horse race. He was on a horse called Lingham Bride, and his one and only adversary, Mark Dwyer, was on a horse called Miss Club Royal. Competing in a two-horse race must be a really bizarre experience and the only thing that could top it from an entertainment point of view is if both horses fell at the same fence. Surely that could never happen. Could it? Well, at the fourth from last fence it did, and because in those days you were allowed to remount your horse if you fell (these days it's forbidden), it was simply a question of who would manage to remount first. Micky did his best but, unfortunately, Mark got to his horse before Micky did and he ended up winning by twelve lengths. Twelve lengths! Where did Micky land – Darlington?

The former jockey Peter Niven, who rode a lot for Micky and was known for being rather careful with his money, was once unseated by his mount at Chepstow and, after remembering that he was due a hundred pounds in prize money should he finish the race, he ran down the final furlong shouting, 'Bring that horse back *now!*' In the end Peter managed to get back on, but he must have finished the race at least five minutes after the winner. What's that old joke? The horse started at 10/1, but it finished at quarter past five.

Stee once had an envelope handed to him by an owner at the races and naturally he thought it was a tip. This used to happen sometimes and it was always called a dropsy. Once the envelope was handed to you you'd wait until you were on your own, open it, and then spend it! Because he hadn't seen the owner for a while Stee was expecting a nice wedge of cash, but instead he got a photograph of the owner and the owner's wife standing next to their other horse that had won last time out. The look on Stee's face was a picture and Jedd, who was with him, almost ruptured himself laughing.

7

A Right Bum Deal

Apart from falling from – or getting kicked by – a horse, the only thing that scared me in those early days was being on the receiving end of either a practical joke or some kind of initiation ceremony. I'd seen dozens of these take place, and I was always terrified of being the next victim on the list.

These pranks ranged from the relatively innocent, such as getting somebody to tack up the wrong horse, to the downright painful, like having your private parts covered in black tar before being strung up naked in the hayloft. Fortunately, that only happened to lads, but the likes of Crooky, Stee and Jedd used to take great joy in filling me in on the horrors that might be to come.

One of the worst I ever heard about took place at another yard, and involved a chestnut horse and a bath. It already sounds awful!

Some poor redheaded girl had only been working there for about a week, and one evening had decided to take a bath. A few of her housemates waited until she'd got out of the bath and left the bathroom, before rushing in and adorning the bath with some hair they'd cut off a chestnut horse's tail.

'Oh my god,' they all screamed. 'Come and look, everyone. She's been shaving her legs and her pubic hair. You could have cleaned the bath out!' they admonished her, as the poor girl returned to see what all the commotion was about.

As Stee was telling the story, I remember tensing up and becoming more and more fearful. It was the only time in those early days that I thought about going home.

'What happened to her?' I asked, open-mouthed.

'Aww, she wasn't bothered,' Stee assured me. 'It was only a bit of fun. They always take the piss out of carrot tops. If you can get through that you can get through anything, and as far as I know she was fine.'

She might have been fine, but I certainly wasn't. In fact, I was mortified.

'Do you think that'll happen to me?' I asked.

'That all depends,' said Stee, being serious for a moment.

'On what?' I whimpered.

'On whether or not you shave your legs and your pubic hair,' he laughed, before patting me on the head and walking out.

Stee was right, though: if you can get through that level of teasing, you can get through anything. Physical strength alone just isn't enough in a yard, and in order to survive you need to be both stubborn and very, very robust. Some people just aren't cut out for the job, and there's absolutely no shame in that. Sometimes it's heartbreaking watching a young person struggle, and many's the time Micky or I have had to call somebody's parents and ask them to come and take them home. The look of relief on the young lad or lass's face when you do that shows you've made the right decision, and it's great that they're no longer suffering. This doesn't happen very often, I'm happy to say, and for every ten who have a wobble, eight or nine will stay. We don't let anyone go without a fight!

That's probably one of the most upsetting things Micky has to do when it comes to staff, but it's not the most awkward. Very occasionally a stable lass will get into trouble, either by getting pregnant or catching a sexually transmitted disease. Sometimes when this happens they'll ask Micky to take them to the clinic, and because he's such a good boss he always says yes, even though he hates going there. That's because, unfortunately for Micky, the turnover of staff at the clinic is almost as impressively low as at his own establishment, and so every time he turns up he's greeted by the same people. Naturally, they all think he's the man responsible, and the looks he receives are severe, to say the least.

It has always been Stee's opinion that girls make better stable staff than lads, and he has never had any problem saying so.

'The girls just get on with the job,' he used to say. 'Whereas lads are a bunch of idle bar stewards.'

Stee has a fantastic way with words. He did have a point, though, and he repeated his argument to me while we were chatting just a few weeks ago. He said, 'If I went around on a night-time and checked to make sure the horses' girths had been brushed or that their rugs had been changed, you could guarantee that hardly any of the lads would have done it, whereas the girls would. That's because there's obviously an element of care involved in stable work, which comes more naturally to the girls. The lads just want to ride out, and generally they couldn't give a toss about the other side of the job.'

Not long after I joined the yard, Stee started fining some of the stable lads for this – and it caused all kinds of arguments. He even had people bawling at him and squaring up to him in the yard, which from their point of view wasn't a good idea. Stee could look after himself, verbally and physically, and had been a decent boxer in his day. They were only making things worse for themselves, and at the end of the day they didn't have a leg to stand on. It never came to fisticuffs, fortunately, but one lad who had a gob on him threatened Stee and was ejected with a rather large flea in his ear and a riding boot up his backside. Since reprimanding them hadn't worked, fining them was the next logical step. The younger lads didn't really earn enough to be fined, and so they were stopped from going racing instead. This approach reaped benefits, and before too long Stee had everyone producing the same standard of work. Some did so grudgingly at first, but they all toed the line in the end.

One day, sometime in 1996, Stee and a jockey called Billy Taylor went to Newmarket to take part in a stable lads' boxing event. Some stable lads might be on the small side, but the vast majority know how to look after themselves, and the two sports have been closely linked for decades. In fact, up until a few years ago, there was even a stable lads' boxing championship that used to attract an audience of thousands in its heyday.

Incidentally, one of racing's most famous pugilists – apart from Stee – is the great Clive Brittain. He used to box when he was an apprentice jockey and in 1950 he even got through to the finals – in the 5 stone 7 pounds division. Some of them used to go down to as low as 4 stone 7 pounds, apparently. That's about a third of a normal person!

I vividly remember Stee leaving for Newmarket because we'd been trying to decide if he would actually fight his opponent or just shout at him. In the end we settled on both. When Stee returned to the yard a few days later, we obviously asked for a blow-by-blow account of his fight but he was having none of it. He had something far more entertaining to tell us.

'Come on, how did you get on?' asked Crooky.

'We both won.'

'Take us through the fight then.'

'Na, bollocks to that. You wait until you hear this.'

I assumed that if a man had won a fight he'd be desperate to tell all, so this must have been good.

'Well,' began Stee. 'After our fights we went out on the lash, and after about ten pints Billy got talking to this lass. One thing led to another and, because the dirty little sod got off with her, I ended up going back to the digs on my own. I wasn't bothered, though. I got the room to myself.

'Anyway, at about four o'clock in the morning I got up for a piss, and when I got back into bed I heard a strange noise coming from outside the window. It sounded like somebody was climbing. I thought, I bet that's Billy.

'The landlady was a right cow and she'd told us that if either of us came back after midnight the door would be locked, and if we tried waking her up she'd call the police. She said she'd had her fill of pissed-up stable lads and jockeys getting her out of bed, and had decided to operate a zero-tolerance policy. Billy wouldn't have been banking on coming back before breakfast, so the only way in was through a window.'

This was already sounding more interesting than any fight; the initial audience of about five had now been joined by most of the rest of the yard.

'What happened next?' I asked.

'I'll tell you if you shut up long enough.'

I pressed my mouth firmly closed and waited to hear the next instalment.

'Because I was pissed I hadn't closed the curtains, so instead of getting out of bed to have a look I decided to stay put and see if it was him. About a minute later, his elbow appeared at the bottom left-hand corner of the window, so he was obviously shimmying up a drainpipe. We were only one floor up. At this point I could have got up and helped him, but I thought I'd watch the wally struggle instead. As long as there was a chance of him pulling a drainpipe off the front of the old cow's house and falling arse over tit onto her lawn, I was going absolutely nowhere.

'Once he was about waist-high to the window, he leant over and tried to open it. Luckily for him it was already ajar and so it slid up a treat. When the window was as far up as it would go,' said Stee, now acting the manoeuvre out, 'he grabbed onto the bottom of it with his left hand and then swung his left knee onto the ledge. He couldn't see me but I could see him and he looked like a right prat. After pulling on the window to make sure it could take his weight, he then pulled back and swung his right knee over before moving his right hand over to join his left. All he had to do now was duck his head and pull himself through.'

Everyone was agog by this time. It was better than renting out a DVD!

'The first part of the move went perfectly,' continued Stee, who was now having trouble containing himself.

'After ducking his head, I could see the little knob-head brace himself, count to three – one, two, three – and then pull himself forward as hard as he could. I hadn't noticed it, but the window had secondary glazing and so, instead of him flying forward and landing on the carpet, he head-butted a massive pane of glass full on. What a bloody noise!'

The memory of this particular juncture was too much for Stee, and he had to stop for a while and compose himself.

'Then what happened?' asked Crooky, who had tears of laughter in his eyes.

'He flew backwards a few feet and then fell back like a sack of shit. It was brilliant!'

After one or two half-hearted cries of concern about Billy's health, which Stee waved off, he continued.

'When I looked out of the window he was lying on his back in the same position he'd been in when he fell. I thought he was doing sit-ups! "What the hell happened to you then?" I asked him. "I couldn't get it up," he said. "Not many people can after twelve pints."'

This brought the house down.

According to Stee, as Billy sat rubbing his forehead, a downstairs light went on. Before Stee could suggest that Billy hide somewhere before making the ascent again, he had jumped up and run off into the night. He obviously preferred to walk the streets for a few hours rather than incur the wrath of the landlady and the local constabulary – and who can blame him?

When it came to pranks and practical jokes, the ones that took place while riders were mounted were obviously the most dangerous. The two I feared most were having my feet pushed out of the stirrups, which is obviously a lot of fun for the perpetrators, and having my bum whacked with a long stick. For the prankster, both these would be administered mid-canter, and while the first one would be designed to give the recipient a bit of a scare, or at worst a tumble, the second could put them in all kinds of pain, and could result in them spooking their own horses. Once that happened, they were no longer in control, and that's when it could get scary. Some people fell foul of this prank on numerous occasions, and nine times out of ten – fortunately – it turned out to be purely painful rather than dangerous.

I had been lucky in being a mere witness to all the pranks and practical jokes up to this point, but one day I was coming off Cross Banks, feeling smug that I'd avoided both the pheasants on the bridleway and the hares, and was looking forward to a run out. Just as I was going into a canter, though, *WHACK!* I felt a hard blow right across my bum. To be honest, that was probably the first time I had ever been hit on the arse before and, as well as my scream being ear-piercing, it was of course just inches away from the horse's ears. The next few seconds are a bit of a blur, but instead of either bucking me off or rearing up, the horse took off at full pelt. This, again, caught me unawares and, despite being less painful than being slapped across the arse, it was much, much scarier. However hard I tried, I just couldn't slow him down, and at one point I actually did a Penelope Pitstop and cried, '*Heylp!*'

Because I wasn't an experienced rider, I hadn't had too many opportunities to gallop. Talk about learning on the job . . . Now I could practise all I wanted, as this horse was absolutely not going to stop galloping, but in this predicament I got none of the exhilaration I might have expected to experience. I was too busy saying my prayers. When my horse eventually came to a halt about a mile away, I was shaking like a leaf, and very nearly collapsed from mental and physical exhaustion. It was then that I started feeling the pain again from the whack, which reminded me of how all this had started in the first place. I knew that the perpetrator was one of two people: Stee or Crooky. I still don't know which, because I never got a chance to look back, but they were definitely the only two people who weren't mounted, and they were the only people I could hear laughing as my horse careered off. Either way, they were definitely in it together, I was sure.

Although I'm certainly no pushover, I'm not often moved to anger, either, but at that moment I became incandescent with rage. Fearing for your life can do that to you.

'You complete and utter bastards!' I screamed, when I finally made it back to the Two Ronnies. 'I could have died on that horse.'

'No, no, no, that wouldn't have happened,' said Stee, nudging Crooky and shaking his head. 'You'd have died *off* the horse. Not on it.'

In hindsight, that was quite a good line, but at the time it passed me by completely. To me, Crooky and Stee were now officially the nastiest, most evil men on the entire planet, and I absolutely wanted them dead! It was the first and only time I ever lost my temper with them – publicly, at least – and whenever I saw them over the next few hours I gave them daggers and repeated my slur on their parentage.

'You really are a right couple of bastards. I could have died!'

'Hee, hee, hee.'

By the end of the day, though, the shock had worn off and I'd started smiling again, and by the following morning I'd even gone as far as recalling the episode in the tack room, much to everyone's amusement. I knew that if I'd carried on being angry with Stee and Crooky they'd have taken me to one side and told me to get over myself. It was a joke, and, rightly or wrongly, that's what people had been doing in yards for donkeys' years. It was a lesson both in how to handle a spooked horse, which I failed, and how to take a joke, which I eventually passed. These days such extreme pranks don't happen, and if they did they would probably result in a tribunal. To be honest, and without wanting to sound like a killjoy, I'm quite glad. It may only have been nineteen years ago, but it was a completely different era really.

Health and safety considerations haven't put paid to all the messing about, though. Other more innocuous pranks that are still practised today include burying people in the muck heap, having purple antiseptic sprayed either inside the front of helmets or around the inside of goggles, or putting dog poo in riding boots. Being thrown in the muck heap usually only happens to the stable lads, but everyone's considered to be fair game for the other pranks. Except the trainer, the assistant trainer or the head lad or lass, of course. It's supposed to be a bit of fun, not professional suicide.

The boots prank, which mercifully I've only been the victim of the once, took place in the tack room sometime during my first winter, and is still one of my least favourite memories of all time.

I was chatting away to Rachel, I think, and as I put my foot into the left boot I felt it sink into something soft and a bit liquidy. Then, just as I was pulling my foot out, the smell hit me like a freight train – a freight train that was covered in dog poo! At first, I screamed, and then, just as I put my foot back on the floor, I was very, very sick. That's when I heard the laugh. 'Hee, hee, hee, hee.' I should have known it. It just had to be him!

Ninety-nine per cent of practical jokes in yards are carried out by stable lads, or, in our case, the head lad! Stable lasses will sometimes get involved in a prank, but they're rarely the instigators. The only prank I ever got involved in was putting a dead rat at the bottom of a bucket, covering it with feed and then asking somebody to go and empty it into a bowl inside a box. This was a year or two after I joined. The bowls are about 5 feet high and so the lucky soul got a nice close-up of the rat as it fell out of the bucket. I was skulking outside when it happened and the scream was blood-curdling. The victim was a stable lad, by the way, not a lass, which made the scream even more impressive. The whole thing worked like a dream.

Before arriving at Micky's yard, the only aspects of the job I hadn't bargained for at all (apart from the practical jokes) were what a huge impact the equine injuries and – in the worst cases – deaths would have on me. In hindsight I wish to hell somebody had warned me. As a person who openly adores horses, it was an appalling baptism of fire, and started to become a reality about two months after I arrived. While mucking out one morning I overheard Micky, Stee, Crooky and Jedd talking about a horse called Clay County. He definitely wasn't one of our current residents and, even though they were talking about him in the past tense, it didn't register with me that he might be dead. The conversation was full of nostalgia and enthusiasm and I assumed that he'd either been retired or was in a different yard. Either way, he sounded like a hell of a horse.

When they all went their separate ways, I ran after Micky to find out more.

'Micky, what happened to Clay County?' I asked.

'He's dead,' he replied sadly. 'We lost him about three months before you arrived.'

For a moment, I was dumbstruck. I didn't know what to say.

'I don't suppose they tell you about this kind of thing at racing college,' he said carefully, obviously realizing I'd been taken by surprise.

'Erm. No, they don't. It had never occurred to me.'

The look on Micky's face was slightly pained, as if he'd broken some bad news to somebody unawares. I suppose he had, in a way.

'Come up into the office,' he said. 'I think we need to have a chat.'

As I followed Micky up the stone stairs into his office, my stomach began to lurch. I didn't know what he was going to say. All I did know was that it was probably going to be quite harrowing.

'Right then,' he began. 'How are you getting on?'

This also took me a little bit by surprise.

'Erm. Fine, I think.'

'Crooky says you're doing well. A bit slow mucking out, mind you.'

Micky sat behind his desk and waved me to the chair in front of it.

'Look, Gemma,' he said heavily. 'This isn't the first time I've had to have this conversation and I dare say it won't be the last. I'm afraid that death is something that you have to learn to accept in this industry.'

Although I found the conversation upsetting, it was something that had to happen, so I sat up and tried pulling myself together.

'Could you tell me about Clay County?' I said eventually. 'I know he's dead, but I want to hear the full story.'

'The full story?'

'Yes please.'

'The end isn't pretty, Gemma,' said Micky.

'As you say, it's something I need to learn to accept. All horses die. I know that. I also know that some of them die either racing or in the yard. It had just never really occurred to me until you told me about Clay County. It sounds like he was a great horse, though.'

This seemed to galvanize Micky, and all of a sudden the atmosphere changed.

'Clay County was the best two-mile chaser I've ever had,' he said, obviously reliving a moment in time. 'In fact, for the whole time we had him, he was the best horse in the yard.'

'What was so special about him?' I asked, latching on to Micky's enthusiasm.

'Well, for a start he was a thrilling horse to watch. One of my all-time favourites.'

'Why?'

'Simple. He used to stand off his fences. Do you know what that means?'

'Yes. It means they take off well before they get to them.'

'That's right,' said Micky. 'Very few horses have the confidence to do that. It's a very special talent.'

Once again, this was something I'd never properly appreciated before, despite already having watched hundreds of races live and on TV. I could obviously imagine it, though, and quickly started trying to think of any other horses that did it.

'The last jockey to ride Clay County before he died came up to me after the race and said, "This is why I do what I do, Micky. What a ride!" Never lose sight of the positives, Gemma,' said Micky, smiling. 'Sometimes you have to look hard for them, but they're always there.'

The end of Clay County's story obviously had a very different tone to it, but as Micky said, it was something I had to get used to. I wasn't looking forward to it, but as Micky continued I tried my best to remain composed.

A few days after that last race, Stee, who looked after Clay County, had opened his box door one morning to find him lying on the floor. The poor boy had suffered a twisted gut and was close to death. Horses are prone to this kind of thing, and it often starts off with colic, which is a general term for gastrointestinal conditions. To try and ease the pain the horse will often roll around on the ground, but unfortunately that can make it worse and often results in a twisted gut. If that happens the results are usually fatal.

Stee and Jedd had rushed Clay County to the equine hospital in Liverpool, but before the vets could operate, he died. Time's a great healer, but his death had obviously left a big hole in the yard and because I was now consciously aware of the fact that suffering casualties was part and parcel of yard life, I began to appreciate how often people talked about them. Not just about how they died, but about how they behaved and what they achieved – like you would a child, I suppose. Every idiosyncrasy would be covered in these conversations, and every time a new horse arrived in the yard, it would be compared to at least one previous resident.

'Flipping heck. He pulls worse than Wise Advice! Nice horse, though. Looks a bit like Norman Conquest.'

'Aye, I bet he's not as daft though!'

One of the saddest stories I ever heard at Tupgill

happened before I arrived, and concerned a four-year-old bay gelding named Reluctant Suitor. He'd been owned by an Italian Geordie called Joe Buzzeo and, according to Jedd, he had the sweetest nature imaginable. He just loved everyone.

One day, back in December 1994, Reluctant Suitor had been running in a novice chase at Doncaster, and with two fences to go he was upside one of Howard Johnson's horses going absolutely hell for leather. He'd only been out six times before that, but already had two firsts and a second to his name. According to Jedd he had bags of talent and loads of promise.

As he went over the next fence, which was a cross fence, Reluctant Suitor hit the orange bar. The sad irony here is that the orange bar is meant to help the horses focus on how high they must jump but in this case, it broke one of his hind legs. Because of all the adrenalin that was pumping through his body, Reluctant Suitor tried to keep on running. It was another furlong or so before the jockey managed to pull him up, by which time he was obviously in a real mess. Within a few minutes the screens had been pulled around him and he was destroyed. This can obviously happen anywhere, so if a horse falls in front of the stands, that's where the vet will be called to. It's something that nobody at a race meeting ever wants to see.

Reluctant Suitor had been looked after by Stee, and when he and Jedd first told me the story they welled up and I cried like a baby. It doesn't happen these days, but back then the groom would sometimes hold the horse while it was being destroyed; but as much as Stee wanted to be there for him, he just couldn't bring himself to do it. Jedd stayed with him instead and Stee went back to the box. Believe me, there is nothing more demoralizing than travelling home from the races in an empty horsebox. Nothing. It's the worst feeling in the world.

A few years ago, we took two horses up to Ayr and both died at the same meeting. I'd rather not go into detail out of respect for the two owners, but I was driving the box that day and, had I been on my own coming back, I can't say for sure that I wouldn't have driven it into a wall. There's no need for exaggeration or poetic licence. That's the truth. This was loss on a grand scale and I must have cried for about two weeks afterwards. Those positives Micky had mentioned were suddenly all too elusive and the experience hit all of us very, very hard. Some people don't get over things like that and, if and when people do leave the industry, you'll find that loss is quite often a contributing factor.

But I'm determined to finish this chapter on a high note, so this is the story of one of the most random horses that ever walked the earth. His name was Norman Conquest and he was a great big chestnut gelding. Normally he was quite a docile animal, but occasionally he'd do something that would make you think, *How on earth are you ever going to win a race?*

To be fair, Norman Conquest was just the latest in a long line of randomly behaved horses. Apparently one of his predecessors, a horse called Burn Bridge, had once approached a birch fence while being schooled and, instead of clearing it, as was expected, he actually stopped and started eating the bloody thing!

There's a big pond up at Tupgill Park that's close to the yard and, one morning as a string of about ten of us were heading off to the gallops, suddenly, and without any warning whatsoever, Norman Conquest left the string and ran straight into the middle of the water. His poor rider, who would rather not be named, hadn't been able to do a thing about it, and now Norman Conquest was in the pond he obviously had no intention of moving. He just stood there, knee-deep in water, looking really pleased with himself! The look on the lad's face was an absolute picture – a mixture of shock, indignation and despair – and, as hard as he tried to move his stubborn steed, he simply would not budge. He was stranded! It was only once Norman Conquest had decided he'd had enough and finished his paddling that they eventually rejoined the string. Needless to say, the lad was reminded of the incident for many years to come.

Oh, sod it. The lad in question was Jedd O'Keeffe.

8

Getting the Wind Up

Once I was up to speed in the yard and had started to prove my worth as a horsewoman, I was put to work on some of the other tasks. One of the most frustrating of these was breaking horses in, and my very first experience left me a nervous wreck. The animal in question was called Joe di Capo and, despite the fancy name, he was actually as dull as dishwater. 'Numb and dumb' would be the best way to describe him.

Ernie Peterson, who worked with Micky part time, showed me how to hold the lunge rope and the whip, and how to encourage Joe di Capo to trot round me in circles. That's basically what lunging is and, although Ernie made it look and sound quite simple, I quickly realized that if the horse you were lunging wasn't interested, you could be in it for the long haul. Joe di Capo was a testament to this, and it took me the best part of a day just to get him to walk a few circles.

Unbeknownst to Ernie and me, Joe's indifference in the lunge ring was masking a rather different characteristic. The roller is what we put on horses to get them used to wearing a saddle and, when we first got it on him, he started grunting and mooing like I don't know what.

'At last,' I said. 'I thought you were actually dead.'

Although it was just a joke, those words very nearly came back to haunt me, because instead of calming down he put his feet together and started bouncing off the ground. That's called humping in the equestrian world, and the more he did it the more terrified I became. This was just for starters, though. After humping for about thirty seconds, he then bolted and – at a full gallop – ran straight into a drystone wall. By this time I was almost in hysterics and, as I ran over to him, I could hear myself starting to scream. The poor boy had completely smashed open one side of his skull; his eye socket was a complete and utter mess and there was blood absolutely everywhere. Until then Joe di Capo had hardly done a thing. In fact, he'd been a complete and utter pain in the bum. Then, out of the blue, he becomes a flipping kamikaze pilot!

That was easily the scariest thing I'd seen thus far, and I don't mind admitting that it scarred me for quite a while. Ernie said he'd never seen anything like it before, and he'd been working with horses for decades. He was the most experienced horseman I knew at the time, and when I saw how shocked he was, I almost fainted.

Extraordinarily, though, the horse made a full recovery. In fact, he even went on to win a race or two. But I couldn't go anywhere near him after that. Unfortunately, you can't legislate for those kinds of incidents, but by the same token you can't go through life expecting them to happen. Racehorses can be massively unpredictable, and we just have to live with it. They are thoroughbreds, at the end of the day.

Some horses take to schooling easily, whereas some, like Joe di Capo, end up taking against it. Or, at least, parts of it. It's all about repetition ultimately, which is what makes the job so tedious. That said, I much prefer tedious to completely unpredictable.

These days young horses are handled so much better than they were, say, thirty or forty years ago. Back then they were kept in a field until they were four and then brought in and expected to take to wearing a saddle, a head collar and having a bit in their mouth. These days, horses will wear a rug, a bridle and have a bit in their mouth from a very early age, and it pays dividends later on. They're also constantly being led from field to stable and back, so by the time they arrive at a racing yard they're ready to be trained. Although there is something quite romantic about the idea of allowing horses to live almost wild for their first few years, fundamentally we want to train a horse to win races, and so the less time we have to spend schooling it, the better. Horses are like humans in that respect: the later you leave it, the harder it is.

As mentioned earlier, colts are by far the worst when it comes to personal hygiene and toilet etiquette. Everything goes absolutely everywhere! In jump racing, colts very rarely feature, as the parts of the body that stop them from being a gelding tend to catch on the jumps, if you see what I mean. As a jump yard that also has a few flat horses, we might just see the odd one occasionally, but they're few and far between. It's only when we're asked to break in a batch of flat horses that we might get more than one or two colts in the yard. The first time that happened was in December 1998, just before the festivities started. What a Christmas present that was. A bunch of badly behaved teenagers with enough testosterone between them to fill a milk tanker!

I think there were four colts in this batch, and one of them was called George the Best. He was every inch a colt and would regularly cause havoc on the gallops.

'He's done it again, Rach,' I remember hearing Stee say one day.

'Who, George the Best?' replied Rachel. 'Aw, you're joking aren't you? How many this time?'

'There must have been at least fifteen.'

'Fifteen!'

Although I remember hearing this conversation, I was about to go out with the second lot and so didn't have time to ask what he'd done. I wouldn't have to wait long to find out, though.

'Stee's had to go racing, Gem,' Micky said the following morning. 'And George the Best needs to go out with the first lot. Take him, would you?'

'Yeah, of course.'

Until then George the Best had always been as good as

gold for me, so I wasn't that worried. He was due to race the following week, so Micky had told me to take him up to the High Moor. There's a large racetrack-shaped gallop up there that runs for about a mile and a half, and it had quickly become one of my absolute favourite places. For a start, the views from the gallop are absolutely astonishing, and if you walk up to nearby Penhill, which is the hill that separates Coverdale and Wensleydale, you can see all the way to Sutton Bank on the North Yorks Moors.

But what made the gallop on the High Moor really special to me was finding out that it had once been used for race meetings. It was Crooky who'd given me the history lesson and, if memory serves me correctly, the meetings had taken place from the mid-eighteenth century until the latter part of the nineteenth.

Apparently everything was going swimmingly until the local 'gait owners', who were the landowners who had grazing rights on the High Moor, fell out with the trainers, and from then on it was used exclusively as a gallop. These days both the High Moor and the Low Moor are owned by Middleham Council, and the trainers have an agreement with them whereby they pay a daily fee for each horse that uses them. I think it's about £1.50.

The only physical remnants from the High Moor's days as a racecourse are what are called the Rubbing Houses, which are basically stables. They were used as part of an old training method called the Yorkshire Sweats. Back then a horse might run four or five times in a day, and so in between each heat they'd be taken to the Rubbing Houses, where they'd have their sweat removed before being wrapped in blankets. It all sounds a bit convoluted to me so no wonder it became obsolete.

Anyway, just as George the Best and I were making our way off the grass gallop, I spotted a string of about twenty of Mark Johnston's horses heading our way. For some reason George started getting a bit jumpy when he saw them, so I tried leading him the other way.

'Come on, George,' I said. 'Let's get you to safety.'

Unfortunately, he had no intention of diverting his course, and because he was still moving forward I had this horrible feeling he was going to try and skittle the oncoming string. Now it all made sense! The conversation yesterday: 'He's done it again!' 'How many?' 'Fifteen.' It dawned on me finally that Stee had been talking about a string of horses.

Before I could do or say anything else, George tensed up, turned himself sideways, neighed a few times, as if to say, 'Oncomiiiiiing!' and then set off. He was either very, very nervous of the string, or he just fancied a bit of fun. Either way, I was horrified.

'What the hell are you doing?' I screamed. 'Oh my god! *Loook oooooout!*'

Within a few seconds pandemonium reigned. As Mark's horses and riders all scattered, I tried shouting out an apology. 'Sorry! He's not normally like this.'

'Yes he bloody is,' cried one of Mark's riders. 'The same thing happened yesterday!'

Give me a nice, quiet gelding any day of the week.

I always knew that the weather in Middleham would be more extreme than the weather in Leeds, and although the most obvious differences would be things like snow and freezing temperatures, it was actually the wind that I found the most alarming.

'High winds are more challenging than the rest of the elements put together,' Micky had once said on a particularly windy day on the High Moor. 'Short-arses have to be really careful, so just watch yourself, Gemma. You think horses are unpredictable? Mark my words. Wind is a lot worse.'

Imagining it was one thing, seeing it in the flesh something else entirely, and in February 1999 I witnessed what is still one of the most bizarre accidents I've ever seen.

It happened on the all-weather gallop, which is on the Low Moor, and involved a young stable lass who was working for Mark Johnston. As well as scaring the living daylights out of everyone, it resulted in the gallop being closed for the day, something that had happened just a handful of times in well over two hundred years.

Middleham Moor, as beautiful as it undoubtedly is, is almost totally exposed, so when the wind is at its most malevolent, anything can happen. In many ways it reminds me of the sea; if it wants to take you out, it will. Catching you unawares is what makes the wind dangerous up there, and this poor lass, who can't have weighed more than about six or seven stone, fell victim to it big time.

The wind that day was bad, I remember, but the day before it had been stronger and more consistent and, because that had been such a talking point, we'd perhaps been lulled into a false sense of security. The difference was that the previous day the wind had been easterly, which is the direction the gallops go, so although it had been fierce at times we more or less knew what we were dealing with. Today the wind was northerly, but it was gusting and erratic.

I'd actually just dismounted at the time of the accident and was about to talk to Micky, who was in his jeep. There'd been a slight problem with the horse I was riding and he'd asked me to fill him in. I remember seeing the passenger window come down so I could talk to him but, just before I started to speak, a gust of wind came out of nowhere. Even the jeep seemed to lurch sideways, and for the next ten seconds or so chaos reigned. The horses nearby, who were either cantering or walking, were all thrown in the same direction, but fortunately they managed to stay on their feet. The riders also managed to stay in the saddle, except for this one girl. She was going at a nice steady canter when the gust came and, as her mount swung sideways towards the rail, she flew into the air, had the reins pulled out of her hands and landed on the other side of the rail. She must have been in mid-air for at least four or five seconds.

Fortunately she was unharmed, but it's still one of the most alarming things I've ever seen in my life. It seemed almost supernatural – like something out of *Poltergeist*. Everyone agreed that it was just too dangerous to carry on under these conditions, so after checking again that the girl who'd fallen, or should I say flown, was OK, we cleared the gallop, and everyone went back to their yards. We were all used to having eventful mornings up there, but that was just extraordinary.

Once the wind had finally finished with us, the rain made what can only be described as a very successful comeback. The average temperature also dropped from about three or four Celsius, which is bearable, to around freezing. According to Stee, the only way to get through this kind of weather was to put your head down and get on with it.

'If this lasts we'll lose three members of staff by March,' he said. 'And I know exactly who'll go.'

For once I actually don't think he meant me, which was refreshing. His prophecy did scare me a bit, though, and I prayed that this cold and wet spell would come to a quick end.

It didn't.

The first time I felt its wrath was on a Monday morning. It bloody would be! When I went out with the first lot of horses I got very wet indeed, and by the time we were ready with the second lot it had started to freeze.

'Why didn't you try drying yourself out in the tack room?' asked Rachel.

'I'd need about three hours!' I said. 'I didn't have time. Have you got any spare gloves? Mine are soaking.'

'I'm afraid not.'

By the time we got to the gallops again I'd started feeling the effects of the change in temperature. My hands, which had been sodden since about six o'clock in the morning, were starting to ache painfully. Although I hated every solitary second of this, there were some who had it far worse. In fact, during that first week of torrential freezing rain, I saw at least five people crying on the gallops, lads and lasses. The conditions you can deal with. They can be depressing at times, but you get used to them. It's the pain that drives you to tears. Everybody reading this will have experienced aching hands before, but not while you're clinging to some reins and trying to control a racehorse for the fourth time that day.

Like all the ribbing and the practical jokes, that's another test of character, I suppose, and although we didn't lose three members of staff as Stee had predicted, we definitely lost one, whose parting words to me were, 'Sod this for a game of soldiers. I'd sooner work in a brothel.'

I was more stoic, but also a bit stupid. That same month I was cantering on the all-weather gallop on the Low Moor one day. As well as having forgotten my gloves, which had been warming by the electric fire, I was also not wearing any waterproofs. I think mine had been thrown out for some reason, probably by mistake, and instead of asking to borrow some, like any normal human being would, I carried on without.

As we were cantering up the gallop, all I could feel was a barrage of sleet hammering the side of my face. As I became wetter, I obviously became heavier. By the time we got back to the yard I must have weighed at least twelve stone and the left-hand side of my face was both numb and red raw. I'd never ridden out in sleet before and, on reflection, I don't think I was really much of a fan.

Crooky was his usual sympathetic self. 'Look at the state of you,' he said, laughing. 'You look like a beaver with a birth mark.'

'Get yourself into the tack room,' said Stee. 'The fire's on.'

When he said the fire, what Stee actually meant was the one electric bar we had between all twenty of us. That was how it was back then, but according to Micky it had been worse when he was an apprentice. A lot worse. For a start, nobody had things like waterproofs, and very few people even had gloves. How they coped, I have absolutely no idea. And there was no option to bugger off and work in a brothel. If you were an apprentice, the trainer effectively owned you, so if you wanted out you had to buy your way out.

How you were treated was down to which trainer you worked for, so it was a lottery, basically. Some of the trainers treated their staff appallingly, and I've heard stories from Micky and Crooky about stable staff living above the stables in rat-infested dormitories. Instead of giving them a meal in the evening, the head lad would just throw up some bananas and crisps, and whoever caught them ate.

When I started out, what kind of gear you had was down to your background more than anything else, and a lot of the kids who came from poorer circumstances didn't have anything; no waterproofs, no gloves, nothing. In fact, a lot of them would turn up with just a carrier bag containing some clothes and a few tins of beans. Thank heavens it's different today.

Bad weather is one of the few parts of the job that still makes me wince a little bit. Sitting here now, I can almost feel my face and fingers becoming numb. So the first few months of 1999 were not an ideal time for me to start doing road work. Road work is part of the schooling process and involves riding a horse on a road for several long sessions so they can get used to it.

The usual route we took was from Tupgill Park up to Carlton via a place called Melmerby, which is a couple of miles away. Melmerby's a sweet little hamlet with a population of about forty. Despite being classed as B-roads, some of the roads in Coverdale are barely wider than the bridle-way at Tupgill, and the majority are flanked by either thick gorse hedges or drystone walls. Behind the walls and hedges lie a multitude of small, irregularly shaped fields that are either used for grazing, silage or hay, and within them you'll usually find either livestock or an old disused barn. Sometimes both. Because they're so small and enclosed the wind tends to rattle down these roads like I don't know what, and sometimes it can take your breath away – not to mention your will to live!

Road work was one of the few tasks I actually dreaded. If you're on your own, which I often was, it can be really boring and, coupled with torrential rain and a force nine gale blowing in your face, you have the makings of some thoroughly miserable mornings. Plodding along in the dark before sunrise, and in the gloomy light that followed, began to really affect me, and I actually think I became a bit down for a time. Sometimes I had to be literally pushed out of the gates, and for a time I absolutely detested Crooky.

'But I don't want to go. I hate road work!'

'If you don't do as you're told, I'll put you in with Broadwater Boy and lock the sodding door.'

I did road work about two or three mornings a week. For the first fortnight or so, I didn't really notice my surroundings at all – partly because the terrible conditions meant I couldn't always see very much, but also because I was lost in my downbeat thoughts much of the time.

Then, one bitterly cold February morning, when I was about half a mile up the road from Tupgill, I suddenly heard in the distance the shrill, urgent call of a barn owl. On any other day it would probably have scared me half to death – but that morning it tore through the cold, pessimistic monotony like a warm knife. It was a wake-up call, I suppose. Mother Nature reminding me how lucky I was.

I brought my mount to a halt and listened intently. 'Where are you, then?' I said, trying to peer through the deluge of rain. Suddenly it called again. It was ahead of me somewhere; somewhere on the left. As I rode on I saw the outline of an old stone barn, and shortly before I reached it the owl called again. Now it was louder than ever. This confirmed its whereabouts, and as I ordered my mount to walk on slowly, I looked expectantly to the left. Despite the sun being reluctant to make a full appearance, there was still enough light for me to see more than just a silhouette.

Although the barn was obviously now disused, it appeared to be in good condition and, through the hatch at the top, which had once been covered by a door and was where they deposited the hay, I could see a beam that led widthways from one side of the barn to the other. The barn itself must have been at least a hundred and fifty years old and there are similar structures the length and breadth of the Dales.

As I continued staring at the oak beam, I suddenly noticed the owl, which was perched at the end farthest away from me. Right on cue it confirmed its presence by letting out another call.

In Middleham we tend to see little owls and tawny owls mainly, but up towards Tupgill you always get a lot of barn owls. I'd heard dozens since I'd arrived, but this was the first time I'd seen one in the flesh. Despite my excitement I was well aware that barn owls are extremely shy creatures, and so I moved on as quickly and as quietly as I could.

For the rest of that winter, whenever I had to do road work, I prayed that I would see or at least hear the barn owl. It never let me down. The task itself was still a right pain in the bum, but those few special seconds leading up to and then passing that old barn transformed it from a despair-inducing bind into an absolute privilege. It made me feel so grateful.

About two years ago I found myself riding up that way one afternoon and, as I passed the bottom of Tupgill Park, it all came flooding back to me: the hours and hours of monotonous road work made truly magnificent by a shy but stunning bird and a barn that seemed as old as the dale in which it sat.

As the barn finally came into view, I felt energized and inspired, just as I had all those years ago, and with the prospect of actually seeing it again a certainty, I tightened my reins slightly and ordered my mount to trot. When we were about a hundred feet away I noticed that the outline of the barn seemed different somehow. I pulled my mount back to a slow walk, part of me actually dreading what I might see. My dad had once said to me, 'Never go back, Gemma. Whatever you do, never go back,' and at the time I hadn't realized what he meant. Now I did.

As I finally came into line with the barn, my worst fears were confirmed. The roof, which had always seemed fine to me, had fallen in completely, and the only thing that remained intact, apart from the four walls, was the beam. Even that had started to collapse, and the far side, where the owl used to sit, was now resting on a protruding stone about a metre below, looking as if it was clinging on for dear life. There was no barn owl, of course, and as I realized that the owl too must be a thing of the past, without warning I just burst into tears. I felt heartbroken.

Fortunately, it didn't take me long to realize that life goes on, and I could appreciate a certain beauty even in that run-down old building. If Dad had been there he'd have said, 'Come on, Gemma love, get a grip. And what the bloody hell were you doing going back?'

9

A Day at the Races

A trip to the races is the fruit of all our labours and is ultimately where we're all judged: horses, jockeys, trainers, stable staff. And it doesn't matter what you aspire to be, the first time you go to the races as a stable lad or lass is something you'll remember for the rest of your life.

The first horse I ever took to the races was a stunning Irish-bred bay gelding called Stash the Cash, who, by the time I arrived on the scene, already had about forty or fifty races under his belt. Or under his girth, to use the correct terminology.

He was another yard favourite, and Rachel and Stee in particular used to love riding him out. If he'd been a child, Stash the Cash would definitely have been diagnosed with having Attention-Deficit Hyperactivity Disorder, as it was impossible for him to do anything at a normal pace. At the yard that wasn't a problem. In fact, it was downright funny sometimes. I'm not sure if I'm the only person who does this (I hope not), but if a horse is behaving in a way that I can associate with humans, I often find myself putting words into the horse's mouth, so to speak. For example, whenever I used to muck out Stash the Cash he would fuss around like I don't know what, and it was as if he was saying, 'Right! Are you supposed to be mucking me out? OK, well you'll have to be quick. The poo is mainly over there and the wee is all over the bloody place. OK? Come on then, chop-chop!'

The only time this became a problem, for me, at least, was when I started riding him out. Not surprisingly he used to pull like mad, and preventing him from taking me half-way across the county seemed nigh on impossible. After a while this became a bit of yard joke, and whenever I set off to the gallops, Stee or Micky would say, 'When you get to West Witton, get us a copy of the *Racing Post*.' There used to be a pecking order, by the way, as to which horses you were given to look after. The girls who were decent riders always got the horses who behaved well, the lads got the rascals, and us newbies shared everything else. These days it's obviously bespoke, with each horse being given the most appropriate rider, but back then it was a bit more formulaic.

When it came to us being sent to the races, I was top of the list once I'd found my feet. Half of this was down to aptitude, and the other half was down to ineptitude. We'll start with aptitude, if you don't mind. Because of my experience with show ponies, I knew how to turn a horse out. And, because I was young and keen, I was always punctual. Good start. Now let's get on to ineptitude. That's simple really. If you're a strong rider in a yard full of horses, you're as close as you can possibly get to being indispensable. After all, the horses are there to be trained, and so if a trainer needs to lose somebody for the day he'd rather lose an inexperienced rider who can only take out two or three lots rather than somebody who can take out six or seven. I wasn't proud. I knew I'd become an experienced rider eventually, and if they wanted to send me off to the races in the meantime, then who was I to argue? Whatever's best for the yard, that's my motto.

When I first started at Micky's, we had a total of eighty horses with us. Forty-five of those were up at Tupgill and the rest were at the Sharp Hill Farm stables, owned by Kate Walton. That was a full quota for us, and so experience was at a premium. Kate, who is a successful racehorse trainer in her own right, has been involved in the business all her life and is the daughter of the late, great Sam Hall. Sam was yet another Middleham training legend and although he died at just fifty-eight back in 1977, he'd already trained well over a thousand winners, and had won the Ayr Gold Cup, three Ebor Handicaps, five November Handicaps, the Lincoln Handicap and the William Hill Gold Cup. It's an amazing record. Twenty or so years on, we still keep roughly half of our horses up at Kate's farm.

The first time I was told I was going to the races was a few months into the job. It was Crooky who broke the news to me.

'You're off with Rachel and the travelling head lass this

coming Thursday,' he said. 'You're only there to help out, mind you, so make sure you take it all in. She'll show you the ropes.'

I didn't want to collapse into a small excited heap, so my response to Crooky's news was bordering on nonchalant. It was the only way I could control myself.

'Yeah, fine,' I said, barely even making eye contact.

I more than made up for this when I got back to my digs. The first thing I did was run to the telephone box across the road and phone Mum and Dad.

'Mum,' I screamed. 'Guess what? I'm going to the races!'

'That's nice,' said Mum, sounding slightly confused. 'You have been before, though, dear. Remember?'

'No, you don't understand. I'm going to the races as a *stable lass* – with the racehorses!'

I'm not sure Mum fully understood the significance of this moment in my career, but to me it was a real milestone.

Having a horsebox is sometimes like being involved in a kind of industry-wide car-share scheme and, as well as sharing rides to and from the races, trainers also tend to share stable staff. For instance, if Trainer A has one runner at Catterick and one runner at Newcastle, and Trainer B has one runner at Newcastle, Trainer A will send his horse up to Newcastle in Trainer B's horsebox and use his own box to take his other horse to Catterick. Suffice to say that cooperation is the name of the game. Cooperation, and confidence. A trainer will only send a horse in another trainer's box if he knows it's going to be looked after, and so the sooner you get some experience under your belt and build a reputation, the better.

These days some of the kids who come to us from racing college have never even been to a racecourse. How strange is that? To me this simply emphasizes the yearning these people have to work with horses, regardless of the end product, and reminds me once again how unique the job is. After all, how many aspiring footballers have never been to a football match?

My first meeting as a stable lass was taking place at Hexham, in the beautiful county of Northumberland.

Obviously the final destination dictates what time of day we set off, but this small detail was irrelevant to me – I used to get told off all the time for coming in too early. Once again, part of this was down to aptitude, in that I was always punctual, and part down to ineptitude, in that I was always very slow at mucking out and so the sooner I got started the sooner we could set off.

Stee was always first in at the yard; when he saw me waiting outside the gates, he had one simple question for me.

'Shit the bed?'

'No, I did not!' I said indignantly. 'You know there's a lot to do.'

'Calm your jets, will you?' he said compassionately. 'You've got hours yet. First job. Get the kettle on.'

Hayley, who was the travelling head lass, had got all the gear ready such as the tack and the rugs, and once I'd finished mucking out and feeding I packed everything into the box. A travelling head lass or lad, by the way, is basically in charge of all the trips to the races. As well as doing the majority of the driving, they're responsible for the welfare of both the horses and the grooms. Hayley had been at Micky's for about a year when I joined and, just like Rachel, she had dark hair and big brown eyes. I thought she was just a tiny bit scary when I first met her; she certainly didn't take crap off anybody. Once I'd packed the box, I got the travel gear onto Stash the Cash, made sure I'd packed the rugs, and then we were away. These days I'll sometimes go and have a kip on the back seat if I've been up early, but during those early trips I was far too excited. Sleep was for sleepy people and, to be honest, I was wired.

Rachel was coming to Hexham too, so I was in very good hands. Both she and Hayley had been good to me since I'd started at Micky's and I think they were amused by my enthusiasm, which even I could see was ridiculous.

As you're travelling to the course, whoever's in charge, though not the driver, obviously, has to fill in the transport forms. As Rachel was filling them in, she very kindly told me what she was doing and why. The first time I got to fill in the transport forms myself was a bit of a rite of passage and, as absurd as it probably sounds, to me it was like Christmas.

'Here Gemma, here's a standard transport form and a pen. Would you fill it in, please?'

'Just you try and stop me!'

One thing that improved immeasurably as a result of all

the form-filling was my spelling, but only thanks to people like Hayley and Rachel. Back then I was absolootly dredful at spelling and some of the journeys would turn into English-language classes. Rachel and Hayley knew what was coming, and after handing over the form, Rachel would look at me expectantly.

'Rachel,' I'd eventually say, at which point Hayley would start to laugh. 'How do you spell Musselburgh?'

'Well, Gemma,' Rachel would say patiently and parentally. 'How do you *think* you spell Musselburgh?'

'Errrrrm, M-U-S-S-L . . .'

'Wrong!'

It perhaps won't surprise you to learn that since leaving racing, Rachel has become a teaching assistant and, although she didn't know it then, I was her first pupil. Things could only get better after that.

When we were about halfway to Hexham, shortly after Rachel had filled in the transport form, I began to notice a very familiar smell.

'Can anyone smell horse poo?' I said, slightly reluctantly.

'I can usually smell nothing else,' replied Hayley.

'No, I mean *really* smell it. It's as if it's right under my nose.'

Rachel looked at me as if I was going bonkers. Maybe I was? The first thing I did was check the bottom of my boots, but they were clean. Well, not clean exactly, but they definitely weren't the source of the stink. Next I picked up my jacket, which was lying over my bag. Nope, that was fine too. The smell was stronger now.

'It must be coming from my bag!' I exclaimed.

Rachel was obviously watching this unfold and, as I picked the bag up, and went to open the zip, I heard her whisper something to Hayley. It sounded like, 'Oh no, not again.'

I'd packed my bag the night before, and inside were some trousers, some shoes, a blouse, toiletries and a jumper. That's what I'd been told to take, and the blouse, which was brand new and one of Dorothy Perkins' finest, had been the last thing to go in.

As I started pulling back the zip, the smell became horrendous, and when I finally plucked up the courage to pull open the bag, instead of seeing the lovely white blouse which my mum had bought for me just a few weeks before, I saw a huge pile of fresh horse manure.

'Stee!' I called out instinctively.

'Or Crooky,' countered Rachel. She was being loyal to her boyfriend and I admired that. She was right, though, it could have been either.

'Aww, what am I going to do now?' I said, staring at the mobile dung heap.

I looked up to see why there'd been no answer to my question, but both Rachel and Hayley were in fits.

'It's the oldest trick in the book,' said Hayley eventually. 'Don't worry. We'll be able to borrow some clothes for you. You'll be fine.'

'Pull over, will you, Hayley,' ordered Rachel. 'I think Gemma needs to deposit something in a hedge.'

Once we arrived at Hexham, the first thing I did was sign in. Like filling in my first form, it was a very special moment for me. These days racehorses are all microchipped, so their details are already logged. Back then they used passports, which gave a detailed description of the horse, and whoever was on the gate had to check each horse against the markings listed.

Back then, although it sounds unbelievable, it wasn't that uncommon for the groom or the travelling head lad or lass to load the wrong horse. Tim once did exactly that. It took me a while to talk him into letting me tell this story, so I'd better hurry up before he changes his mind.

To be fair to Tim, it was as much the travelling head lad's fault as it was his. On the day in question, just before they were ready to leave, the travelling head lad, who was called Martin, had instructed Tim to go and fetch the horse.

'Overoski,' he said. 'I think he's in box ten. Chestnut gelding.'

'Chestnut gelding' is the equivalent of the name 'Smith' in horse terms so, unless you were absolutely sure about the box number, which Martin wasn't, it was a disaster waiting to happen. Had Overoski been one of Tim's he'd obviously have realized if there was a different horse in box ten, but unfortunately he didn't. All he saw when he arrived at the box was a chestnut gelding, so in his eyes he was following orders correctly.

After arriving at the racecourse, the man on the gate did his checks against what was listed in the passport and, lo and behold, one of the horses was an imposter.

'Erm, excuse me,' said the man on the gate. 'It appears you've loaded the wrong horse. This isn't Overoski.'

'Eh?' said Martin. 'Of course it is.'

'I'm afraid it isn't. None of the markings match.'

'What? Oh shit! Are you sure you went to box ten, Tim?'

'Of course I am. There's a big 10 outside it!'

'Which horse have we got, then?'

'I don't bloody know! The wrong one, obviously.'

'Any idea who looks after it?'

'Joe's got a few on that side of the yard. He'll know. Try him.'

After a quick telephone call to Joe, who was obviously sworn to secrecy, it appeared they'd taken a horse called Barley Meadow.

'Overoski's in box twelve,' said Martin.

Apparently Barley Meadow was due to run at Catterick, which is where they were, but not for another two weeks!

'Right,' said Martin. 'We've got to get ourselves out of the shit. What time's the boss arriving?'

'He's going to Sedgefield first so he'll probably be here in about an hour and a half.'

'Really? OK, quick. Get him back on. If we hurry we can get back, do the swap, and be here before he arrives.'

Fortunately for Tim and Martin, Catterick is only about ten miles away from Middleham, and so a disaster was narrowly averted. Imagine if they'd been going to some-where like Ayr or Perth! It's too awful to think about.

In all seriousness, the consequences of taking the wrong horse to the races, should you be further away than Catterick and actually get found out, would be absolutely catastrophic – after the owner, the trainer, the jockey and the clerk of the course had finished with you, the chances are you'd have to change your name and move to a different continent!

Apparently, the man on the gate swore he wouldn't tell anybody about the faux pas, so imagine if it appeared in a book?

Once we were through the gates at Hexham, Rachel went off to declare the horse and hand over the jockey's colours. The first thing I did, after borrowing some clothes, was plait Stash's mane and tail. There's a prize for best turned-out horse, but some stable lads or lasses don't care about win-ning it and so, as opposed to plaiting, etc., they'll simply brush the horse down and then lead it out. The prize money can range from about twenty-five quid to over a hundred, but money was never my motivation. I would never turn it down, of course – I'm a Yorkshirewoman, after all! – but I was in it for the aesthetic mainly, and if a horse of mine ever failed to win best turned-out I was not a happy bunny.

Whenever the prize money is upwards of a hundred quid, the stable lads will sometimes offer to pay the plait-happy stable lasses to plait their horses up, with a promise of a share of the spoils if they win. We got an allowance of about twelve quid a day for going racing but an extra fiver, plus the possibility of a bit more, was always welcome. Some stable lasses would be daft enough do it for nothing and, unless they had a prior agreement in place with the stable lad, they rarely got a cut of the prize money. That used to drive me mad! Funnily enough, Stee was one of the few lads I ever worked with who could plait his own horses. In fact – and he'll love me for saying this – he was a damn sight better than Rachel.

Although he was gorgeous and had a lovely character, Stash the Cash was, not to put too fine a point on it, a bit of a sweaty mess, and so once I'd done his mane and tail I gave him a quick wash. This was in winter, so you can imagine what he was like in the summer!

After plaiting him and washing him down, I had a cup of tea and something to eat in the canteen and then got changed into the poo-free clothes I'd borrowed. After that I went back to the boxes, scraped all the sweat off again (I told you!), and then brushed him down.

As I left Stash's box, I couldn't help noticing all the different horseboxes parked up. The one that stuck out the most was an enormous blue horsebox that from a distance looked like a cross between an articulated lorry and a Winnebago. I was drawn to it like a car enthusiast would be to a vintage Ferrari and, when I got closer, I saw the word 'Godolphin' written on the side.

I bet that cost as much as a house, I thought.

Since 1992 Godolphin (who are based in Newmarket)

have had over four thousand winners, and they are the biggest producer of thoroughbreds in the world. It doesn't happen often, thank god, but when they decide to enter a horse somewhere like Hexham it causes a real stir.

When I found Rachel I told her what I'd seen.

'Oh god,' she said. 'What are they doing here? They haven't got one in our race, have they?'

'Why,' I said. 'What's the matter?'

'What do you think? They don't turn up just for fun, and you can guarantee that whatever horse they're running will have cost hundreds of thousands of pounds. *And* it will possess a rather illustrious parentage.'

Godolphin are known as 'The Boys in Blue' within the industry, and these days if I ever see one of their boxes turn up at a meeting I instinctively echo Rachel's words. 'Oh god! What the hell are you doing here?' Professional jealousy, I suppose.

As much as I admire the likes of Godolphin and all the big, rich industrial outfits, it's just not my thing. A couple of years ago a former jump jockey I knew saw me in a pub and, after saying hello, he asked me what I was doing.

'I'm still working for Micky Hammond,' I said.

'Really?' he replied. 'How sad.'

Before he could say anything else, and before I had time to kick him in the nuts, I decided to walk away. Some people make the rather annoying error of confusing loyalty or contentment with a lack of ambition, and this berk was a prime example.

If you work in a smaller yard, every single win, regardless of the prestige or the prize money, is like a group one. Once again, some people might confuse enjoying sharing the pleasure of winning with workmates and colleagues as lacking individual drive and competitiveness, but nothing could be further from the truth. As well as being addicted to speed, I'm also addicted to winning and, of course, that's prevalent throughout the industry. At Micky Hammond Racing we have some fantastic horses, some fantastic owners and some fantastic people working for us, and as well as being confident in our abilities, we are as ambitious and forward-thinking as the next yard. The difference is that unlike all the big outfits that have hundreds of horses and hundreds of people working for them, we're able to retain a family atmosphere. In my opinion, that makes for a much nicer working environment. I'm not saying we don't have issues. Of course we do. Also, because everyone tends to know everyone else's business, these can have more of an effect in a smaller yard than they would if they happened in a big yard. Familiarity can certainly breed contempt, but I'd far sooner be small and imperfectly formed than large and industrial. But it's each to their own, of course.

Back at Hexham, about half an hour before the saddle was due to go on, I put the bridle on Stash the Cash, led him out and let him stretch his legs for a few minutes before leading him up to the pre-parade ring. The pre-parade ring gives racegoers the opportunity to assess a horse's fitness and also helps the horse to remain warm and focused.

Before being gelded, Stash the Cash had been a half-decent flat horse and Frankie Dettori had won twice on him: once at Sandown and once at Newbury. Since being de-nutted he'd been even more successful, but hadn't won for the last eighteen months. A week earlier he'd had what's called a racecourse gallop around the track at Aintree, and the jockey who'd ridden him said he'd been awful. Since I'd been riding Stash he'd felt great, so I was gutted by the jockey's reaction. A racecourse gallop, by the way, is when you allow horses to run a course after a meeting, like a kind of dress rehearsal. Back then we never really worked them off the bridle so a racecourse gallop was a great opportunity.

Next up was the parade ring, and I'm not going to insult anyone's intelligence by explaining what that is! Even if you're not a racegoer, it's fairly self-explanatory, and it's something I felt nervous about but was also really looking forward to, in a perverse way. That sums up the whole day, really.

Walking Stash round the parade ring was the first time I had to face the public and, although they were going to be looking at Stash rather than me, it was still a nerve-wracking experience. Since the previous October the only people I'd really spoken to other than my colleagues were a vet, an owner and a couple of friendly walkers I'd met on the gallops.

There's usually a nice buzz of excitement in the parade ring prior to a race, and that first day at Hexham was no exception. The crowd surrounding the ring must have been three or four deep, and as Stash and I started our first lap I could hear people whispering to me, 'Is he fit?' 'What do you think his chances are?' Obviously I couldn't say anything so I just smiled and blushed. Best of all I heard one racegoer say, 'Look at that number two. He's pretty. She's done a good job with him.' I couldn't have been any prouder! You do occasionally get derogatory comments, but only from people you know. Sometimes family or friends might be in the crowd, and if that's the case you're almost guaranteed to get some stick. 'Those plaits are a bit wonky, aren't they?' 'Not very well turned out, that one.' Once again you can't say anything, but I have been known to fire off the odd evil stare. That's all the ammunition we can carry, unfortunately!

Once I'd led Stash the Cash around the parade ring a couple of times and had soaked up all the comments on how beautiful he looked (and he did), I handed him over to Micky, who was in the centre of the ring with his jockey that day, Brian Harding. Brian had recently won the Queen Mother Champion Chase at the Cheltenham Festival on a horse called One Man, and so to have him riding the first horse I'd taken to the races was a huge thrill. Although Brian had ridden Stash previously, it had been almost three years ago, and that time out he'd come second. Obviously I was hoping for one better this time, although to be honest I wasn't holding my breath.

After the parade ring the groom, as we're referred to on the day, will find somewhere to watch the race; in this case it was in a stand close to the finish line. I'd just found a place when the announcer told the crowd who had won best turned-out. The prize money on my first day was fifty quid and, guess what, I won! That was without doubt the proudest moment of my career so far and I still had the race to come. Going racing with Mum, Dad and Becky as a spectator had always been one of my favourite treats, but my involvement in proceedings took the experience to a different level. I still get the same feeling today. It's totally addictive.

Although the race started at the far end of the course, I watched it on the big screen and Stash was one of the last to set off. Bugger!

For the first ten fences, Stash was stuck firmly in fifth place and, after what the jockey had said about the gallop, I gave up hope. I wasn't too downhearted, though. It had been a fantastic day, and knowing there'd be more of this to come made the smile I'd been wearing all day feel like a permanent fixture.

After they'd jumped the second to last fence I was about to go down to the finish line when I suddenly realized that he was up into second place, and by the time he got to the final fence he was a length clear.

'*Come on Stash!*' I screamed. '*Come oooooooon!*'

I might be quite small in stature but I have a mouth like the Tyne Tunnel.

Somebody must have had some money on Stash, because the noise as he came over the line was absolutely incredible.

I remember welling up at this point, and the hairs on the back of my neck weren't just standing on end, they were doing a jig. It's hard to describe the feeling really. It was pure joy.

For the next few seconds I just stood there with my mouth open, trying to take it all in. Best turned-out – nailed it! The race itself, and the reason we were all there – nailed it! Because of the amount of adrenalin I had pumping through my body, I could have built a brand new racecourse there and then, but instead I had to settle for jumping up and down a few times. You know these animals inside out, and because you get so involved with them you often spend more time thinking and worrying about them than you do your own family. When I collected that horse from the finish line and led him towards the winner's enclosure, I felt like a proud parent. Fortunately, there were no TV cameras present, as if there had been they'd have recorded the fact that as well as feeling super-proud of my horse I was also crying my eyes out. How on earth could I not?

By the time we reached the winner's enclosure I'd just about sorted myself out, but when the crowd started clapping him it set me off again. A small teary mess leading in a large sweaty mess. What a pair!

The atmosphere in the winner's enclosure, regardless of race or meeting, is always warm and positive, and it's something I'd like to try and bottle one day. As well as the punters who've backed the winning horse, it also tends to attract the racing enthusiasts, and so socially it's just a great big love-in.

I do remember an exception to this general rule, however, when the atmosphere definitely turned a bit sour. Very sour, in fact. It was March 2000, and I was leading a horse at Bangor called Peradventure. Once again Brian Harding was the jockey, and as the 11/4 favourite we were expecting good things. Unfortunately, he got beaten on the line by a horse called Ashman. I can't remember the details but I'm pretty sure he just ran out of steam. Anyway, when we were in the winner's enclosure, which is where all the placed horses go after the race, not just the winner, some Welsh bloke who'd obviously bet his house on Peradventure started having a go at Brian, and even tried leaning over the rail and pulling him off the horse. I forget what he said exactly but, because this idiot wouldn't back off, Brian ended up whacking him with his whip! I was trying to hold on to the horse at the time and I was terrified. I was properly shaking. The security staff were on the scene pretty quickly, but not before Brian had given the bloke a mouthful and another whack. What a moron.

After smothering Stash with kisses, I gave him a drink and a nice long wash. He was so sweaty, bless him! After that I put a rug on him and then took him to the vet's box, which is where they test all the winners and any horses they think might have been got at, such as odds-on favourites who don't win or 100/1 outsiders who did. They are looking for a painkiller that might enhance performance or a sedative that might do the opposite. Fixing a race happens very rarely these days, but that's partly down to the checks.

Stables have to be so careful. Horses are often given a drug called Bute, an extremely powerful painkiller that's administered for a variety of knocks and injuries. It can stay in their system for anything up to two weeks so if a horse that's been given the drug is due to race within that time-frame, it's always best to withdraw them.

How long we hang around in the vet's box depends on how long it takes the horse to have a wee. Sometimes that can take a few minutes and sometimes it can take over an hour. Usually, if it's longer than an hour, they'll take blood instead, but if our horse was in the last race at Ayr and we've got a five-hour journey ahead of us, the hanging around can be torture. While the vet's wandering around the box with his pouch waiting for the horse to pee, we're peering over the box door willing it on. *Get a move on, will you? For heaven's sake, pee!*

Fortunately for us, Stash the Cash was busting for a wee, and we were in and out of the vet's box within about five minutes. We still waited for about an hour before leaving, though. It's best to give horses time to relax after a race, and it gives us time to groom them properly. It's often different with flat horses. If the horse has been in a five-furlong sprint and hasn't tried, then you can get out a bit sooner, but I'd far rather be there longer with a horse that's done well.

The drive from Hexham to Tupgill took about two hours.

Instead of winding down after a hard day's racing, Rachel and Hayley had to put up with a blow-by-blow account from me about exactly what had happened. They'd been there for most of it, of course, but I didn't care. I needed to vent, and vent I did! As with Micky after my first trip to the gallops, they took my enthusiasm with good humour and even managed to stay awake.

After putting Stash the Cash to bed, Rachel gave me a lift back to Castle House. The moment my head touched the pillow, I was gone. I think I must have had the best sleep ever that night because when I woke the next morning I felt brand new. I was in such a good mood and, bearing in mind it was dark, wet and cold, I must have been seriously annoying that day.

Back then it didn't matter what time you got back, you had to be at the yard at the normal time. In fact, the following week I went racing at Musselburgh and, even after getting back at one in the morning, I had to be up at about five. After feeding and mucking out all my horses I was off again to Perth. The bed in the back of the box was very welcome on the way up.

These days it's different, and if you get back from the races at arse o'clock in the morning you're always given time to catch up. Sometimes you might be racing four or five times in a week. That can be really hard sometimes, and it tends to separate the boys from the lads and the girls from the lasses.

They decided to draw stumps on Stash the Cash when he

was about eleven years old; as far as I know he went on to do some hunting. 'Draw stumps' is what retirement is known as in horse-racing circles; I've no idea why the cricketing analogy is used.

Ever since then, whenever something bad happens, I always use that first day at the races as a reminder of how wonderful life can be.

Somebody once told me that you should never meet your heroes, and this was proved to me a few months after my maiden trip to Hexham. The hero in question was the jockey Adrian Maguire, who, in addition to amassing over a thousand winners during a glorious career, had the dubious honour of being the first jockey Becky and I both liked, featuring prominently within our scrapbooks. One of the reasons we both liked him was because sometimes, if one of his horses was misbehaving, he'd ride in a kind of mushroom position. Becky in particular used to love this, and whenever a pony of hers misbehaved, she'd scrunch up and say, 'Look, I'm doing it like Adrian Maguire!'

The meeting in question took place at Newcastle Racecourse while I was accompanying a horse called Heidi III, who was actually a boy! He'd just won the Great Yorkshire Chase at Doncaster, which is a really good handicap race, and he was easily one of our best horses. Looking after him was a bit of a privilege, I suppose, although at times he could be quite difficult: as well as being a bit shy, he only liked being around certain people. When it came to the yard, that was either Stee or me, and nobody else got a look-in. Not that they'd have wanted one.

Heidi III was due to race in a Class B handicap chase and the jockey who was booked to ride him was . . . Adrian Maguire! When Micky told me I was cock-a-hoop. The race was going to be on Channel 4, so it felt like all my childhood dreams were coming true. A slight exaggeration, I suppose, but that's how it felt.

Heidi III had been second in the betting to a horse called Lannkaran, which was being ridden by Richard Johnson, and because it was so well fancied I didn't think Heidi III would have a chance. Fortunately for us, Lannkaran made a mistake about five furlongs from the finish and, even though Heidi III also made a few errors, he led at the last and managed to hang on. This was unbelievable! One of my favourite jockeys ever had just won on one of my favourite horses, and I was about to go and lead them into the winner's enclosure. Did I mention it was all being shown live on Channel 4? Life really couldn't get any better.

If TV cameras are present at a meeting, they always follow the winning horse from the finish line to the winner's enclosure, and these days they'll have a presenter in tow who'll interview the jockey as the groom leads the horse in. Back then they weren't allowed to interview the jockey until he or she had dismounted, and so on this occasion it was just a camera.

As they came in after the finish, I went to grab Heidi III,

but before I could offer Adrian my congratulations he started laying into me.

'Put that sweat sheet on, will you? Don't you know what the hell you're doing?'

I was mortified.

While all this was unfolding, a friend of mine called Geraldine had been watching at home. She used to work for a trainer called Ferdy Murphy, who was also based in Middleham, and years earlier Adrian Maguire had worked for him as a stable jockey. She knew Adrian of old, and when she saw him shouting at me on TV she went bananas. The following day she called Adrian at home, gave him what for, and then called me.

'I'm not having that,' she said defiantly. 'I tore a right strip off him! Having a go at you live on Channel 4. It's disgraceful!'

The thing is, Geraldine has quite a lethargic Cumbrian accent and I couldn't for the life of me imagine her tearing a strip off somebody. She obviously had, though, and the next time I saw Adrian at the races he came up and apologized. Very graciously, I might add. So all was well that ended well, and Adrian had earned his right to return to my scrapbook.

10

Middleham and Me

I loved working at Tupgill Park, so when I found out that the owner, a man called Colin Armstrong, had given Micky notice on the yard, I was heartbroken. Colin wanted to diversify into things like restaurants and tourism and with our yard being the first place you came to when entering Tupgill Park, it was the obvious place to develop. There were still three other trainers in situ, so for the time being its racing heritage would remain intact.

'We could never replace Tupgill,' I declared dramatically when Crooky broke the news. 'It's the most gorgeous place on earth.'

'What a load of bollocks,' said Crooky. 'We're completely surrounded by places like this, and if we move to the yard I think we're moving to, you'll be able to walk to work in about thirty seconds.'

Almost instantly my affection for Tupgill Park evaporated, and with the prospect of my commute being cut from ten minutes to less than a minute, all thoughts turned to the nearby sprawling metropolis of Middleham.

'Which yard?' I asked hopefully.

'Oakwood, I think. Walter Bentley's old yard. The one on the East Witton Road.'

Oakwood Stables, which is where we are based today, is on the road leading towards Masham and is about two hundred yards off the square. It's a bit smaller than the yard at Tupgill and, instead of having two long rows of stables, it has three shorter ones that run parallel and another row running across one end. At the other end of the stables sits Micky's house, and immediately in front of that, built into the middle row of stables, is the office, which is upstairs, and the tack room, which is below it.

Crooky's estimation as to how long it would take me to walk there from Castle House was wildly optimistic. It would take me at least two minutes.

A few days later the move to Oakwood Stables was confirmed, and because the vast majority of us lived in Middleham, everyone was thrilled. Since arriving I'd spent the majority of my waking hours at Tupgill, so as well as cutting my commute down, it meant I would finally have an opportunity to settle into the town properly and make it my home.

For someone who loves horses, Middleham is a Mecca. Racehorses have been trained in the area for just over two hundred and fifty years, and there are daily reminders of the town's history. The first man to train in the area was a former jockey called Isaac Cape, who is credited as being the first professional trainer in the history of horse racing.

He has a lot to answer for. Isaac first set up shop in 1765, and, like Micky, he started off at Tupgill. The yard Isaac Cape trained out of is where James Bethell is now based so, despite the yard's age, it's as busy and successful as it ever was.

One of the most successful trainers during that early period was a man called John 'Crying Jackie' Mangle. He'd been Isaac Cape's apprentice jockey, and used to cry whenever he lost. One day, after a blazing row with Isaac, Crying Jackie jumped ship to a trainer called John Hoyle who was based just around the corner at Ashgill Stables, where Crooky now trains. When Hoyle eventually died in 1786, Crying Jackie took over the yard and went on to pull off a remarkable hat-trick by both training and riding the winners of three St Legers in a row: Paragon in 1786, Spadille in 1787 and Young Flora in 1788.

In the years since then, we've had hundreds of trainers settle in and around the town, and between them they've won every major race in the country. Captain Neville Crump, who I mentioned earlier, turned out three Grand National winners from his stables and also trained five Scottish and two Welsh National winners. He died in 1997 aged eighty-six, and is buried in the cemetery surrounding St Alkelda's. Captain Crump's stables are now part of Mark Johnston's training establishment, so the quality of horses has obviously been maintained. Mark, who was actually a vet before he went into racing, had recently moved to the town from Lincolnshire where he'd had his first yard, and he was already making a name for himself when I arrived in the town.

One of the more established Middleham trainers back then was Chris Fairhurst, who had taken over Glasgow House Stables from his father Tommy, a local legend. Tommy served his apprenticeship under Dicky Peacock's father, Matthew – which is when he earned his nickname 'Squeak'. Back then a favourite initiation ceremony involved plunging the apprentices into a large water trough until they were on the point of drowning. Nice! I was always told that you had to make your own entertainment in those days, but I have to confess that I didn't think it involved waterboarding! When it was Tommy's turn, he squeaked as he hit the cold water.

Like the vast majority of stable lads, Squeak's initial ambition was to become a jockey, and on 20 May 1955 he rode his first winner for Captain Jack Fawcus on a horse called Chanlana. After five more winners for Fawcus, Squeak decided to go freelance; he had limited success, however, so he went to work as head lad and second jockey for the Tupgill-based trainer Ernie Weymes. Then, in 1969, Squeak finally took the plunge and embarked on what became a twenty-five-year career in training.

Based at Glasgow House Stables, which is right in the heart of Middleham and just a few yards from Castle House, Squeak started off with just a dozen horses. During his first year he trained eighteen winners. When Squeak finally handed over the reins to Chris back in 1993, he did so not only as one of the most popular racehorse trainers in the north of England, but as one of Middleham's favourite characters. That's the reason I've singled him out. Despite almost being drowned on his first day, Tommy 'Squeak' Fairhurst went on to be a success as a stable lad, a head lad, a jockey and a trainer and, in my opinion, he epitomizes the spirit that makes the people in this industry unique.

As embarrassing as I used to find the subject of men, I did actually have a boyfriend when I arrived in Middleham. I'd first met him when I was helping out Georgie in the town at weekends, and his name was Paul. He too worked in a yard but, because he shared digs with Georgie, I got to know him socially as opposed to professionally and we rubbed along OK. I certainly wasn't looking for a boyfriend, but when he asked me out one day I just heard myself saying, 'Yes.'

It was pretty low-key while I was in Leeds and at college, but once I was living in Middleham we started seeing a bit more of each other. It was still a fairly innocent relationship, though, and consisted of little more than having tea – as in dinner – at the Richard III pub. Back then it was called the Commercial Inn – or the Commie, to the locals – and 'tea at the Commie' once a week was about the closest we came to going out. Sometimes, if we were feeling daring, we'd ask Rachel to give us a lift over to the One Stop shop in Leyburn so we could rent out a DVD. So it was hardly *Love Island*.

Not long after moving yards, which happened in April 1999, I became friends with a local lad called Tim Hogg. As well as being Stee's brother, lucky bloke, Tim was also an aspiring jockey at the time, and was assistant head lad to a trainer called George Moore. He was about 5 feet 6 inches tall (a giant in Middleham), had blond hair, which I quite liked, and he smiled a lot. As well as being a few years older than me, Tim was also quite fit (do people still use that term?).

When Paul was away racing, Tim and I would get together for a drink. Nothing ever happened, but we got on really well. Our conversations, far from being a little bit stop-start, which they can be when you're young, often extended into the wee small hours as we yapped away to each other. That's not a good idea when you have to be up at five o'clock, but neither of us minded.

When Paul eventually left to work in Jersey and our relationship fizzled out, Tim suggested a date.

'Fancy going out one night?' he said one afternoon over a cup of tea.

'Suppose so,' I replied nonchalantly. 'What did you have in mind?'

The reason for my indifference wasn't because I didn't want to go out with Tim – far from it. It was because I was expecting him to suggest one of the following: a DVD from Leyburn, courtesy of our chauffeur Rachel, or tea at the Commie. As much as I enjoyed both, their charms had palled a little over time.

'Actually, I was thinking about something a bit different,' said a now slightly haughty and confident Tim.

'Really,' I replied, pretending to almost spit out my tea in surprise. 'Don't tell me. A bus to Hawes Dairy?'

'I was thinking of a tea room in Reeth. If you think you can handle the excitement?'

'Come on,' I urged him. 'What have you really got planned?'

When Tim suggested a double date at the pictures in Darlington followed by a KFC, my brain almost exploded. It wasn't programmed to take in such radical departures from the norm, and it took some time to process his proposal.

The two people lucky enough to be sharing in this momentous occasion were Simon West, who worked with Tim, and a girl I knew from home but who also worked in Middleham, Leanne Steade. They were already going out with each other, so actually it was a good idea, if a little bit wild and adventurous.

What I remember most about that night was the speed at which Tim ate his chicken burger. Apart from watching a horse gallop, it was the closest thing to perpetual motion I think I'd ever seen. He actually inhaled it! That was one of my first impressions of my future husband. When we arrived back in Middleham, Tim walked me back to Castle House. I think he was hoping for an invitation up to my room. Instead, he got a quick snog, a 'thanks very much for a lovely evening', and a pat on the bum. After that we were officially dating.

Despite being in a relationship with Tim, my life outside of work at this time was very sedate – a stark contrast to the lives led by the majority of stable lads and lasses. There was, and still is, a very healthy pub culture in Middleham; after closing time, stable staff would often pile into nearby Castle House. There were always lots of people living there and, even if none of them had been to the pub, there would usually be somebody who was up for a party. Having a room front centre meant that I heard everything that went on, and I mean everything! Some of it was downright filthy but, fortunately for me, I'm one of those annoying people who can sleep almost at will and irrespective of what's going on around me. Sometimes I'd stay awake, though, if something exciting was happening, like a big row. That used to happen a lot, not surprisingly, and some of them could get quite interesting. The lads would have rows about anything really – horses, football, girls or whatever – and they'd often result in a punch-up.

When it came to stable lasses, their rows were usually about the lads. They too could get a bit unruly at times (they still can), but after a slap and a bit of hair-pulling, they'd usually get split up. If ever there was a lad and a lass having a row, it would almost always be as a result of an accusation of flirting, or, best of all, infidelity! Sometimes the third party might be in attendance, and if that happened, things would go nuclear. They were like mini soap operas, I suppose, and I remember lying in bed some nights, clutching the hem of my duvet cover and shouting instructions at either a wall or the ceiling.

'Go on, just hit him. He's obviously been playing away.'

The best row I ever heard at Castle House was on a Saturday night. Because it was summer it was still quite light, even after the pubs had closed. Back then, summers in the Yorkshire Dales seemed to go on forever.

Because it was warm I had my window open, and at about eleven fifteen I could hear a row spilling out from one of the pubs. Here we go again, I thought. I'd become quite adept at recognizing the specifics of a row: how many people might be involved, who they were, and whether or not it might turn violent. This one was a proper barney! There must have been at least five or six people involved – maybe more – and my immediate instinct was to get out of bed, stick my head out of the window and find out what was going on.

Naaaa, I thought to myself. *I'd better not. If somebody saw me looking they might have a go at me.*

As the row carried on I lay in bed (bum touching the floor), closed my eyes and tried to tune into the commotion. It was quite far away still, so my internal radar told me that it had probably started inside the Black Bull, which was at the bottom of the square and the furthest pub away from Castle House, and had spilled out onto the road.

After I'd strained my ears for a few minutes, the noise seemed to get louder, and it soon became clear that those involved were now moving up the square towards Castle

House. Many of the digs in Middleham are based north of the town square, and so with any luck they'd go past me on their way home. God, how exciting! *Emmerdale* had nothing on this.

By now I'd managed to get the gist of the quarrel, and it was as follows: two men had been vying for the attentions of the same woman. The woman in question wasn't interested in either, but a second woman, who appeared to be a friend of the first woman, was interested in one of the men, and as well as being annoyed with the first woman, she was also annoyed with the man she was interested in. Does that make sense?

Instead of the row passing Castle House and moving north, like I was hoping it would (very slowly!), it came straight inside and immediately began moving up the stairs. By now I'd pulled the duvet over my head but, as far as I could make out, there had already been some hair-pulling and a slap. The woman who fancied the man, but now hated the other woman, had declared undying love (for the man), whereas the man who fancied the woman who didn't fancy him, had declared undying lust. Everyone was drunk, nobody was happy, and in the end the police were called.

'I f****** haaaate you, Sandra. You always get the men I'm after.'

'Piss off, Janis. I do not! What about whatshisname from Leyburn? I never got anywhere with him.'

'I reckon he's a puff.'

'Oh, shut yer gob, Brian!'

'Don't speak to him like that!'

'Oh, here we go.'

'I luv 'im! You don't.'

'How can you love a prat like that? You just think you do. And besides, yer rat-arsed!'

'Right, I'm going to tear your bloody hair out!'

By the time the police arrived things were in full swing but, instead of the officers pouring water on the flames of love and lust that were now engulfing Castle House, they appeared to chuck about half a gallon of rocket fuel on them.

'If you don't get out of my way and let me slap her, I'll kick you in the balls – officer.'

'I wouldn't advise that, madam. It's a ten-mile drive to Richmond, but if I have to arrest you and put you in the cells, I will.'

'Awww, piss off!' SLAP!

'Right! You're under arrest for assaulting a police officer. Anything you say may be—'

'Brian! Are you going to let him take me away like this? Brian! BRIAN!'

'I suggest the rest of you go back to your respective homes.'

'Can I come back with you, Brian?'

'Don't you dare! Brian. You go anywhere near that slag and I'll kill myself. I love you, Brian. Don't go back with her!'

'Mind your head as you get in the car, madam.'

'Aww, piss off.'

By the time Janis had been taken away, there was a crowd of about twenty people standing outside my window, and although it had got a bit scary towards the end, it was a fabulous form of entertainment. Free things always go down well in Yorkshire, but I'd have paid money for that.

This kind of thing was a regular occurrence in Middleham, especially at the weekends. We never usually had the coppers here, but you were guaranteed at least one catfight and sometimes you'd even get a mass brawl. That was only letting off steam, really, and when I say mass brawl, what I really mean is six or seven stable lads throwing a few punches over whose round it is.

By this time I'd just about found my voice in the tack room (I've never been as confident socially as I am professionally), and so whenever a big fight took place I'd make a mental note of it and then retell it the following day. I think I did this partly because I liked a gossip (don't we all?), but also because it helped me feel part of the crowd.

The most outrageous thing I ever saw or heard during this period – even more outrageous than hearing Janis slap a policeman – took place when there was a French contingent working in the town. This used to happen quite a lot, and there'd often be a big group of Irish lads or French lads working at a yard. They were always a good laugh and, as well as giving us all something to gossip about, it was interesting to see or hear how they worked. The French, for instance, were very laid back, apparently, and the effect they had on the yard they were working at was, shall we say, quite calming.

Tim, Rachel and I were at a party one evening at a place called Colt Cottage, which is just a few yards from the square. This was yet another place full of stable staff and, although I hadn't been keen on going, Tim and Rachel had persuaded me. Some of the French contingent were there and, just as I was cracking open a can of Diet Pepsi, I spotted one of them holding what looked like a very long cigarette. Actually, it was huge!

'What the hell's that?' I whispered to Tim.

'It's wacky backy,' he replied. 'Those French lads are mad for it.'

'What's wacky backy?' I asked innocently.

'You know. Drugs!'

'*Oh my god*,' I shouted. '*They're doing drugs!*'

Like most parents back then, Mum and Dad were very anti-drugs, and before I came to Middleham they'd given me a lecture on what would happen to me if I ever took them. Actually, it was probably more like a diatribe, and by the time they'd finished with me I was terrified of the whole idea. I knew that drugs would probably kill me, and that if I was ever caught taking any I'd end up in jail. I didn't know what they looked like, and I certainly didn't know there were hard and soft drugs. All I knew was, they were bad!

My initial reaction after seeing the 'drugs' was to get up and leave, but Tim and Rachel managed to persuade me to stay.

'Just calm down, will you,' said Tim. 'It's only a bit of fun.'

'Fun? *Fun?* There's nothing "fun" about taking drugs, Tim,' I said wisely.

'How do you know?'

'Mum and Dad said.'

'And how would they know?'

Awkward bugger.

Tim and Rachel had no intention of getting involved in the drug orgy themselves, but they were a little bit more enlightened than I was, and were happy to let the French lads get on with it. To me, it was even worse than Crooky and the travelling tack man. He hadn't even lit the damn thing, yet I still felt as if I was in a hippy commune.

The only other time I've seen anybody smoking a 'spliff' or a 'doobie', as I believe they're called, is at a Take That concert, and this time I was offered a puff. 'No thank you very much,' I said haughtily. I couldn't believe it! If that's what happens at a Take That gig, I dread to think what goes on when Bruno Mars is on stage.

I've no idea what the French lads were like with horses as they never worked in our yard, but in addition to turning Middleham into the drug capital of Wensleydale (a mantle the nearby town of Leyburn had been desperately clinging on to ever since some secondary school pupils got caught sniffing marker pens), they also set the hearts of at least two females aflutter. Not me though. I didn't fall for the Gallic charm. And besides, I couldn't understand a word they said.

I did sometimes get a good idea of how they were faring in the bedroom stakes, though, and they weren't as successful as you might assume. I think they were expecting every woman in the town to immediately drop her drawers every time one of them showed an interest, but I'm afraid they got short shrift. Although they were a novelty and sounded quite romantic, as young women I don't think we were aware of that old cliché about all Frenchmen being sexy. And even if we were, I don't think we'd have subscribed to it. We liked our men just like we like our horses: quiet and obedient!

That said, there was one girl I knew who made full use of the contingent, so at least someone was happy.

There used to be another French lad who worked in the town about ten years ago. He was called Pascal and worked for Mark Johnston. The reason I mention him is because he always claimed to hate the French with a passion. Stee reminded me of him the other day and I could almost hear him talking.

'A fucin 'ate zee bludy French. Zay get on ma fucin tits!'

'Why, Pascal?'

'A dunno. Zay just do. Zay bore me to fucin def. A lack it 'ere best. No fucin French!'

It's only very recently that I've become a pub or a party

person; back then it just didn't interest me. I wasn't keen on alcohol at the time, and instead of going for a pint or a glass of wine in the evening I always preferred a walk or a DVD.

There were a few other girls in the town who were my age at the time, and they too preferred something a bit healthier – or a bit more boring, depending on your viewpoint. Looking back, it was all a bit rural and girlie, I suppose, and the only thing preventing my social life from being just a long succession of sleepovers was a pair of pink pyjamas and a copy of *Beaches*! We weren't even old enough to drink – legally. Not that that ever stopped anybody. Only the horses and one or two of the lasses drank water in our yard, and it would have been the same all over the town. I'm not saying it was a prerequisite to drink alcohol seven days a week, but it wasn't far off.

It was definitely the walks that I looked forward to the most, and we always managed to find a dog that needed walking. Dogs *are* a prerequisite in racing, I'm pleased to say, and every trainer I know has at least one.

Working in a racing yard can obviously be quite boisterous at times, and either walking over Middleham Moor or down towards the River Cover was a perfect contrast. I'm certainly no paragon of virtue, but all that shouting, swearing and carrying on – not to mention the work itself – could really get to me sometimes, and after six or seven hours of it I tended to crave a bit of peace. Some people think it's always quiet in the country, but I promise you it's not. There may be fewer of us, but we've all got well-trained gobs.

I always describe where we live and work as being a little piece of heaven, and although it sounds a bit clichéd it's the best description I have to offer. It's the Yorkshire Dales, for heaven's sake! In my view the Yorkshire Dales National Park's best kept secret is Coverdale. It's like Polo Venture really, small but perfectly formed, and its largest village, Carlton, has a population of a whopping 232 people! That, and a gorgeous little place called West Scrafton, where James Herriot once had a cottage – population, circa seventy – are the only two villages in the entire dale, as every other settlement falls into the category of a hamlet.

Its main industries are farming, first and foremost, followed by tourism, and then horse racing. There are only two pubs in the dale: the Thwaite Arms in Horsehouse, which is only open in the evenings and at weekends, and the Foresters Arms in Carlton, which is a community pub. A friend of mine, who was born and bred in West Scrafton and went to school in Carlton, once told me that, back in the day, when the pub was used almost exclusively by farmers, if, at the end of an evening, they ever wanted a bit of 'after hours', they'd buy the deeds to the pub from the landlord for a nominal fee, so if the police paid them a visit he wouldn't lose his licence. This meant that the farmers owned the pub and so – legally speaking – they were drinking what was theirs. Most importantly, no money was changing hands. Once the farmers had had their fill, the deeds were sold back to the landlord for the same amount (I think they missed a trick there), and the following day during licensing hours they'd settle up for the night before.

One landlord in times past would apparently fall asleep during these sessions; because he used to snore very loudly, the farmers would pick up his chair, take him outside, and lock the door.

11

Box Twenty-Six

Settling into Oakwood Stables didn't take us long at all, and although we didn't have as much space as we did at Tupgill the advantages were obvious. For a start, racing is a very sociable industry and, as stunningly beautiful as Tupgill Park is, being in the centre of Middleham brought us all to life a bit. From the hours of about 7 a.m. to midday there was a real buzz about the place, and in addition to the hundreds of horses and riders coming to and from the gallops, we were now part of the general hubbub as everyone went about their daily business – farmers, shopkeepers, publicans and schoolkids. I absolutely loved it. I'm obviously biased but, in my opinion, it's the horses that make Middleham special. The horses and the castle.

The only thing I took exception to at Oakwood Stables was the loo. Yard loos are notoriously disgusting – dangerous, even – but the one at Oakwood brought a whole new meaning to the words. Nobody ever wants to clean them, so they can often go months without seeing a brush or even a squirt of bleach. The one at Tupgill did get a bit iffy at times, but generally people managed to clean up after themselves so, providing you didn't do anything silly like breathe, you were OK. By the time we got to Oakwood, everyone seemed to have forgotten how to clean a loo, and whenever one of the lasses went in there you'd hear a scream followed by a cry of, 'Back in a sec. I'm just off to the public loos.'

The only reason I mention the 'loo of doom' is because about two weeks after we moved in it was subjected to what can only be described as a dirty protest. One of the lads, who will have to remain nameless, came in one morning after a very heavy night on the tiles and, after doing some truly unspeakable things in there, he walked out of the yard and was never seen again. He just disappeared! Stee's theory is that he was too embarrassed to face us. Either way, nobody went near the loo for weeks.

The one thing we were a little bit short of at Oakwood Stables apart from space was grass. Up at Tupgill we were surrounded by the stuff, but all we had at Oakwood was a strip outside the yard that separated us from the road. A paddock it was not. This meant that if we wanted to give our horses a pick of grass, we had to go to an area called the Busks, which is some common land on the road to Leyburn. It's only about half a mile away from the yard, and once there we could dismount and let the horses graze for ten minutes. We couldn't do it every day, but we'd try and make sure every horse got down there at least twice a week.

About a month after we moved to Oakwood Stables, I

came home for lunch one day and decided to go for a walk. The person whose dog I usually took with me was away on holiday, so I started thinking about finding one that needed a permanent home. We always had dogs back in Leeds and the one we had at the moment was called Benji. He was a typical black Labrador – caring, friendly and inquisitive – and I'd missed him almost as much as I'd missed Mum and Dad. Later that day I gave Mum a call and told her about my plans.

'Why don't you take Benji?' she said immediately.

I was taken aback at first. Upset, even. 'Why? Don't you want him anymore?' I asked.

'Don't be daft!' she replied. 'With everyone out most of the day he's spending too much time on his own.'

This was a great idea. I could take him out before I went to work and again in the afternoon and the evening. I might even be able to take him to work with me sometimes!

After talking it through a bit more with Mum and then Dad we decided to give it a try, and so the following weekend they brought Benji up to Middleham. There was another dog in Castle House, so I knew it wouldn't be a problem having him there. I also knew at least five people who'd look after him when I had to go racing.

I think it took Benji about four or five minutes to settle in to Castle House and he absolutely adored Middleham. He was also a horse lover, which helped, so if I ever took him into work with me he'd always behave himself. From then on my walks around the dale became even more of a joy and having a dog to come home to, especially one I both knew and loved and who knew and loved me, was exactly what I needed.

While I was delighting in my first Dales summer in 1999, the season threw up a problem I'd not encountered before. Horses with hay fever. These days horses have inhalers, the same as humans, but if you work in a yard that's close to something like rapeseed you could be in for trouble. We had a horse once who, as well as having an inhaler, had to sleep on shavings as opposed to hay. He used to sneeze all the time and he also came out in blotches. Some people tend to confuse a horse sneezing with a horse snorting but, mark my words, there's a world of difference. When a horse sneezes you know about it. It's rapid, noisy, and often very, very messy!

Being summer in Yorkshire, the weather was far from predictable. Like most humans, horses are OK with all kinds of weather really, providing it's not either overly changeable or extreme. What they hate most of all is having two hot days followed by two cold, although that doesn't happen too often in Middleham – usually it's just cold. The only time I ever see them get annoyed is when it becomes really hot. Once again, that doesn't happen too often where we are, but when it does millions upon millions of flies suddenly appear and everyone starts to sweat. Us and the horses. In this weather we usually hose the horses down and then scrape the excess water off before leaving them to dry in the sun. Most horses love that, but you do still get the occasional complaint. We have a horse at the moment called Fat Rascal and he won't go anywhere near the hosepipe, even to have his feet washed. He's such a namby-pamby. He's definitely not alone, though. Lots of horses have an aversion to water, and they're all very adept at letting you know.

We once had a large bay gelding who was the polar opposite. Whenever he came to a big puddle, whether it be on the road or the moor, he'd get down on his knees, roll over and start thrashing around in it. If you were a spectator, I'm sure this would have been cuteness personified, but to his poor unfortunate rider, i.e. me, it was anything but. Eighty per cent of the time I'd manage to spot these puddles before he did, which meant I could pull him away in time. Sometimes, though, if I was deep in conversation – or gossiping, as it's sometimes known – I'd suddenly get thrown, and while I was picking myself up, wondering what the hell had gone on, he'd be having a bath! He was the same at the races. I remember hosing him down after a race one day and, before I got the chance to scrape the water off, he was down rolling on the floor. It didn't matter if it was concrete, mud or grass: if it had water on it, he'd be down.

One thing I've never been able to do on a racehorse is jump on. Most of the lads can do it, and so can some of the lasses, including my sister, Becky. She's got plenty of bounce. I can climb trees, walls and fences, no problem. Spider monkey, yes. Gymnast, no! Because I always needed a leg up, I was always first to get on, and one day after coming back from the gallops, just as I was getting back on Polo after we'd given our horses a pick of grass, he suddenly reared up and started going crazy. Given his usual demeanour I was flabbergasted by this.

'What on earth do you think you're doing, young man?' I said sternly. 'Pull yourself together this instant!'

I couldn't see anything that might have spooked him, and I simply thought he was misbehaving. But instead of calming down he suddenly started running backwards and ended up going straight into a tree. Whatever it was that had spooked him in the first place had nothing on this, and as soon as his bum hit the trunk of the tree he sped off and started rearing and bronking up the road into Middleham. At least he was going in the right direction for home, I thought wryly.

Because Polo was quite a narrow horse, his tack wouldn't always fit properly, and whenever we went down to the Busks I'd let the girth straps out a bit so he could relax. Unfortunately, I hadn't managed to get the straps back up again before he started going bonkers and I thought my saddle would go at any second. How I managed to stay on my errant mount I have absolutely no idea, but it was a good five minutes before I got him back under control. As he was bucking up the road I could hear an even bigger commotion going on behind us, and when I looked back I saw two other horses doing exactly the same thing. The rest didn't seem at all bothered. That's what I mean about the herd mentality being selective and not exclusive. They're like humans, I suppose. There are those who like to feel part of something, and those who aren't really fussed. That was a proper squeaky-bum moment, though!

Because we were now based on the opposite side of the moor, our route to and from the gallops had obviously changed. This brought to light an equine eccentricity that as far as I know is unique to one animal – the animal in question being The Wiley Kalmuck.

By the way, one of the things that really amused me was the variety of names the horses have, ranging from the predictable to the downright odd. The most bizarrely named horse we had – to my mind – was The Wiley Kalmuck! The first time I heard it, I honestly thought it was 'cow muck'. According to the Collins dictionary, the name Kalmuck was 'a member of a Mongoloid people of Buddhist tradition, who migrated from West China in the seventeenth century'. Perhaps they migrated on bay geldings? Who knows.

The Wiley Kalmuck was owned by an Irish gentleman called Mr N. O'Sullivan. Although he didn't turn out to be the best racehorse in the world (he eventually became a great point-to-pointer), my colleague Ashley had his first and only winner on him. Actually, I think it was the only time either of them won!

Despite not being very fast, the one thing The Wiley Kalmuck was good at was walking. Or power-walking, to be exact. As soon as we were in sight of the moor he'd get excited, and as the rest of the string carried on as normal he'd be off like Billy Whizz. You couldn't fault him for his enthusiasm. Galloping, no. Walking, yes! The only problem with this was that it made it almost impossible to sit with him, and the last half a mile or so before we reached the gallop was an absolute boneshaker of a ride.

Right at the bottom of the moor, about half a mile from Middleham, there are some lunge rings on the right-hand side. Lunging is when you walk a horse in a circle on the end of a line to teach it obedience or to burn off excess energy. I should try it with my sister. One morning, not long after we moved, I rode The Wiley Kalmuck past these rings while one of them was in use, and the moment he clocked the horse that was being lunged he went absolutely bananas, rearing up, snorting and refusing to move on. I'd never seen anything like it. It lasted for about five minutes and, in the end, I had to ride him away. Rachel was with me the first time it happened and she couldn't believe it either.

The following day he was fine on the way up as there were no horses being lunged, but on the way back there were two rings in use and once again he started throwing a massive wobbler. He was fine *being* lunged, by the way. He just couldn't bear to watch it.

Sometimes he wouldn't clock that the rings were in use until the very last minute and, just when I thought we'd got away with it, he'd look over.

I could almost hear his mind whirring. *Why are they here? Why are they going around in circles? Good god, they're wearing white socks! I'm sorry, but this just isn't right. I'm afraid I'm going to have to go bananas!*

We almost took out a couple of walkers on the way back from the gallops one day; they desperately flung themselves against the wall separating the lunge rings from the moor.

'So sorry, he has a lunge problem!' I managed to blurt out.

I dread to think what they thought I meant.

By far the worst thing to happen to me during those first few months at Oakwood, apart from going near the loo, was being told by Micky that Polo Venture was going to be sold. That was a day I'll never, ever forget.

He was owned by a syndicate called the Million in Mind Partnership. They usually had at least five or six horses in training at any one time, and at the end of every season they'd have what's called a dispersal. At the time, I had absolutely no idea what a dispersal was, and when it was explained to me I almost died.

'I'm afraid it means that Polo's going to be sold at the Doncaster sales,' said Micky.

This would have been in August 1999, and the sale was taking place in October.

'You mean Polo's leaving us?' I asked him, flabbergasted.

'Looks like it,' said Micky.

I think that was one of the first times I'd ever had any bad news broken to me and, unfortunately, I started to cry. Micky knew I was close to Polo Venture – everybody did – but I don't think he was expecting waterworks.

'Come on,' he said, patting me on the shoulder. 'I know it's easy for me to say this, Gemma, but you shouldn't get too attached. I told you that at the start.'

'I can't help it though,' I sobbed. 'I'm going to miss him so much.'

Not everybody becomes attached to the horses they look after, and because they don't belong to us, that's probably quite wise. Micky had indeed warned me about this and, unfortunately, I hadn't listened. I think they call it selective hearing! But honestly, I doubt it would have made a blind bit of difference. From that very first day, Polo Venture and I had been inseparable. He'd been so good to me. So incredibly patient. When I'd walked through those gates on that wet October morning in 1998, I'd been a novice with a capital N. I'd never galloped before, and the only kind of racehorse I'd ever ridden had been a retired one. By this point Polo Venture had already won a race, so he was the one with all the experience, not me. He was the one who showed me the ropes, and I couldn't have wished for a better teacher. It might sound a bit fanciful to some people, but I'm a great believer in the theory that horses and humans can cooperate like this. I obviously can't prove it, but I believe it, and to me that's all that matters. Polo Venture knew that I was inexperienced and a bit scared, and he took care of me. I'm sure of it.

When October arrived, what I should have been doing was commemorating my first year in racing, but instead I was tearing my hair out at the prospect of losing Polo. I'd had several weeks to mull it over and, in that time, I'd managed to turn it from being a rather unfortunate situation – which is what it was – into the worst thing that had ever happened in the history of the world. To my colleagues it probably looked as though I was being a sulky little sod, but I was already in mourning for my best friend. I suppose I did prefer horses to humans at the time, but I wasn't the only one. These days it's a bit more even stevens. I still adore horses, but I quite like people too.

The only possible solution to this dilemma – the only one I was going to be happy with, at least – was to find an owner in the yard who wanted to buy Polo Venture. Somebody had mentioned this to me one day, and when I realized that it might be a solution, I ran off to find Micky.

'Do you know if any of our owners might be interested in buying Polo?' I asked hopefully.

Bearing in mind I'd only been in Micky's employment about a year, I might just have been speaking out of turn.

'I beg your pardon,' he said, visibly taken aback.

'I said, do you know if any of our owners might be interested in buying Polo? If you do, would you mind having a word with them? I'd really appreciate it. He's a fantastic horse and in his last five races he's finished—'

Micky didn't allow me to finish the sentence.

'Believe it or not, Gemma, I am well aware of Polo Venture's recent form, and what our owners might or might not wish to buy is none of your business. Do I make myself clear?'

'Yes, of course. I'm really sorry. It's just—'

'Never mind, "It's just". Now go and get on with your work.'

I felt like I'd crossed a very big line, and so instead of moping around I forced a smile and got my head down. It wasn't difficult finding a few positives to cheer me up and, although I knew I was going to miss Polo Venture massively, I also knew that I had a job to do and life had to go on.

To save myself from grief I ignored the sales, and when Micky returned from Doncaster I didn't even ask him who had bought Polo. I was desperate to, obviously, but he was right: it was absolutely none of my business what ours or any other owners spent their money on, and so I bit my tongue and tried to remain professional. It wasn't easy, but it was the only way.

After an hour or so Micky stuck his head around the tack-room door.

'Gemma, can I see you upstairs in the office for a minute?'

'Yes, of course,' I said.

The tack room at Oakwood is directly below the office so, unfortunately, we were there in a flash. I was dreading what was to come.

'Right then,' said Micky, sitting behind his desk. 'Polo Venture has a new owner, and I thought you should be the first to know.'

'It doesn't bother me,' I said, respectfully but dishonestly. 'He's not my horse.'

'Yes, I know he's not your horse Gemma, but you've looked after him for almost a year – very well, as it happens – and so I thought you might like to say goodbye before he moves.'

As he said the word 'goodbye' my heart sank into my boots. *Come on, Gemma*, I thought. *Try and keep it together.*

'OK,' I said quietly. 'Where's he going?'

I remember thinking, please let it be local. Please . . .

'Box twenty-six,' said Micky. 'As you know, he's in box fifteen at the moment and I've decided to give him a change.'

'What?' I said, suddenly finding my voice. 'You mean he's staying with us?'

'That's right,' said Micky, smiling. 'When you gave me your sales pitch the other day I'd already been asked to bid on him by an existing owner, and we got him. He was never going anywhere.'

I didn't know whether to kiss him on the cheek or kick him between the legs, but to err on the side of caution I just gave him a quick smile and then ran off to find Polo. What a truly amazing day that was.

By the way, I wasn't the only one enamoured by Polo Venture. Crooky has two daughters called Amy and Emma, and they used to come and help me during evening stables. Like everyone else, I had four or five horses to care for, but even they gravitated to Polo and, just like me, they fell head over heels in love with him. While I was brushing him down they'd take it in turns to sit on him, and the reason they both became obsessed with horses is because of Polo Venture. That horse has been the subject of a lot of first loves.

He always won best turned-out at the races. I made sure of that! I would scrub those white socks of his like you wouldn't believe, and he wasn't allowed anywhere near puddles. You should have seen us weaving around to avoid them as we made our way to the pre-parade ring.

What Polo loved most about going to the races was being plaited. He could not get enough of it. I used to look after another horse called Karo de Vindici, and if you didn't plait him at the races he used to sulk and run like a donkey. Honestly! He was a bright bay horse and, although he was small like Polo, he could jump fences like Desert Orchid. Jim Crowley, who was Champion Flat Jockey in 2016, used to ride him over the jumps. Nobody else was brave enough. I remember one day when I was getting him ready to go racing, he nudged his box door open and started going walkabout. I was only halfway through putting his tail bandage on, and so as he wandered out into the yard I was following him and calling for help. Stee wasn't impressed by that, I remember.

'Drop the bloody bandage, you idiot,' he said.

'No way!' I replied. 'I'm over halfway through. Just stop him, will you!'

Like the fillies I mentioned earlier, Polo Venture would always poo, wee and sleep in exactly the same place. This meant that, because there was never any moisture when I turned his box over, it always became very dusty and I used to get told off for it.

'Why's that box so dusty?' Crooky would demand.

'Because he always pees in the same place,' I'd tell him.

'That horse isn't normal!'

'What horse is?'

If I hadn't seen Polo's perfect piles of poo with my own eyes, I would never have believed it. He must have actually positioned himself in exactly the same place every time he went. It was amazing! On the few occasions when I did turn up to work with a bit of a hangover it was so, so easy. *There's the poo, there's the wee, give the straw a fluff, and we're off!* Mucking out boxes and having to shift lots of horse poo when your body's trying to process several pints of something alcoholic can often have an interesting effect at six o'clock in the morning. Back then, hangovers were commonplace, and never a day went by without somebody succumbing to the fatal mix of the after-effects of the night before and the smell of the horse manure. One Monday morning at Tupgill we had three or four people hoicking their guts up, and I was so naive that I thought they had all got food poisoning.

'What's wrong with them?' I asked Rachel. 'Have they eaten something they shouldn't have?'

'No,' she said, grinning at me. 'But I think they might have drunk something they shouldn't have.'

I'm afraid I still didn't catch on.

*

I think Valiant Warrior would be disgusted if I didn't give you at least one more example of his unorthodox behaviour, so here goes. He is, after all, still a legend in our yard, and really should have arrived with his own government health warning.

A few days after I got the good news about Polo, Micky received a telephone call from a TV production company.

'We'd like to film some of your horses on the gallops, if that's OK? It's for a documentary we're making.'

Ever the marketeer, Micky agreed to the request, and the following week a camera crew arrived complete with a presenter and a sound engineer.

'Why don't you go out with the second lot?' suggested Micky. 'They'll be ready soon.'

One of the only people who ever managed to stay on Valiant Warrior was Stee (who said only opposites attract?), and – as luck would have it – he and Weasel were due out.

'What sort of mood's he in, Stee?' asked Micky.

'A shit one,' Stee replied. 'Somebody's obviously told him what happened to his bollocks.'

'There'll be a camera crew following you to the gallops and back, so try and make him behave.'

'That's all I need.'

'You'll be fine. Have fun.'

With that Micky walked off to the office and Stee, me and the rest of the string made our way out of the yard and onto East Witton Road. The camera crew, who were all very friendly, followed the string in a pick-up and were filming from the back.

'He doesn't like this,' said Stee.

'Doesn't like what?' I asked.

'All this bollocks behind us.'

'You mean he's camera shy?'

'I don't know. Look at him though.'

Stee was right. Something was bothering Valiant Warrior. It seemed as if he'd taken a big dislike to being filmed.

'Why don't you move to the front?' suggested Rachel.

'Good idea.'

Although this placated him a little bit, Valiant Warrior was still as mardy as hell on the way to the gallops, but that was nothing to what he was like once we were on them. From the moment he set hooves on the Low Moor he started bucking violently – god only knows how Stee managed to stay on. Not surprisingly the camera people absolutely loved this and, just as Stee managed to get Valiant Warrior under control, they moved in for a better view.

'Piss off, will you,' shouted Stee. 'You'll spook him.'

Before the cameraman could respond, Stee rode Valiant Warrior away to safety.

Valiant Warrior's speciality on the gallops was what we call whipping round, which is when a horse turns anything up to about one hundred and eighty degrees, mid-canter and without warning. It's absolutely terrifying to watch but is also amazing! His pièce de résistance, if you weren't already off and shouting for an ambulance, was to buck a couple of times. He was just a complete and utter nut-job.

A few minutes later, Stee and Valiant Warrior were coming back down the gallop, and once again the cameramen moved up to the rail. Valiant Warrior took exception to this, and just as they reached the rail he stopped, whipped round about a hundred degrees and then started bucking on the spot. God knows how, but Stee actually managed to stay on.

This is one of the key points about the job. Regardless of how docile or amenable our mounts might seem to be, we are always on the cusp of danger and the job takes a lot of guts. Paradoxically, that's one of the reasons we do it and love it so much; if all the horses we worked with ran at the same speed and shared the same temperament and personality, I dare say we'd all have proper jobs. How many sports do you know where the competitors are actually followed by an ambulance? I can't think of any others.

I should point out here that Valiant Warrior was actually an excellent racehorse, despite only costing about four thousand guineas. As well as finishing in the top ten of the Grand National one year, he won eleven times in all and grossed over £70,000 in prize money. He'd probably have won more if it hadn't been for an injury that ultimately ended his career. He was due to run in what's now called the Topham Chase at Aintree in the spring of 2001, and he was favourite. This would have been one of the biggest moments in Micky's training career, and there was a real buzz around the yard. Valiant Warrior may have been a mildly psychotic, cantankerous old git, but he was *our* mildly psychotic, cantankerous old git and we loved him. Unfortunately, a few days before the race, he suffered a tendon injury and had to retire. Out of sixty-two starts, he finished in the top three twenty-seven times. That's not bad going.

According to Stee, Valiant Warrior is still very much alive, although no longer kicking, thank god, and since retirement he's been living in Wetherby with a donkey called Desmond! Apparently, they're a right couple of miserable so-and-sos and are probably the equine equivalent of Statler and Waldorf from the Muppets. He's got hardly any teeth left now, bless him, so although he's still valiant, he's less of a warrior.

12

Bully for Me

From a professional point of view, one of the best things about moving to Middleham was being able to take part in Middleham Open Day, which traditionally takes place every Good Friday. For one day only, racing yards throughout the town open their gates to the general public and, in doing so, allow racing fans to see what goes on behind the scenes. Up to five thousand people can attend the event, which raises thousands of pounds for Racing Welfare, the charity that supports racing's workforce and now organizes the event, and the Yorkshire Air Ambulance.

If you're proud about what you do, and most of us are, it's great to be able to show off your side of the industry and demonstrate just how much passion and hard work goes into making racing what it is. Of course, it helps if the horses cooperate, but ultimately, they're a law unto themselves.

One of the horses we had at the time was Minster York, a big, obstinate chestnut gelding who used to bite like buggery when he was in his box. You had to be really careful.

His favourite manoeuvre was ambushing people as they walked past. His head would suddenly appear and he'd go for you. To try and prevent any injuries, Stee had prepared a sign that he'd pinned to the box door saying, DANGER! THIS HORSE BITES! Had it been up to him he'd have put something like, THIS HORSE IS A RIGHT MARDY GIT SO IF I WERE YOU I'D TROT ON, but Micky was having none of it.

After pinning up his sign, Stee stood there admiring his handiwork, and just as he turned to walk away Minster York came flying up to the door, stuck out his head and bit the skin in the middle of Stee's back. He was quick as lightning!

'*Aaaaaah, yer bastard!*' cried Stee.

Hoist by his own petard.

Stee wasn't the only one to be ambushed by Minster York that day. Some people are convinced they have a natural way with horses, and so when they see a sign saying DANGER, THIS HORSE BITES, they think it doesn't apply to them. 'Horses have always loved me,' I remember hearing one man saying to his wife as he approached Minster's box. To be fair to him, he managed to get his hand within an inch or so of Minster York's nose, but just as he was going in for a stroke – SNAP!

'You bugger!'

He obviously couldn't say anything, because there was a sign there telling him exactly what was going to happen. I promise you I did try not to laugh.

Choice Challange, meanwhile, used to enjoy pinching people's hats, and the open day that year gave him a bonanza. Good Friday can be perishing up in the Dales, and April 2000 was no exception. As a consequence, a fair amount of people were wearing hats, and Choice Challange had nicked about twelve before ten o'clock. One boy wearing a yellow bobble hat didn't even notice he'd lost his! It became a joke after a while and people started walking past his box deliberately, hoping he'd snatch them and take them inside.

As well as being a demon hat-nicker, Choice Challange also had a talent for falling at fences, and he'd come a cropper in four of his last five races. A few weeks earlier, a conditional jockey by the name of Andrew, who was based at the yard, had begged Micky to let him ride the horse, and after a lot of badgering Micky agreed. (A conditional jockey is what we call an apprentice national hunt jockey.)

'I'm a horseman, Micky,' Andrew had said. 'I won't cock it up like those other idiots. You just watch me, Micky. I'll get him over the line.'

He didn't half talk a good game, this lad, and in the end I think we were all hoping he'd make it five out of six!

Shortly after the start of his next race, which was at Perth, Andrew started patting Choice Challange down the neck. I was Choice's groom that day and when Micky saw him do this he went bananas.

'What the bloody hell's he doing that for?' he said.

Then, as they were approaching the first fence, Andrew

started stroking the horse's ears. I could see Micky was fuming.

'He's stroking his bloody ears now!' he bawled. 'What's he going to do next? Get off and give him a fetlock massage!'

About ten feet before the jump, while Andrew was still mid-stroke, Choice Challange stopped dead. To be fair, Andrew cleared the jump beautifully, but the only ears he could stroke now were his own. It was almost as if Choice Challange had said, 'Look mate. Don't do that.'

'What an absolute dickhead!' said Micky. 'Horseman my arse.'

Getting on well with Micky, and having Crooky as an ally, definitely paid dividends when I first entered the industry. But then, as I started becoming more confident and proficient at my job, one or two of the other girls mistook this for arrogance. One such was Kim and, not long after the open day, she decided to declare war on me. She'd been working for Micky a few months longer than I had, and because of her big mouth she was somebody I'd always avoided.

Had I spoken to either Micky, Crooky or Stee, they would obviously have done something about it, but I'm afraid it wasn't quite that simple. To be honest, at first I didn't even realize it was happening, and that's so often the case. If you want to make somebody's life a misery in a small, tightknit community, you have to do it carefully. Kim knew exactly what she was doing and, by the time I caught on, I felt too embarrassed to say anything. I think the culture was also very different at the time; as opposed to grassing somebody up, you were expected to keep your mouth shut and fight your corner, which is easier said than done. I'm often told by people older than I am that things were better in their day, and I'm probably guilty of saying the same to those younger than me. But when it comes to bullying, that is most definitely not the case, and I shudder to think what it was like in the years before it happened to me.

The best way of describing Kim's approach was a drip, drip effect, and she started by trying to get me into trouble and making me look stupid. Apparently, this is textbook bullying in the workplace, and for a girl who was only a year or so older than me she seemed like an old pro. I'd seen people like her at school but had always managed to avoid them. Now that was impossible.

The first example happened in a box one day. Because it was quite chilly I'd decided to put an extra rug on one of my horses. He didn't like the cold and so I thought it was the right thing to do. Kim must have been watching me and she went straight to Stee.

'Why have you put another rug on that horse?' he said, coming into the box.

'Who told you that?' I said.

'She did,' he said, pointing to Kim.

'I put it on because he doesn't like the cold,' I replied. 'You know he doesn't. It's just a thin one underneath.'

'Oh, OK, fair enough,' said Stee.

As he left the box I could see Kim standing a few metres away from the door, and the look she gave me was pure hatred. She'd tried to get me into trouble and it had bitten her on the bum. Why do it in the first place, though?

The following day she went to Crooky and told him I hadn't washed and brushed the girth on one of my horses. Crooky was obviously red hot on that kind of thing and so he came straight over.

'Is it true you haven't done the girth on that horse?'

'Who told you that?'

'Kim did.'

'I've just done it now,' I said. 'We've only been back five minutes. Give us a chance!'

'Oh, right. OK, good enough.'

This time Kim was standing over the other side of the yard, and once again she had a face like thunder. Or, to be slightly more accurate, like a bulldog chewing a wasp. Two attempts at getting me into trouble and making me look like a prat, and two bites on the arse. I still had no idea what was happening, though, and simply put it down to a bit of bitchiness. It was schoolyard stuff as far as I was concerned and, because it hadn't worked, I forgot about it.

Sticking with the drip, drip approach, Kim then decided to start making up lies about me. I've no idea what they were exactly, but over the next few weeks people who I'd always got on very well with started blanking me, and that's when her campaign started gaining ground. I had no problem working on my own, but one thing I didn't like was a bad atmosphere, and because the girls were blanking me and giving me daggers all the time, that's exactly what we had. Even Rachel and Hayley were different with me, so goodness knows what she told them.

Now that Kim had successfully turned some of my colleagues and friends against me, which was upsetting enough, she started trying to undermine my confidence. Yet again a drip, drip effect was employed, and the first instance I can remember took place in the tack room.

There's a board inside the tack room that says which horses you're down to ride, and occasionally you would see some potentially interesting pairings. On this particular morning I was down to ride the dreaded Valiant Warrior, which I was not looking forward to, and just as I turned around to leave, she stopped me.

'You don't stand a chance on that,' she snarled. Actually, it was more of a grunt. 'It'll kill you in seconds.'

I'll say this for her, she was convincing. Even so, I just walked away.

Normally, if you saw somebody paired with a horse you thought they might have trouble with, as opposed to wishing death upon them you would wish them luck. Or, if you knew the horse, you would pass on some advice. 'Drop your irons and keep your hands down on that one, it can be a bit dodgy,' I remember somebody saying to me one day. It's the decent thing to do, and, nine times out of ten, it's exactly what happens.

Kim was obviously taking the opposite approach. At first her campaign was restricted to the yard, but eventually it spilled out onto the road and even onto the gallops. You remember how I mentioned that people often split into their little cliques as they're riding to and from the yard? Well, because I'd become persona non grata with some people I was often alone, and she would use this opportunity to have a dig.

I remember riding past Dicky Peacock's house one day on the way to the Low Moor when all of a sudden Kim came alongside me.

'This is going to be a right mess,' she said. 'I'll see to that.'

This was the first time she had actually threatened me, and it frightened me.

Unfortunately Kim, myself and another lass were down to do a three-furlong gallop that lot. Just before we set off, Kim sidled up to me, leant over and punched me in the ribs. Not hard, but enough to know that it wasn't a bit of fun.

'Careful you don't fall,' she said.

Before I could decide how to react, Micky gave us the signal to go, and so while she was sitting there posturing, I gathered my reins, gave my horse a quick kick and set off.

'You fucking cow,' she shouted.

The other girl, who'd deliberately kept her distance, had set off at the same time as me and we finished together. Kim, on the other hand, who'd obviously been taken by surprise, had taken an age to get going. Micky wasn't happy.

'What the hell was that?' he said to her.

'Sorry,' she said. 'I was daydreaming.'

'That horse is supposed to be running at Sedgefield next week and I need to have a proper look at him. Go again, and this time, concentrate.'

As the other girl and I made our way back to Middleham, Kim made her way to the start. I didn't dare make eye contact with her but she must have been fuming.

About fifteen minutes after we arrived back at the yard, in rode Kim.

'You'll pay for that,' she hissed.

'Pay for what?' I said as calmly as I could.

'You made me look like a right twat.'

What I should have said at this point, had I been brave enough, was that she didn't need any help in that department and was already the high priestess of twats. Instead I just got on with my work and tried avoiding her. It didn't work, though, and because she kept following me around, I stayed as close to Micky, Stee or Crooky as I could.

I cannot tell you how hard I fought not to let her think she was getting to me, but the fact is, she was. By now it was an everyday occurrence. I'm not sure if it was related, but after about three months I came down with what I later discovered was a really bad case of glandular fever. Because of what was happening, I hadn't been eating or sleeping properly, so was probably a lot more susceptible to infection.

Once the glandular fever had taken hold I was in all kinds of pain, but I still went to work. I promise you I'm no martyr, but it was all part of me not giving in, and in hindsight it was a ridiculous thing to do. I should have said to her, 'Look. Do you mind if we cease hostilities for a bit? I feel like death warmed up!' Either that or just stayed in bed.

If anything, she actually became a lot worse once I was ill; as opposed to just making professional jibes, she started getting personal. For some reason, I found these a lot more difficult to take, which just compounded everything. It was hell.

The personal digs started one Monday morning. I'd worn jeans and a jumper on Saturday and, because they weren't dirty, and because I'd been too ill to do my laundry, I wore them again. Everything else was clean, by the way! Unfortunately, Kim picked up on my fashion faux pas and decided to use it as a stick to beat me with.

'Weren't you wearing those clothes the other day?' she said. 'My god, you're disgusting. How can you wear the same clothes day after day?'

She was obviously trying to get a reaction, but as much as I wanted to tell her I hadn't been wearing the same clothes day after day, I managed to walk away.

Because of everything that was happening, I probably looked a bit ropey at the time and about an hour later she started on that.

'What the hell's happened to you?' she said. 'Do you always look this appalling? Some people like to take pride in their appearance.'

Two new girls were in earshot when she said this and,

because they were obviously scared of her, they started to laugh.

'Yeah, you look like shit,' one of them said.

Making other people hate me was obviously high on Kim's bucket list, and once she saw the newbies were onside they immediately became her Crabbe and Goyle.

The following Saturday morning my parents arrived to take me out for the day, and when they saw me they seemed a bit shocked.

'What's wrong, sweetheart?' asked Mum. 'You look dreadful.'

There was no use arguing with her. I'd just been to powder my nose and Mum was right, I looked awful.

'I just feel a bit run down,' I told her.

'Your Mum's right, love,' said Dad. 'You look like crap. Have you discovered alcohol at last?'

'Norman!'

At Mum's insistence, Dad drove us straight to A&E at the Friarage Hospital in Northallerton, and after waiting an hour or two I was told I had glandular fever. One thing the doctor couldn't understand was how I'd managed to work through it. I was just stubborn, I suppose. After urging me to rest up, which I ignored, he sent me away and within a few days I started feeling better. Physically, at least. Mentally, I was still going through the mill.

The following Tuesday, at about two in the afternoon, I was doing the washing up in the bath at Castle House when Tim came to see me. The sink in my room was too small and, because I was too tired to go to the kitchen, I used the bath instead. That morning at the yard had been horrible and she, Crabbe and Goyle had barely left me alone. This had rendered me on the brink of tears, and when Tim asked how I was feeling, Mount Gemma just erupted. I ended up telling him everything, and, once I'd finished blubbering, he sat me down, gave me a big hug, and said he'd speak to Stee on my behalf. What a relief! Stee might have been tough sometimes, but he would always do the right thing and I knew he'd nip it in the bud. Or, if I was lucky, kick her up the arse.

As it was, Tim didn't even have a chance to speak to Stee, as just three days after me telling him, Kim had left Micky Hammond Racing and was on her way back under whatever stone she'd crawled from. She'd become pregnant, apparently, and had decided to go back and live with her parents.

Once Tim had updated the girls at the yard on what had been going on, everything went back to normal. Nobody said anything, which was fine, but a lot of smiles came my way and that was good enough for me. This may sound a bit melodramatic, but during that time I had completely forgotten how good life could be and finding my feet again was an absolute joy. In fact, it was just like starting over.

Like Micky, my dad had once said to me that regardless of how bad a situation gets you should always try and find something positive to take away, and although it took me a few years, I now know exactly what that is. Apart from a bit of a complex, which I got over, I came away with an ability to spot the early signs of bullying. Which, now I'm an assistant trainer and partly responsible for the welfare of the stable staff, is massively beneficial. Getting it wasn't fun, but I'm so glad it's there.

A slightly more immediate plus after my bout of Kimitis was being sent on my first overnight stay at the races. Whether or not Micky sent me deliberately after having endured a few crappy months, I'm not sure, but when he pulled me to one side and told me that I was going to be spending a night in Musselburgh, I felt elated.

'Really?' I said to him. 'Aww, that's amazing!'

'You're going to Musselburgh, Gemma,' said Micky. 'Not Dubai.'

'I don't care,' I said, beaming at him. 'I've never been overnight before.'

Micky just shrugged. 'It's the little things, I suppose,' he said. 'Have fun.'

Staying overnight when you're racing was a privilege and was something that was normally reserved for either the lads or the more experienced riders. Why? Because they wanted to go out on the lash, that's why! The lads especially used to absolutely love going overnight, so the fact that I'd even got a look-in was amazing.

One of my favourite stories regarding stable lads on an overnighter came from Stee, not surprisingly. He too had been to Musselburgh with a jockey and a stable lad and,

Dante, the last northern horse to win the Derby, seen here a few minutes after his famous win in 1945 with his jockey Billy Nevett and, standing on the far left, his trainer Matt Peacock.

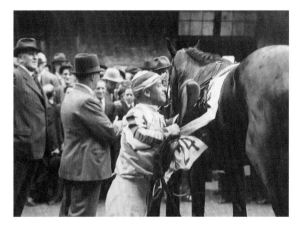

Dicky Peacock in 1981 with his King's Stand Stakes winner, Fearless Lad.

The completely random Norman Conquest, doing what he does best.

Heidi III was the first big winner I looked after. Here he is shortly after winning The Great Yorkshire Chase at Doncaster.

Heidi III in action at Newcastle.

With Heidi III after he won the BWD Securities Hurdle in Newcastle.

Some of the residents at Oakwood
Stables, the current home of
Micky Hammond Racing.

Lovely Benji at Wren Cottage.

Micky out on the gallops.

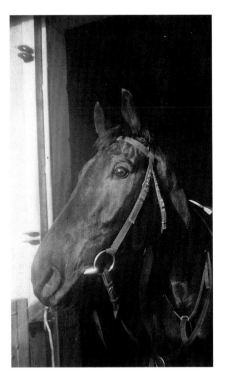

The horse with the most amusing name – The Wiley Kalmuck.

The Rubbing Houses up on the High Moor – a remnant of its racecourse past.

Leading Polo out at Kelso in April 1999, where he won by a good two lengths. The jockey that day was my old friend Nathan Horrocks, and if you look to the right you'll see Micky wearing a tie.

The beautiful Polo and I at Kelso Races in April 1999.

Alderbrook Lad, who had the tack malfunction, at Aintree.

My home with Tim at Wren Cottage.

Tim and Stee at Ripon Races, with me in the background.

My win on Charlotte Vale!

Charlotte Vale with her first foal, Margo Channing.

Riding out with my sister.

A trip to a point-to-point. From left to right:
Micky, me and Micky's daughter Kierra, the groom Ryan Clarke,
Maxwell the horse, Catherine Walton and my dad, Norm.

after coming back to the B&B from the pub, the jockey, who I'd better not name, decided he was hungry.

'You should have got a bloody kebab,' said Stee.

'Naaaa,' said the jockey. 'I'll raid the kitchen here. They won't mind.'

'They bloody will!'

'Naaaaa, they won't. It'll be fine.'

A few minutes later, the jockey had put the deep-fat fryer on and had emptied the entire contents of the freezer onto the worktop. There were chicken nuggets, burgers and chips. He got the lot out. Once he'd decided what was on the menu, he left the rest of the food on the side and, after throwing his selections into the fryer, he went through to the living room for a sit-down. About an hour later he was woken by the B&B owner. As well as ruining a freezer full of food, he'd burnt the rest and had all but ruined the deep-fat fryer. Needless to say he was about as popular as a non-runner. We used to hear dozens of stories like that. Most involved alcohol and all involved at least one person getting into a lot of trouble!

These days the trainers tend to put you up in Premier Inns and Travelodges, but back then you were shoved into a random B&B and you could have been sharing with anyone. Just like the horseboxes, the accommodation was run like a car-share scheme, and so who you were sharing with was often a bit of a lottery. All I knew for sure was that I'd be sharing a room with a female, which was a blessed relief. I just hoped she wasn't called Kim.

The reason we were staying overnight was because the horse was running at 11.30 a.m. the following morning, and by the time we arrived at the B&B having deposited the horse at the racecourse it was gone six o'clock. The person accompanying me on this momentous trip was Bob, Micky's stepdad. He used to drive the box full time for Micky when he first started out. Now he was a bit older, he'd just fill in now and then. Bob's no longer with us, unfortunately, but he was an amazing character and was one of the best story-tellers I've ever known. As well as being very knowledgeable about racing, he knew absolutely everyone. I think most yards probably have a Bob, and although I only knew him for a relatively short time, he became a kind of surrogate grandparent. He was only about 5 feet 6 inches tall; he had a ruddy, reddish face and he always wore a flat cap. Actually, that's a pretty accurate description of nearly all the men I know in racing who are of a certain age! Red faces and flat caps are almost as common as horses.

As it was just the two of us on this journey, Bob had a very captive and appreciative audience and, although it took us a good four hours to get to Musselburgh, it absolutely flew by. The first thing he said to me as we turned out of the gates was:

'Do you know, Gemma, this bloody box has turned into a knocking shop lately.'

Normally, if we were chatting, Bob would regale me with a story or two about his career or about a jockey he used to know, so I have to admit this caught me unawares.

'How do you mean?' I replied cautiously.

We were passing through East Witton at this point and, after turning left into the village and passing the Blue Lion pub, he gave me a disapproving look.

'What's that for?' I said.

'It's for what I'm about to tell you. Honestly, Gemma, the things you young 'ns get up to these days.'

'Go on then,' I said, becoming slightly impatient. 'Tell me!'

Before carrying on, Bob took a quick look behind him.

'Don't worry,' I said. 'There's only me here. And I don't suppose the horse will be all that interested.'

'All right, all right,' said Bob. 'Anyway. Last week I went up to Perth for the two-day meeting and I had two of your colleagues with me.'

'Yes, I know. It was Sharon and Michael.'

Bob seemed somewhat peeved that I was aware of this, but he carried on anyway.

'Well. On the way up there they had a rug over their knees and it kept on . . .' He paused for a second. 'Moving.'

'How do you mean, moving?' I said.

'You know. *Moving!* Up and down and that.'

Suddenly I could feel myself going bright red.

'Oh! That kind of moving.'

'Exactly. In the end I got fed up with it and I said to them, "Now look here, you two. If you want to fiddle around with each other's privates, get off and do it in the back because I'll tell you what, I'm sick of it!"'

'Quite right too. And did they?'

'Yes, they bloody did!'

'Well, that's good, isn't it?'

'No it is not! I meant go to the back seat, not the bloody bunk! They closed the curtains and that was it, they were off.'

Now I was shocked. I hadn't been expecting that.

'What happened?' I asked.

'What do you think happened? After five or ten minutes I stopped the box and threatened to throw a bucket of cold water over them. I wasn't listening to that all the way to bloody Perth. It's the best part of five hours!'

'I didn't even know they were at it,' I said to him.

'Well they are. And at every given opportunity!'

Sharon and Michael were both fresh out of racing college and, after giving it a bit of thought, it all made perfect sense. They were always disappearing off here and there.

'Well I never,' I said, probably sounding old before my years.

Since then I've learned that fornicating in horseboxes is as much a part of racing as placing a bet, and if it doesn't happen on the journey to or from the racecourse, it almost certainly will when you're there.

About seven or eight years ago I was at Newcastle Racecourse for a night meeting and was travelling with a girl called Gillian, who, as well as having a healthy sexual appetite, had a habit of disappearing at race meetings. This hadn't got her into trouble so far, as she'd always arrived back in time to do her job, and although we never asked her what she was up to, we knew full well.

About an hour and a half before our race was due to take place, the owner of the horse we had running came to have a word.

'Have you seen Gillian?' she asked.

'Yes, she's just gone to get changed,' I replied. 'She's in the box.'

The same horse, which Gillian looked after, had won the last time out, and the owner had a dropsy for her.

'I'll just pop over and give it to her,' said the owner.

'OK,' I said. 'See you in the parade ring.'

Without wanting to sound crude, somebody was already giving Gillian more than just a dropsy, and when the owner opened the side door to the horsebox, the sight that greeted her made her scream out loud. The moment I heard her I ran towards the box. Nobody had ever caught Gillian at it before, and I was determined to be one of the first. As it was, the sight that greeted me exceeded even my worst imaginings.

'Oh my god!' I said when I arrived.

Fortunately I'd missed the 'action', but Gillian hadn't just been entertaining one guest in the box. She'd been entertaining two: a man and another woman, both jockeys. It wasn't so much *un ménage à trois*, more *un box de cheval à trois*.

'Do all your members of staff embroil themselves in gangbangs?' asked the owner. Fortunately she was laughing. She'd been in racing a long time.

'Only ones with names beginning with G,' I said.

'Ooh, you devil,' she said, giving me a shove. 'Give her this when she's sorted herself out, will you? See you in the parade ring.'

To be fair to young Gillian, she hardly batted an eyelid when she eventually emerged from the box, and when I handed her the envelope she just winked at me. I thought, *you cheeky little madam!*

When I saw Micky the next morning I told him what had happened. 'Well, Gem,' he said, grinning. 'You know what they say. If the horsebox is a-rockin', don't come a-knockin'.'

There's many a true word said in jest.

The other story involves another young lady called Deborah, whom I've only ever known by reputation. She was based in a flat racing yard down south somewhere, and, like Gillian, she would often disappear for some 'fun' at race meetings. The difference between the two temptresses was that, unlike the elusive Gillian, Deborah used to enjoy having an audience when she performed, and once she'd chosen her co-star – she wasn't fussy, so I heard – she'd invite all and sundry to come and watch. Some people would watch inside the horsebox, which was obviously the orchestra stalls, and the rest would peer through the windows, which must have been the dress circle. Or, in this case, the undress circle.

If Jilly Cooper is ever stuck for ideas, she should try knocking on the door of a few horseboxes. Especially at race meetings. The problem is, she might get invited in.

Once Bob had dispensed with being outraged, he proceeded to tell me a story that had been told to him recently by the jockey Martin Foster.

Martin had been riding a horse for Martin Pipe at Ludlow and he'd been thrown at the far end of the course, away from the stands. Unfortunately, the horse managed to find its way out of the course perimeter, but instead of just leaving it to run, Martin got up, nicked one of the groundsmen's pushbikes which was lying against a fence, and gave chase! He was still wearing his silks, of course, and he even had his whip with him. I forgot to ask Bob if he used it on himself.

The reason Martin went after the horse was because it was off in the direction of Ludlow town centre, and with lots of cars around, anything could have happened. According to Bob he got within about fifty feet of the horse before it came to a halt, but he chased it for at least a mile. Best of all, he managed to stay on this time! You can just picture it, though; a fully tacked-up horse running freely down a street with its jockey giving chase on a pushbike. Brilliant!

By the time Bob and I had deposited the horse at the racecourse it was about 6 p.m. and we didn't arrive at the B&B until about ten past.

'I'll see you downstairs at seven thirty,' said Bob. 'We'll go and get something to eat.'

The person I ended up sharing a room with was a girl called Beth, who was Peter Beaumont's travelling head lass. It was a twin room, but, as opposed to having a bath or a shower in a separate bathroom, it had a shower in the corner of the bedroom. It still had a bathroom, quite a large one, actually, but for some reason they'd decided to put the shower in the bedroom. How strange.

Although I knew Beth to say hello to, I didn't know her well, and when she said she was going to have a shower I started to panic. Even though I was now twenty, I felt hugely embarrassed, and the scene itself wouldn't have looked too out of place in a Victorian melodrama. 'Oh, good gracious. Nudity! Allow me to avert my eyes, madam.'

It was such an awkward moment but, instead of leaving the room, I just sat there facing the wall and pretending to read my book. I forget what it was now but – given the circumstances – it should really have been something by Jane Austen.

My reluctant roommate was quite a bit older than me and, once she'd got herself dressed, she sat on her bed and picked up her book. She's waiting for me to have a shower, I thought. I didn't know what to do. I wanted to have a shower, but I couldn't do it.

After about ten minutes of me generally being very uncomfortable, she leant over and said, 'Gemma, would you like me to go for a walk so you can have a shower?'

'Oh, yes please,' I gushed. The relief I felt was astonishing; partly because I was a bit prudish and would probably have covered up piano legs if I could have, but also because I stank to high heaven and was having problems escaping my own smell.

Once I'd had a shower, in private, I met up with Bob in

the lobby and, after having a quick drink, we met up with a friend of mine called Kieron and went for a Chinese meal. Kieron worked for a trainer in Malton and, because we'd crossed paths so many times, we'd become friends.

The reason I remember this night so much is because it was the first time I ever drank wine. Liebfraumilch, to be exact. I felt very posh. Because it was quite sweet, it was like drinking something soft, and I ended up downing over a bottle. I felt so rough the next day. My first – and only – Liebfraumilch hangover!

At about seven o'clock the next morning, I met Kieron at the racecourse to feed and muck out our horses.

'How're you feeling?' he said.

'Bloody horrible. I keep having Chinese and Liebfrau-milch burps!'

'Me too. Not nice, is it?'

'Not at all. After mucking out, should we let them out for a pick of grass?'

'Why not? See you in a bit.'

As we led our respective horses down to the paddock next to the course, I noticed that Kieron's seemed a bit jumpy and, just as we went through the paddock gates, we got the shock of our bloody lives. Suddenly, and without any warning whatsoever, Kieron's horse took off at full pelt. And because Kieron didn't let go of the lead rope, he went with him. Kieron ran at first, but after about twenty feet he gradually became airborne. It was like something out of a Disney movie. And, just like Polo Venture's perfect piles of poo, if I hadn't seen it with my own eyes, I would never have believed it.

'Let go of the rope, Kieron,' I screamed to him. 'Let go of the bloody rope!'

I don't know how long in seconds it was before he let go, but in terms of distance it must have been at least two or three hundred yards. When he did drop the rope, the horse soon lost interest and started grazing. 'Huh! That's no fun anymore.'

I'll tell you one thing, it definitely cured Kieron's hang-over.

13

Losing a Friend

Almost two years into my tenure, in August 2000, Crooky trusted me to travel with Polo Venture to a race meeting on my own. The venue was Perth racecourse, and to say that I was excited would be a huge understatement. We actually had three runners at Perth that day, and so Jedd was in one box with two of the horses and I was in the other with Polo.

Polo was, as I've probably said a dozen times, my first real friend in racing, and by now we'd developed not only an understanding, but a kind of extrasensory perception. If you've had horses or ponies you might understand this, but I swear he knew how I was feeling and what I was thinking – and I felt the same about him. OK, maybe it was more of a mood thing, but he could definitely tell when I was nervous, excited or upset, and he'd always react in some way. I'd once had a right dressing down from Crooky about something, and when I went to tack Polo up to take him out, he immediately came and started shoving me very gently, as if to say, 'Come on. It's OK.' I wasn't crying or anything (for a change) and I wasn't even mouthing off. I was just a bit upset. Things like that used to happen all the time, and after two years everything had become effortless but wonderful with him.

Anyway, that day we were both a bit distracted, and on the way up to Perth I must have stopped off at least four times to make sure he was OK.

The race itself was a two-mile championship hurdle, and as a first race venue for our endeavours going together unaccompanied, we couldn't have wished for anywhere better. Perth is a beautiful course and the setting even more so. It's situated within the parklands of Scone Palace, one of Scotland's finest stately homes, and is the UK's most northerly racecourse. I'd been there several times already, but each time I arrived I fell more and more in love with the place.

I can't tell you how proud I felt leading Polo Venture around the parade ring that evening. I don't have kids myself, but it was probably akin to watching your four-year-old appear in the school nativity play. No donkeys here though, thank you very much. Thoroughbreds only, and preferably ones with nice white socks! His reaction surprised me more than somewhat.

'Ta-dah,' is probably the most accurate translation. 'OK, everybody look at me!'

What a transformation. I couldn't believe it. Polo wasn't exactly a shy horse, but I hadn't thought he wasn't an extrovert either.

'You bloody tart,' I whispered to him. 'Where did that come from?'

He just nodded.

Though we were all confident he'd do well at Perth, I was nervous when it came to handing him over to the jockey, Brian Harding. Once again, if you had to equate this to a parent–child experience, I'd probably say it was like dropping your child off on their first day at school. Polo was happy enough, though. In fact, he was in his element. I wasn't. Far from it. Something was making me feel anxious, but for the life of me I couldn't put my finger on it. Perhaps it was seeing him so self-assured that unnerved me; although, given the circumstances, that was ideal.

Viewing isn't brilliant at Perth, especially for somebody my height, so instead of being out front I decided to watch the first two thirds of the race on a TV behind the main stand. All being well, win or lose, this was going to be the climax to a very special day, and, as they came under starter's orders, I remember tapping the table I was standing at. I sometimes do that when I'm nervous.

That's my boy, I said to myself. Then, as they set off, I took my gob out and shouted, '*Come on Polo!*' as loudly as I possibly could. Two men who were standing in front of me turned around and looked at me as if I had three heads, but I didn't care.

Polo started the race full of confidence, and he must have cleared the first hurdle by at least a foot and a half. Perhaps he didn't want to get his socks dirty? Actually, that would be typical of Polo.

Watching him clear the first hurdle helped settle me and,

after that, the unwelcome sense of foreboding was con-
quered by Polo's now infectious confidence. He was no
novice, by the way. This was his fifteenth time out and
although he'd only had two firsts so far (one over the jumps
and one on the flat), he'd never finished outside the top
three.

The second, third and fourth hurdles were taken almost
in his stride and, as he approached the fifth, I remember
looking round at my fellow spectators, my air of pride now
garnished with just a smidgen of conceit.

'I ride him out daily, don't you know,' was what my
expression said. 'Taught him everything he knows.'

And then it happened.

Once again Polo took the fifth hurdle as he had the rest,
and was at least a foot over the sticks, but for some reason
he seemed to land awkwardly on his left side and, as Brian
tried his best to straighten Polo up, he stumbled and then
his front left leg just seemed to snap.

People often assume it's the jump itself that puts the horse
in danger, but actually it's the six or seven strides it takes
afterwards that are most crucial. That, in effect, is when the
majority of racehorses live or die.

That image of Polo Venture mid-fall is as clear in my
mind today as it was when I saw it broadcast, and I've now
given up trying to wipe it from my memory. It's always the
same with the bad stuff – the harder you try, the more vivid
it becomes.

'Oh no,' were the only words that would come out of my

mouth, and as I stood there clinging on to the side of the table, I began whispering it to myself like some kind of spiralling mantra – 'Oh no, oh no, oh no', each one sounding a little bit more desperate.

The silence at the back of the stand was eventually broken by a racegoer standing directly behind me.

'They'll have the screens round that one,' he said sadly.

'Aye,' said another. 'It's not getting up, is it? It'll be dog meat by morning.'

'It's those who travel with them I feel sorry for,' said the first one. 'Fancy having to go home in an empty horsebox.'

That brought me round. What did he mean, empty horsebox?

Before any more thoughts could enter my head, I tried to prise myself from where I was standing. These days I know exactly what to do if one of your horses falls: go to the gate and wait for news. But at the time I didn't know what to do. I was in such a state.

Micky, I said to myself. *Got to find Micky.*

Micky had travelled to the meeting with Jedd and another stable lass called Jessica. It was futile, though. I probably knew at least a hundred people at that race meeting, but for some reason nobody seemed familiar.

I couldn't find Jedd, so in the end I decided to make my way down to the track. As I looked to where Polo had fallen I saw the screens arriving, just as the racegoer had predicted. Part of me was desperate to run over there, but there was something holding me back. Fear of what I'd see, most probably. Instead I ran towards the weigh-in room, hoping to find Brian. He seemed to have been unhurt by the fall, thank god, and providing he wasn't injured in any way, he would have been taken there by the ambulance. He'd know what to do. But as I made my way over to the weigh-in room, which is right next to the pre-parade ring, I suddenly saw one of the stewards talking into a walkie-talkie. He was bound to know what had happened.

As I started walking towards him, the steward looked up, and as he caught my eye his expression suddenly changed. He'd looked concerned as he spoke into his walkie-talkie, but on seeing me that expression morphed into one of sympathy. It was then that I knew Polo Venture had died.

Even so, I still stopped in my tracks when I saw his expression change, as I had the strange feeling that if I let him tell me the news of Polo's fate, I'd be as good as signing his death certificate. I was compelled not to move. How mad is that? In the end a steward came up to me.

'I'm sorry,' he began. 'I really am. The vet was with him almost immediately so he wouldn't have been in pain for long. Look, I know it's hard, but you'll get over it.'

I'm afraid that was the wrong thing to say.

You'll get over it?

People handle bad news in different ways, I suppose, but at that particular moment in time I'd boarded the angry bus. I wanted to throttle him, and if you actually could kill another human being just by looking at them, I think he'd probably have exploded right there in front of me.

You absolute bastard, I thought to myself. How dare he say that? That horse had been my life since the first day I walked into the yard.

I was determined not to cry, but as a fairly green eighteen-year-old who'd never really experienced loss before, the emotions I was feeling were completely overwhelming. So much so that – as opposed to keeping my big mouth shut – I drew myself up to my full five foot nowt and began to protest.

'Do you know something,' I blurted out, becoming a gibbering wreck almost immediately. 'For the last two years I've probably spent more time with that horse than I have my boyfriend. In fact, I know I have. I've ridden him out five times a week. I've fed him, mucked him out, brushed him down and cared for him when he's been ill. He's my best friend, for heaven's sake, and you reckon I'll just get over it? How the hell could you possibly understand!'

Of course he understood, and the look he shot me said as much.

In truth that steward at Perth racecourse probably understood better than anyone else, for the simple reason that he would have seen it happen all too frequently. What's more, he'd probably had the same conversation with hundreds of sobbing stable lasses.

'You'd be surprised,' he said finally.

What got my attention was that, as the steward spoke, it was almost as if he was looking straight through me. As if he was reliving every fall he'd ever had to contend with.

'I'm so sorry about that,' I said, trying desperately not to read his mind. 'He's the first one I've lost.'

'Really?' he said. 'I wish I could promise he'll be your last. You will get over it,' he said again, his gaze now fixed on mine. 'You've got no choice.'

Tim, who was an aspiring jockey at the time, had a ride at the same meeting, and as soon as he heard what had happened he came looking for me. When he found me I was in bits. Tim was hugely sympathetic, of course, but at the same time I think he knew it was something I had to experience. An unfortunate rite of passage, if you like.

'It's the worst part of the job,' he said to me. 'But if you're going to stay in racing, it's something you have to accept. You'll never get used to it. If you did you shouldn't be working with horses. But you have to learn to accept it. Now come here and give us a hug.'

The moment he said the words 'give us a hug', I completely broke down. All I could think about was the fall and Polo Venture's last moments; the ground staff pulling the screens around him and the vet arriving. I had so many questions: who was with him when he was shot? Was he in pain? Did anyone try and comfort him? The poor boy must have been terrified.

In truth, yes, he probably was in pain but, as the steward had pointed out, it wouldn't have been for long. And, according to Tim, he would have been comforted by the ground staff.

I'd wanted to be there for him, but even if I'd been able

to it would have been a terrible idea. Micky told me as much later on.

'Not even I attend terminations any more, Gemma. Not unless I have to. Trust me, it can scar you.'

Until then I think the most upsetting thing I'd experienced in my twenty months as a stable lass had been mucking out a slovenly colt whilst hungover. I'd also had a couple of falls, not to mention one or two rollockings from Micky, Crooky and Stee. The last one, which had happened a couple of weeks before, was when I'd lost my temper with Stee and had told him to bugger off in the earshot of Micky and an owner. That was like signing my own death warrant, and the moment the words came out of my mouth I knew I was in massive trouble.

'I'll let you deal with this, Stee,' said Micky, walking away. He looked so pissed off.

To my surprise, Stee didn't actually shout at me. In fact, he didn't say a word. He just looked at me regretfully and walked away. The contrast to what I'd been expecting was a lot more powerful and I felt absolutely appalling. I desperately wanted to run after him and apologize, but I knew that would be the wrong thing to do. What Stee was saying by remaining calm and walking away was, 'You go away and think about what you've just done. Then let's have a chat.'

The following morning I came in a bit earlier and asked if I could have a word with Stee in the office. The queen of contrition was about to speak.

'I am so sorry,' I said. 'I promise you that will never happen again.'

'It'd better not or I'll have your tripes out,' he said, laughing. 'Now sod off and make us a cup of tea.'

I'd never been so happy to be sworn at in my entire life!

Coming to terms with Polo's death was hard at first. After all, he'd been the first friend I'd seen and spoken to every day for almost two years, and in equine terms he was the love of my life. He was also the first horse I actually dreamed about, and I can remember those dreams to this very day. They're nothing very remarkable, I'm afraid. Just me and him doing what we always did. I did once have a dream about him running in a race, and funnily enough, that's the one I remember most. He won, of course.

14

The Winter of My Content –
and Discontent

In December 2000, I left Castle House and moved in with Tim. Actually, I didn't so much 'move in' with him as just not go home one day. This used to happen quite a lot in Middleham; as opposed to couples sitting down, talking it through and getting giddy over things like Ikea catalogues and soft furnishings, they'd just get on with it.

'Eh! I see you haven't been home for a bit. Does this mean you've moved in?'

'Erm. Yes, I suppose it does.'

'Fine. You'll be paying half the bills, though.'

Oh, the romance!

These days, a big announcement would be made – on Facebook, obviously – after which some cards would appear, followed by a few annoying but well-meant recommendations as to what colour you should paint your loo. Give me the seamless transition approach any day.

At the time Tim was having quite a good run as a jockey,

and since the summer he'd had five winners and a few seconds. The majority of his successes had been on an Irish horse called Orange Order. This popular chestnut gelding had originally been owned by Prince Khalid bin Abdullah of Saudi Arabia, and the first jockey to ride him more than once had been Conor O'Dwyer – funnily enough, about the same time I planted a smacker on his cheek.

Like so many jockeys, Tim often struggled to make the weight when he had a ride, and that Christmas he took his abstinence to extremes. On 22 December he was offered a ride at Sedgefield on Boxing Day, but he would have to lose about five pounds for it. Instead of politely declining the ride like any sane person and then enjoying his Christmas, Tim accepted it and went about losing the weight.

'I take it the horse stands a chance?' I asked him.

'No, not really,' he replied. 'It just needs a run-out.'

I couldn't believe it!

'Then why did you accept?' I asked him, flabbergasted.

'You never turn down a ride, Gem. Not unless you can afford to.'

So in between 23 December and Boxing Day he consumed nothing but an apple a day and a few glasses of water. I remember looking at him while the rest of us were having Christmas dinner, and he didn't seem bothered at all. I'd never seen willpower like it. I would have been chewing my hand off!

Tim's first win as a jockey had been in 1997, but instead of it being down to either his or the horse's performance, it was the result of one of the most bizarre finishes ever seen at a British racecourse. The course in question was Catterick, and earlier in our relationship Tim had described the finish in detail to me as I had listened, wide-eyed.

It was a national hunt flat race, and with a mile to go, Tim and his mount were about twelve lengths back in third place. 'The two horses in front of me were first and second favourite so I wasn't too concerned,' he said. 'I also had about five lengths on the horse in fourth so, with a bit of luck, I thought I'd manage to hang on to third.'

Tim smiled to himself and continued. 'Suddenly, the second favourite veered violently to the left and because the jockey wasn't expecting it, he fell. *Get in*, I thought. *I'm on for second!*

'With about half a mile to go the jockey-less second favourite lurched to the left once again and went straight into the other horse. I couldn't believe what I was seeing! This horse's jockey absolutely shat himself and, after becoming unseated, he fell to the horse's left. At first, I thought he'd gone, but instead he'd managed to get hold of the bridle and was actually hanging in front of the horse. If he'd fallen then he'd have gone straight under it.'

This was miles better than smoking wacky backy!

'By this time, we only had about a furlong to go and, after taking a quick look back, I saw that the rest of the field were nowhere near. As long as the jockey had hold of the bridle as they went over the line he'd win, and I almost shouted, "Jump, you bastard!" I obviously didn't want him to get hurt but he was the only thing separating me from my first win.

'What I couldn't believe was how this jockey was managing to hang on while his horse was going full pelt. I know they obviously have strong arms, but this was ridiculous!

'So, about two hundred yards before the line, he managed to pull himself around and grab on to the saddle, and that's when I thought he'd made it. But when he was literally no more than a few yards away, his horse tripped slightly and he fell to the ground. Meanwhile, I rode over the line to win the race. You should have heard the cheer from the crowd. They'd never seen anything like that before!'

The predominant noise you hear at the end of most races is obviously cheering, but at the end of this particular one there was quite a lot of laughter too. Tim didn't mind, though, and when he and his horse were eventually led into the winner's enclosure, they got a hero's reception.

My new home, which Tim had been living in for about a year, was Wren Cottage; a gorgeous-looking but minuscule one-bedroomed abode situated right next door to Manor House Stables and just a couple of hundred yards from the castle. Manor House Stables is where Matthew Peacock, the laid-back Dicky Peacock's father, used to ply his trade, and is just around the corner from where Atty the mad poodle used to ply his.

By far the most famous horse to be trained by Matthew Peacock at Manor House Stables was Dante, the last northern horse to win the Derby and the first Middleham horse to do so since Pretender in 1869. These days Dante is better known for the Group 2 race at York that was named after him in 1958, the Dante Stakes, but in 1944 he was the country's top-rated two-year-old and had won all six of his races. He'd actually been bred just across the road at Matthew's stud farm, so was very much a Middleham horse.

One afternoon, a few weeks after moving into Wren Cottage, Tim got permission from Patrick Haslam, who was then training out of Manor House Stables, to show me around the yard. It was one of those places I'd heard so much about and, because it was situated so close to Tim's family home, he knew it very well. There are actually two yards at Manor House Stables: one that's situated next to Wren Cottage, and another one almost parallel that faces the castle. Some people might argue that all yards look the same, but I completely disagree. These places are often teeming with history, and when Tim started telling me about Dante I was fascinated. In addition to this there were about forty horses in each yard, so I was in my element.

When we got to the yard facing Wren Cottage we came across a large bell hanging above one of the stables.

'What's that for?' I asked.

'It's called Peacock's bell,' replied Tim. 'It's rung every time the Peacock family either train or breed a group winner. The first time it was rung was way back in 1880 when the stables were first built.'

Although the Peacock family still owned Manor House Stables, they hadn't trained there since Dicky died back in 1984. The stud farm, however, was still going strong, and although the bell looked a bit rusty it was still very much in use.

'When was the last time it was rung?' I asked, not thinking for a moment he'd know.

'Twice in 1990,' said Tim immediately. 'When Tirol won the English and Irish 2,000 Guineas.'

Somebody needed to get out more.

A few years ago, the bell was moved over to the stud farm. It was rung again in March 2017, when a six-year-old chestnut gelding called Redkirk Warrior won the Lexus Newmarket Handicap in Australia, and no doubt it will clang again soon.

According to Tim, who I was beginning to think knew everything about everything, Wren Cottage had been built sometime in the eighteenth century, from stone that had been liberated from the castle. Sounds like Crooky's ancestors must have built it.

'It's a bit of a shithole,' Tim said when he first took me there. 'But it's home.'

'I think it's lovely,' I replied.

It really was very 'chocolate box'. Well. From the outside. Inside it looked like a bomb had hit it.

'I take it your cleaner's on holiday?' I said to him, stepping over a pile of dirty clothes.

Having seen the inside of my room at Castle House, Tim

knew I was in no position to criticize, and the look he gave me said as much.

For the first month or so I loved living at Wren Cottage; mostly because I liked living with Tim, but also because it was the first time I'd felt like an adult outside of work. Despite only being nineteen, I'd already come of age professionally, but domestically I still hadn't a clue.

The realization that I was actually now living with somebody had been difficult to take in at first, for the simple reason that I had no idea what to expect. I mean, what were you supposed to do? I was no domestic goddess, so what if Tim was expecting me to do the housework? Even some of the housework? He'd be in for a very nasty shock. I did try getting involved with that kind of thing, but if I'm honest Tim ended up doing about eighty per cent of it. Nothing's ever changed in that respect.

Then, in mid-January 2001, the moment I'd been waiting for during the past two winters finally arrived. We had snow!

The thought of seeing Wensleydale and Coverdale covered in a thick blanket of white had become a minor obsession with me. A crisp, clear, snowy day would be so much nicer than the cold, wet and miserable winters I'd had so far in Middleham. Although, to be fair, they had been character forming. On a few occasions I had really had to drag myself out of bed, but generally I'd been surprised by just how well I'd coped. Everyone had been in the same boat so, although it had been what the lads would always call a 'ball-ache', I hadn't seen anyone else complaining.

Something that had occurred to me halfway through that second winter was that if I managed to get through this then surely I'd stand a better chance of getting a ride? Working in the pouring rain might not be a pre-requisite when it comes to becoming a jockey, but experience definitely was, and – regardless of what was falling from the sky – I felt that I was still moving in the right direction.

Paradoxically, it's this time of year that can often turn would-be jockeys into pretty bitter human beings, and understandably so. Once you realize that you're not going to make it (and, let's face it, the vast majority of us don't), you can start to resent working in such testing conditions, and it's been known to turn people away from the industry completely. All that pain and misery – and for what? I sup-pose it's yet another part of the ongoing and fairly brutal selection process.

What we'll do these days, if we spot something like that happening, is to try and set them on a different career path; either by helping them to become a head lad or lass, or a travelling head lad or lass. Unfortunately, this doesn't always work: the realization that your dream is finally over can be devastating, and can often result in people making knee-jerk decisions to leave. Some who go do come back after a while, but – sadly – a lot don't. These stable lads and lasses are all talented horse people, and the industry is a lot poorer for losing them.

That first morning when I awoke to find snow on the ground is something I will remember for as long as I live. There was no street lighting around Wren Cottage, and I didn't realize until I opened the front door.

'Tim, it's been snowing!' I said excitedly.

'And?'

Tim's eight years older than me and, after living in Middleham all his life, he'd already had more than his fair share of arctic training.

'Have you never seen snow before?' he said, locking the door behind us.

'Not like this.'

There must have been at least three inches on the ground, and it was still coming down apace.

'So, I take it you've never ridden out in it before?'

'No, never.'

'Well, it's dry at the moment and not too cold. Pray it stays that way.'

This made me stop for a second. 'Why?' I said, calling after Tim.

'You know when it got cold last winter? You know, when it was wet?'

'Yes, of course I remember.'

'Well, if this goes like I think it might, you can times that by ten.'

By the time I got to the yard, I'd forgotten all about Tim's doom-laden prophecy and just got on with my job as usual. The only thing we had to be careful about, early on at least, was slipping on the snow, so until the first lot went out everyone walked very gingerly indeed. The first person to go arse over tit would be the one everyone remembered, and I was determined it wasn't going to be me.

'Get some salt down while we're out, will you?' Stee had said to a lad before leaving the yard. 'If it starts to freeze we're screwed.'

Once again, I didn't take heed of Stee's warning. I was too busy staring at the winter wonderland in front of me. Middleham's a stunning little town whatever the weather – even when it's raining – but in the snow it's absolutely amazing, and because it's built on a hill you always get to see a lot more than you would if it were flat. The view that greeted me as I rode up from the yard very nearly had me in tears. It was now clear and the snow had stopped. Daylight was almost here, and all that accompanied the thankfully familiar view of the beautiful Georgian buildings in the ancient cobbled square – now augmented by an almost translucent layer of fresh, dry snow – was the gentle sound of horses' hooves. I had never experienced anything like it.

'What are you smiling about?' asked Stee, who was riding alongside me.

'This!' I said, gesturing at what lay before us.

'You're mad, you are,' he said. 'It's only a bit of snow.'

Stee too is Middleham born and bred, and somewhere

along the way the novelty of seeing the town in the snow had worn off.

'Well, I like it,' I said, giving him a smile.

Everything with the first lot went fine. Middleham Moor suited its new look just as much as the town it was named after and, because the snow was nice and fine, I didn't experience any problems. In fact, the only thing I found difficult was keeping my eyes on what was in front of me. It was impossible!

'You're smiling again,' said Stee on the way back.

'Just leave me alone, will you?'

By the time we got back with the second lot, the temperature had started to drop, and by the time we went out with the fourth it must have been at least minus five degrees. That's when I first started to experience a real Yorkshire winter.

Before I left that day, I fell flat on my arse at least three times. Fortunately, so did everyone else. It was funny at first, but once it started hurting a bit it didn't seem quite so amusing, and that's when the arguments started. Freezing your arse off is no fun whatsoever, especially when said arse is covered in bruises and you've got a bunch of morons laughing at you.

By the end of that week I had fallen completely out of love with winter. Visually stunning it might well have been, but the pain it inflicted on me was like nothing I had ever experienced before. The worst day was Thursday. I was riding up with the third lot, and by the time we got to the moor I was in so much pain that I'm afraid I started to weep. Every single bone in my body ached like mad and gripping the reins had become agony. I'd simply gone beyond my pain threshold. I remember being massively embarrassed but I just couldn't help it.

What made it slightly comical was that my facial expression had frozen in place and was exactly as it had been before I started blubbing, and when I got back to the yard I looked like I'd had a face-lift. Either that or I'd been injected with a gallon of Botox. I wasn't the only one, though, and until we'd all warmed up a bit, the tack room looked as if it was full of rich Californian housewives.

Since landing from Leeds I'd heard tales about snowdrifts that were at least ten feet high, especially from some of the farmers. Tim and Stee's late granddad had been a sheep and dairy farmer in West Scrafton and, according to Tim, he'd spend days on end on the moor during the winter trying to dig his sheep out of the drifts. The only time he came back to the farm was to have a quick meal or to grab a couple of hours' sleep, and in some years this went on for many weeks. He really did risk life and limb for his stock.

I'd never seen a snowdrift close up, but that was about to change. There's a track on the Low Moor called Wall Corner Side, which is close to a tarn called Pinker's Pond. The great Willie Carson served his apprenticeship up at Tupgill Park under a trainer called Captain Gerald Armstrong, and on 19 July 1962 he had his first ever winner on a horse called Pinker's Pond. The equally great Lester

Piggott used to spend his summers up at Tupgill Park and, according to a reliable source, he did nothing but eat salad leaves and smoke cigars.

I hadn't been down that way for a while, so had forgotten about the gradient of the lane. All I saw before me was a flat bed of snow on an incline. As we started off, the snow covered the horse's ankles almost immediately. Then, a few steps later, it had gone up to his knees. This didn't register, I'm afraid – I have no idea what I was thinking of – and it was only when the snow had touched the horse's belly that I realized I might have misjudged the lie of the land. By then it was too late, and just two or three steps later it was up to my waist and to the horse's neck! To say it took me by surprise would be a huge understatement, but the horse just kept on going. In fact, he seemed to be enjoying himself.

'Whoa!' I shouted, grabbing the reins. Luckily, he came to a halt. By now the gradient of the incline had started coming back to me and I'd worked out that in just another step or two we'd probably become submerged. This wasn't a life-or-death situation – the snow was too thin for that – but it certainly wasn't ideal, and after carefully backing the horse up a few metres I rode him to safety. He appeared to be in his element, though, and once I had him back on the moor he gave me the fright of my life. Suddenly, and without warning, he fell to his knees, dropped to one side, and after lying there for a second started rolling around like a huge, demented dog. I could have sworn he tried to do a snow angel! In all my years in racing I had never seen anything like that before, but there didn't seem to be any harm in it. It was just really sweet. *You go for your life*, I thought. *I'll just stand here freezing my bum off.*

Conversely, we once had a horse for a few years who wouldn't leave his box if it was snowing. All he did was shake his head and walk back into his box, and it didn't matter how sneaky you were, he was wise to it.

Nope. Not going. And you can put your stupid sugar lumps away. I'm not interested.

Despite what I've just said about forgetting where I was on the Low Moor, one of the most important rules when you're riding in the snow is to stick to places you know. Veer off course and you could encounter things like rabbit holes, and there are no prizes for guessing what can happen when a horse steps into one of them. A friend of mine runs a stud farm nearby, and he and his staff spend half their lives filling in rabbit holes. It's a constant fear for them.

The change at Wren Cottage, once the snow and ice came, was unbelievable. The windows, which I believe may have been the original ones, were about as much use as a chocolate fireguard and because there was no heating in the house, we used to get dressed and undressed in bed. There was a storage heater on one wall, but that had given up the ghost sometime in the 1960s and so, unless you lit a fire, which we only did for a few hours in the evenings, you were left to the unforgiving mercy of Jack Frost.

In February 2001 Becky came up to help us during the

half-term holidays, and it was so cold that me, Tim, Becky and even Benji, who was never usually allowed upstairs, ended up sleeping in the same bed! I remember the four of us peeping our heads out from underneath the mountain of blankets first thing in the morning, and it looked like a cigar smoker's convention. Never before had I been less keen to get out of bed.

It never got that bad in Castle House, which didn't have any central heating either, but I think that was because of all the hot water pipes that were running under the floor-boards. It could get cold sometimes, but it was never arctic. Wren Cottage only had one bedroom, and, just like a tomato, it must have been made of at least eighty per cent water! Most of those old cottages were damp, but our place was sodden. Mum used to say that it was at least three degrees cooler in Middleham than it was in Leeds but, because I now felt a loyalty to my newish home, I'd always try and dispute it. The only person I was fooling was myself, I'm afraid, and – if truth be known – the difference was probably more like ten.

There's one more snowy scenario that to this day puts the fear of god into me, and it's when the snow starts to ball in horses' hooves. If the snow is light and powdery, it's never a problem, but the moment it becomes wet and heavy you start to worry. The trigger for it becoming troublesome is when your bum goes up and you break into a canter. All of a sudden, there are lots and lots of hoof-shaped snowballs heading your way at about thirty miles an hour, and the ones that don't hit you in the face, which is pleasant, will probably hit the underside of the horse. Because the assault is so incessant, that can seriously spook them. Either way, it's going to result in at least one of you becoming scared or pissed off, and nine times out of ten it's both. Trying to control a spooked horse is difficult at the best of times, but when you're also being pelted in the face and on the arms by a couple of hundred icy snowballs, it becomes damn painful and more than a little bit alarming. The trouble is, the faster the horse goes, the worse it all gets. The only upside, I suppose, is that if you get thrown you'll most likely land on something soft.

That said, over the years I've seen some awful falls, and several have required ambulances. The worst one I ever witnessed happened on the gallops one morning a couple of years ago. The stable lad who was riding the horse ended up breaking his collarbone, several ribs and one of his arms. The horse wasn't used to the snow and the moment it started peppering its own belly it stopped and began to buck like mad. The stable lad, who was only about seventeen, must have landed at least ten or fifteen feet in front of the horse. Luckily the Yorkshire Air Ambulance got to him within about twenty minutes and they took him straight to James Cook Hospital in Middlesbrough.

Before the Yorkshire Air Ambulance was introduced in 2001, it was always a bit of a lottery for us if there was an accident. The nearest ambulance is based in Bainbridge, which is about seventeen miles away, and even if it was available it could take a good forty-five minutes to get to you. The Yorkshire Air Ambulance has been a godsend as far as we're concerned, and must have saved hundreds of lives around the county.

Nothing spooks a horse more than being hit on the belly by something it can't see (apart from being screamed at by a stable girl who's just been hit on the arse), and early in 2017 we had an incident that almost ended in tragedy.

The horse, Alderbrook Lad, was doing a routine seven-furlong canter and, just after he'd finished, he threw his rider. It happens.

Micky and I were parked a little further down the gallop at the time, and when Alderbrook Lad eventually came into view his saddle had gone right around underneath him, and his bridle, which was still connected to the girth, was hitting his belly. As tack malfunctions go this was a big one, and because the bridle was hitting him he became spooked and that just propelled him forward.

So as not to scare him, we tried to maintain a safe distance, but as he cantered off towards Middleham, we lost sight of him for a while. As we followed on we realized quite quickly that his journey so far had been far from uneventful, and just before we reached the town itself we saw some fresh hoof marks on the road.

'He's hit that drystone wall,' said Micky. 'Look.'

The skid marks from Alderbrook Lad's shoes went right from the centre of the road to the far left-hand side and, because they stopped at the wall, he'd obviously hit it at speed.

As we went around the next corner we caught sight of him again; just as we did, he skidded onto his side and went right underneath the front of a Range Rover. Fortunately, the Range Rover was stationary, but when he pulled himself up and started off again we could see cuts and abrasions all over his body.

'Jesus Christ,' said Micky. 'We've got to stop him, Gemma. He's going to kill himself.'

Unfortunately, the saddle and the bridle had started hitting him again, and as soon as that happened he was off at full speed into the town. This was where things became dangerous and we prayed that there were no children playing or prams being pushed around.

Once again, Micky and I tried to maintain a safe distance in the jeep and, as we turned past the castle and then down towards the square, we saw him heading off in the direction of the yard. Hannah, who is Micky's racing secretary, had been made aware of what was happening and had gone out to try and flag him down. No chance! He was now going at about thirty miles an hour and so Hannah ran back into the yard, kept the gates open and hoped that he'd run in.

Unfortunately he didn't, and as we passed the gates in the jeep one of his shoes came off and hit the windscreen. That was absolutely terrifying and, as well as cracking the windscreen, it made such a noise that Micky almost drove off the road and into a wall. Because of the speed at which he was going, his three remaining horseshoes were generating some massive sparks and some of these were hitting him on his neck. For some reason this slowed him down for a bit, but eventually they all went the same way as the first shoe and, once the sparks had stopped, he was flying again. At one point we got close to him by mistake and it felt as if we were in a chariot race. Ben Hur comes to Middleham!

The next potential problem we had was Cover Bridge, which is about a mile and a half from the yard. This is a blind humpback bridge that runs over the river Cover, and if he didn't run into an oncoming vehicle, which was entirely possible, he'd be on the road leading up to East Witton and that's a mile straight. We wouldn't be able to stop him and – because he had no shoes on – this could do his feet untold damage.

In order to go over Cover Bridge, you have to veer right on the road, but if you go straight ahead you'll end up in a yard. That is, if the gate is open. Fortunately for us, it was, and instead of veering right he went straight into the yard and came to a halt. Had he gone over the bridge he'd have run straight into the path of the oncoming van we saw cross the bridge moments later and, if that had happened, obviously he wouldn't have stood a chance.

When we got out of the jeep we walked over to him very slowly. The poor boy was absolutely petrified and his feet were in a terrible state. There was blood everywhere. A few minutes later the horsebox arrived, but because he was so traumatized we had to wait two hours before he was ready to travel.

This horse had been due to race at Cartmel the following week, but naturally we had to pull him. He did run a month later, though, in May 2017, and I'm pleased to say he won! He's actually a really promising horse and, looking back, I think it affected Micky and me more than it did him. I still have nightmares about it.

15

A Cup of Ambition

In May 2002, Micky decided to take a sabbatical. As opposed to becoming disillusioned with the industry, I think he was just exhausted, and because his marriage had recently broken down he needed a change of scene. It was still a massive shock, though, and we had no idea when he was coming back. As well as giving me a job – my dream job – Micky had taught me so much; not only about horses, but about the industry itself. I couldn't have wished for a better mentor. He'd already trained over five hundred winners by this point, and you don't achieve that by accident.

Although Micky's internship was different to mine (very different, in fact), his introduction to the sport had been extremely similar. His father and his uncle Fred had been racing fanatics, just like my dad, and each Saturday they used to bet on something called the ITV Seven. This was an accumulator bet where vast sums of money could be won if you correctly predicted the winners of all seven races shown on ITV. It was racing's equivalent of the football pools, basically. In addition to watching this with his dad and his uncle, Micky and his family also went to the races occasionally: either Kempton, Sandown or Epsom. That's where he got the bug, so to speak. What made Micky want to work in the industry was the fact that when he left school he was just five feet tall and weighed seven stone. Opportunities for people of that build and stature were few and far between, and if you lived close to any racing yards it was often suggested that you might want to give it a go. That said, by the time Micky had made his decision to work in racing, he still hadn't sat on either a horse or pony. In fact, he hadn't even sat on a seaside donkey!

You don't find it so much these days, but back then a lot of people would turn up at a racing yard on spec, having never even seen a horse in real life. It sounds ridiculous, doesn't it? At least Micky had been to the races. That was how the industry operated then, though, and the recruitment policy was that if a trainer liked the look of you, he or she might give you a try. Providing, of course, that you didn't have a tall mother. This is quite bizarre but, back in the day, if your parents dropped you off and your mother was over a certain height, the trainer wouldn't hire you. Boys were always expected to be taller than their mothers and so if yours was tall and you were assumed to be still growing, you were stuffed. Providing that wasn't the case, and you had no experience, the chances were you might be in luck. It was assumed that being inexperienced meant that you had no bad habits or preconceived ideas. All racehorse trainers do things differently, and training a member of staff from scratch and to your specifications was probably preferable to re-training one from another yard who had been trained to somebody else's.

Incidentally, the worst kind of people you get applying for jobs in racing are ones who've already tried working in two or three different industries. It's not exclusively the case, but because they're not necessarily interested in racing, they don't have any affinity with the animals and that's something you simply cannot teach. Some staff turn out to be OK, but that's a happy accident more than anything else. If somebody doesn't have a natural affinity with horses it can put the animals on edge, and as we already know they can sense things like fear and nervousness a mile away.

By his own admission, Micky rather naively thought that riding a horse would be easy, and he's certainly not the first person to make that mistake. I knew a couple of lads at racing college who shared that opinion and I was lucky enough to be there when they went for their first hack. One of them actually screamed! Micky too ended up having a bit of a baptism of fire and had three bad falls on his first morning. When he left the yard that day he had a newfound respect for both the animals and the profession. Newfound, but essential nevertheless.

Apparently, the pay was awful – just fifteen pounds a week at the start – and two thirds of that was gone within the first few hours. There'd be five pounds for his bed and board, five pounds for the hire purchase on his motorbike, and five pounds to spend. This was the late 1970s, although given the figures involved you'd have thought it was the 1940s. I know stable work isn't the best-paid job in the world even now but, considering how hard the job was, what they got paid then was an absolute pittance. Regardless of whether you've been to racing college or not, riding horses and preparing them for the races or the sales is a skilled job, so how they got away with paying so little for so long is beyond me. Thank god, it's changed! Micky always makes the additional point that – as well as only earning sixty quid a month – he only got one day off a fortnight. But he follows that up by saying it was just as well, as that was as often as he could afford to go out on those wages.

The first trainer Micky worked for was a man called Buck Jones, and the person who taught him to ride was Buck's father, Davy Jones. He wasn't the Monkee, by the way, although – believe it or not – Davy Jones from the Monkees did work in Middleham for a time as an apprentice jockey. He was rather good, apparently, and had also worked in Lambourn. This Davy Jones, who had also been a jockey, had once ridden in the Derby and the Cheltenham Gold Cup in the same year. Being taught to ride by such a consummate horseman was an opportunity that wasn't lost on Micky. Before too long he was having a few rides on the flat, which had always been his ambition, but before he had a chance to make a name for himself, he started growing again. This meant that if he wanted to continue as a jockey he'd have to go over the sticks, which he wasn't keen on.

When he finished his apprenticeship with Buck Jones, Micky took his first sabbatical and spent eight weeks cleaning windows while he learned how to drive and tried to decide if he wanted to stay in racing. Fortunately, he did, but when he went to work for trainer Hugh O'Neill, he only went in as a stable lad. It was Hugh O'Neill who managed to persuade Micky to apply for a jump jockey's licence, even though Micky himself wasn't bothered one way or the other. He just wanted to work with horses.

Micky's first ride as a jump jockey took place at Fakenham in a conditional jockey's novice hurdle and, in the same race, also having his first ride as jump jockey, was Karl Burke, who now trains at Spigot Lodge. They've been friends ever since.

Even by this point, Micky was still having second thoughts about staying in the industry, and the only thing stopping him from going back to window cleaning was the fact that stable work was marginally less dangerous!

'I had one or two bad experiences, Gemma,' he'd said when I once quizzed him about it. 'Painful experiences! Mark my words, falling off a horse is easy compared to falling off a ladder.'

His first year at O'Neill's was the same year that Walter Swinburn won the Derby on Shergar, so we're certainly going back a few years.

Micky had his first winner over the jumps at Windsor on a horse called Excelsior, beating none other than Bob Champion into second place. Excelsior was owned by a notorious ticket tout called Stan Flashman, who became chairman of Barnet Football Club, and Micky won on him a couple of times. Excelsior, not Stan. Two hundred and thirty winners later, he decided to go into training.

When Micky went on his sabbatical, Crooky took over as trainer, and so to all intents and purposes everything stayed the same: same horses, same staff, same owners. To me, though, things weren't quite the same, and for the eighteen months Micky was away I felt as if I was treading water. In fact, I probably *was* treading water a bit.

Racing may have gained a new trainer when Crooky took over, but as far as I was concerned I'd lost my head lad. I'm not saying I didn't like Crooky as a trainer – far from it – but because he'd only just started, he was as busy as hell. For the first time in his life, Crooky had had to remove himself from the tack room and, with him being stuck in the office, and with Micky not being around, the yard seemed slightly soulless. Part of my reason for getting up in the morning had been to impress Micky and Crooky and learn from them. There were still plenty of people I liked and admired in the yard, but I no longer had a mentor. Don't get me wrong, I was still living the dream – riding out thoroughbreds twenty times a week and going to the odd race meeting. Something was missing, though, and once it all changed I think I went into my shell a bit. At least at work.

At home everything was fine. More than fine, in fact. Wren Cottage was still cold, small and damp, but with Tim and Benji there to keep me company I was never stuck for stimulation. They were perfect housemates, really. Admittedly one needed walking twice a day and smelt a bit, but the other was a cuddly dog with an adorable wet nose.

It was actually about this time that Tim decided to give up being a jockey. He'd had his first ever ride on 16 December 1995 on a horse called Twin Falls and had finished sixth out of a field of fourteen. Tim used to say he'd finished fourteenth out of a field of six, but he always does himself down! Since then he'd had a further eighty rides as a conditional and then a stable jockey and, as well as shedding a similar number of stone in weight just to make them, he'd also had almost as many injuries. OK, so perhaps I'm exaggerating a bit with the weight and the injuries, but you see what I'm getting at. The sacrifices you make, even as a conditional jockey, are ridiculous.

Over the years Tim had broken his wrists, his fingers, and his ribs, which is just about inevitable if you're going to ride horses over jumps. But in addition to these 'inconveniences', he'd broken his collarbone, which happened a few years before I met him, and his back, which happened about a year after, and with his original ambition now waning a bit, and his love of food and hatred of saunas and glasses of water on the increase, he thought it was the perfect time to stop.

'I'm buggered if I'm going to spend another Christmas eating apples and drinking glasses of bloody water,' he said one day. 'I can't be arsed with all that any more.'

Breaking your back obviously sounds a lot worse than breaking your collarbone, yet Tim was in hospital for four weeks after breaking his collarbone and only four days after breaking his back. The difference was how long he had to convalesce for. With his collarbone, it was another three weeks after he left hospital, whereas with his back it was over three months. I didn't see the race, fortunately, but I'll never forget receiving the telephone call telling me it had happened. We'd only been going out together a couple of months, but we were already close. Although I knew plenty of people who'd had horse-related accidents, none of them had been serious. I think it was Rachel who gave me the news, and when she said he'd broken his back my immediate thought was that he must have been paralysed. It was an awful moment and I remember feeling incredibly cold. Apparently, Tim had been thrown from his mount halfway through a race and had landed with his legs over his face like a sandwich board. Basically, he'd snapped his back and, had it happened a millimetre or two further down, he would have been paralysed like I'd feared. I remember going to see him in hospital and I was amazed when he said he was going to discharge himself.

'You can't,' I said in a panic. 'The doctors won't allow it.'

'I'm not bothered about them,' said Tim. 'I want to go home!'

Typical man.

In the end the doctors said it was OK for him to go home providing he had complete bed rest for at least three months.

He had no choice but to agree, really, and without wanting to sound selfish, it played havoc with our social life! It was back to DVDs as opposed to KFC in Darlington, and even tea at the Commie was off the cards. At least he could eat what he wanted for a change.

One slightly more extreme example of jockeying finally getting the better of you involves a jockey I read about just the other day called George Chaloner. In three years he'd suffered three very bad falls, and the last one, which happened at Newcastle in 2017, was his comeback ride from the previous fall. As well as breaking his foot at Newcastle, George suffered a similar injury to Tim's, and his T8 vertebrae was just millimetres away from being paralysed. After having further scans they also discovered he'd injured other parts of his back, and all this at the age of just twenty-five. Apparently, George had been having nightmares about the fall before that, so I'm not surprised it broke his resolve. Fancy having to retire at twenty-five, though. It's heartbreaking.

A lot of people assume that stable staff and jockeys must go through life worrying about being injured, but in my experience that's not true. It's the friends, relatives and loved ones who go through the mill, and for the first two or three years my mum would ring me at least four or five times a week to make sure I was OK.

'You haven't fallen, have you?' she would ask me in a panic.

'Of course not. I'm talking to you!'

'I do worry about you.'

'Yes, I know you do, Mother.'

It's different when you're the one doing the riding. I was always told not to worry about things you can do nothing about, and I think that's the general philosophy in racing. We all know the dangers involved and, providing we keep our wits about us and do our jobs correctly, then we've done as much as we can. You can't legislate for most of the accidents that happen, so all we can do is try and eradicate human error.

Shortly before Tim told me he was going to quit being a jockey, I'd fractured my wrist at work after falling on the gallops and, although it wasn't the most serious injury ever, it was unbelievably painful. I think the most serious injuries I've ever had are a kick in the face and some nice ripped ligaments. The kick in the face happened about ten years ago and, as with Tim's back, had the horseshoe landed just a few millimetres further down I'd have lost the sight of my left eye. As it was, I ended up with half a horseshoe indented on my forehead and about fifteen stitches! The snapped ligaments happened as a result of a fall, and I couldn't walk properly for months. Despite the above, I think I'd still prefer an injury – or at least a minor one – to having to fast for several days, and if I'd been Tim I would have knocked it on the head years earlier.

As far as I'm concerned, wasting, which is what they call the process of losing weight for a race, is a form of masochism, and even the thought of it scares me half to death. It also requires willpower, which I'm afraid rules me right out. When a jockey wastes depends on when they get told about the race, so sometimes it can happen gradually, which is the lesser of the two evils, and sometimes rapidly, which is purgatory, and is what happened to Tim when he rode at Christmas. Over the years, I've known dozens of professional jockeys, and the majority try and remain at least two stone below their ideal weight. That's obviously not natural, and how they don't end up killing anybody is beyond me. What's far more natural is what happens to them once they retire, and I know the perfect example.

Years ago, well before my time, Micky used a jockey called Peter Niven, or Niv, as he was known. Stee used to mention him all the time, and nearly all the stories he told me about Niv involved him being a bit of a grumpy so-and-so.

Before the season started, Niv would come into the yard to school some of the young horses. However, during the off-season he would often become a stone or two above the weight required, i.e. his normal weight, which meant that by the time he started schooling he'd been wasting hard for a good while.

'Boiled eggs and Silk Cut was Niv's regular diet,' said Stee. 'No man could be happy on that.'

One day, Niv had arrived at the yard to school Burn Bridge, the horse who enjoyed nibbling on fences. I'm not sure if it was because Burn Bridge was eating better than he was, but it was clear from the start that they weren't going to get on. When Niv walked Burn Bridge down to the first fence, which is what you normally do in order to generate a bit of enthusiasm, he might as well have given the horse a pipe and a comfy chair. He just wasn't interested.

'Niv was fuming by this point,' said Stee. 'He didn't like lethargic horses, and if Burn Bridge had been any more so, he'd have collapsed and died.'

After getting back on, Niv walked him back to the two other horses that were being schooled. They were standing about a hundred yards away and were being ridden by two of the lads.

'Right then,' said Niv. 'Let's go.'

With that, the three horsemen of the schooling apocalypse immediately set off towards the first fence. 'You need to pick up the pace,' Niv shouted to the lads, and so they did as they were told. Seconds later the three popped over the plain fence without too much drama. Niv still wasn't happy with the pace, though, so he decided to give Burn Bridge a slap behind the saddle with his whip.

'Schoolboy error, that,' said Stee. 'He only gave him a quick slap, but Burn Bridge hated the whip. Hated it!'

As they approached the ditch, Burn Bridge slammed on the brakes and went from roughly 25 mph to zero in about thirty inches. Niv, however, carried on, and went head-first over the fence without the horse. He was furious!

'I'd never smiled as much in all my life,' said Stee.

For balance, and Stee always reiterated this, Niv was an exceptional jockey, and from the moment he retired and started eating normally again he became fat and happy. They're Stee's words, Mr Niven, not mine!

About eighteen months after Micky left, I heard a whisper that he was thinking of coming back into training. He'd been working for William Hill Radio since giving it up, and had been living in Ripon. I forget who told me now, but when it was finally confirmed later that week that Micky was coming back I felt absolutely elated.

Because Micky owned the yard, he gave Crooky notice and eventually Crooky moved to Tupgill, which is where he is today. Because Crooky was now established in his own right, some of staff went with him, as did some of the owners. I made it clear that I wanted to stay on at Oakwood, and Crooky respected that.

I think it was expected that the owners who didn't move with Crooky might keep their horses at Oakwood, but unfortunately that didn't materialize. I think they felt anxious that Micky had spent time away from the industry and wanted to see how he got on. Micky would be the first to admit that this was a big blow to his ambitions, as he was now caught between a rock and a hard place. He obviously wanted quality horses again, but in order to get those into the yard he'd have to prove himself. His response to this dilemma was to take on poorer-quality horses, and pretty soon we had a full yard.

During his first month back we had three or four decent winners, and so everyone quickly began talking about the triumphant return of Micky Hammond. It was all over the racing press and the mood in the yard was obviously buoyant. Unfortunately, instead of capitalizing on this and carrying the momentum forward, we stalled, and for the next few months we couldn't win a race – or even get a placing – for love nor money. It had obviously been a false dawn and we'd been punching well above our weight. This, it appeared, was normality! What compounded our problems was the fact that some of the owners hadn't been paying us, and it got to a point where Micky was having problems paying the wages. The situation in the yard had gone from good to bad to absolutely awful, and the mood had followed suit. We all knew what was happening with regards to the results, and now the payment issues, which I'm sure Micky had hoped to keep quiet, had started filtering out. It's not easy keeping a secret in a racing yard, and once that news began circulating, the mood dipped even further. Now, everyone was nervous about their future and, to be honest, they had good reason to be.

Not being paid on time – or even at all, in some cases – also meant that Micky was unable to buy horses at the sales. Trainers will often buy horses at the sales and then sell them on to owners. Not at a profit. They do it because they know what to look for. It's all part of getting the right horses into the yard and, even if an owner can't be found immediately, at least you have the horse. For that, though, you need capital.

These days our owners will often give Micky and me a

budget and ask us to buy a horse on their behalf. I absolutely love this part of the job, although it's a massive responsibility. They're entrusting you with tens or even hundreds of thousands of pounds. That's when it goes beyond being a business relationship. From then on, it's a partnership.

With mounting debts, poor horses and a few months' worth of bad results, Micky knew something had to change. One morning he called everyone into the office.

'I've made a decision,' he said. 'I'm going to start again from scratch.'

'How do you mean, from scratch?' asked Stee.

'I'm getting rid of all the crap. All the bad horses and all the owners who don't pay.'

'How many horses will that leave us with?' Ashley asked.

'About ten,' said Micky. 'It's going to be hard, but we can't carry on like this. This isn't what I came back for.'

Although I obviously appreciated the seriousness of the situation, the prospect of starting again with two or three quality owners and ten decent horses excited me far more than plodding along with a yard full of no-hopers. I don't think Micky was quite so excited. After all, he had the full SP with regards to the financial situation and, as bad as some of the owners were at paying their bills, our income would nevertheless be dropping dramatically.

To me this was the ultimate challenge and, as well as locking me into the industry, it sparked my ambition to begin moving up the racing ladder. Just because you work for a trainer, it doesn't necessarily mean you have faith in their methods. I thought Crooky was brilliant, but I'd missed working with Micky and wanted to start learning from him again. When you have absolute faith in somebody and they leave, unless you can emulate them and start practising what you've learned, you're left frustrated. If Micky ever left again I wanted to be in a position where I could potentially carry on where he'd left off and integrate his methods with my own.

My first move up the ladder came courtesy of both Stee and Rachel, and the position itself was a hybrid really of travelling head lass and assistant head lass. When Micky came back, Stee and Rachel had stayed on at Oakwood Stables – Stee as head lad and Rachel as travelling head lass. But about six months later the two of them decided that they wanted to leave the industry for good, and that left two massive gaps. They wanted to start a family and didn't believe racing was the right environment in which to do it.

'If we're having a kid together, we're definitely not working together,' was Stee's logic. I think he was right.

Fortunately, Stee and Rachel are family, so although they left racing they didn't leave me.

Ashley took over as head lad and, because we worked well together, I became his assistant. I also took over Rachel's job. This made sense as, with just ten horses in the yard, trips to the races were going to be weekly rather than daily. At least for the time being.

I quickly had to learn how to delegate, how to give

instruction, and, most importantly of all, how to keep everything to a very high standard. You can't really achieve the third of these objectives unless you've mastered the first two and, although I'd had some experience in instructing people and giving out orders, it had only been very recently. Before Micky made the decision to cut back and start again, we'd had staff issues, and I'd been given the task of bringing some newbies up to speed.

Now I was having to do it all the time, and at first I found it quite daunting. Not because I had difficulty communicating with people. Anything but. It was what I was having to communicate. First of all, I had to make sure my instructions were in alignment with Micky's wishes. Secondly, because everything was second nature to me, I'd do it without even thinking. Now I had to verbalize everything I did – and believe me, it's not as easy as it sounds. In fact, it can be downright infuriating sometimes, especially when people don't get it right.

I'd found the delegation side difficult when I was working with the newbies, for the simple reason that a lot of the time they didn't do as they were asked. That probably makes me sound like a bit of a disciplinarian, but unfortunately some of the staff we'd taken on fitted into the category I mentioned earlier: they were only in the job because they'd failed at something else. As more and more horses came into the yard, we had to get bums on saddles and hands on forks, and unfortunately for us they had been all that was available. This meant that very few of them either cared or listened, and it made for quite a strained working environment. They were decent riders, but that's only part of the job.

At first, I became exasperated by these members of staff, and would shout and bawl at them. I cared, they didn't, and to me not caring was a cardinal sin. Fortunately, it didn't take me long to realize that this approach simply made them worse, so after having a quick word with myself I changed tack. For every two or three rubbish members of staff, we had somebody decent, and so instead of worrying about the idiots I focused on the good people. Leading by example, I think they call it. We all had to work a bit harder, but while one group thrived, the staff who weren't on board eventually got the message and one by one they left. Off to try somebody else's patience. Going forward, we tried to be very careful about who we took on. We employed the same approach that we eventually did with the horses and owners, I suppose. For me this was a valuable lesson as, later down the line, when I became Micky's assistant, it taught me what to ask and what to look out for when interviewing. It's not an exact science, of course, but these days it's very rare that somebody slips through the net.

I hope he doesn't mind me saying this, but when Micky came back into racing he was a lot more talkative and approachable than he had been. I mentioned earlier that some people prefer horses to humans, and generally I think that was the case with him. One of the many things I admire about Micky, both as a horseman and as a trainer, is that he likes to take time to get to know the horses. That's something I've always tried to emulate and it obviously pays dividends when it comes to training. Talking to the lad or lass who looks after the horse on a daily basis is essential, but when the trainer too has some first-hand knowledge of the horse, everything joins up and comes into its own. That's not why he does it, though. Micky does it because he's fanatical about horses – plain and simple – and in a racing yard you couldn't wish for a more positive role model. Now Micky also seemed to be a lot more interested in people and, once we had the right staff in place, the whole set-up was just about perfect. All we needed now were more horses and a few winners.

Once Stee and Rachel had left and we'd got rid of all the time-wasters, we had just six members of staff. Bearing in mind we had almost eighty horses when I first started, and about twenty members of staff, you can really appreciate the difference. Staff-wise there was me, Ashley, a girl called Katie Dowson (who had a few rides as a jockey and is now racing secretary to Sir Mark Prescott), our conditional jockey, Joe Colliver (he's now a professional jockey), Allen Nutter, who now works for the trainer Ann Duffield, and later on a lad called Wayne Hogg (no relation to Tim), who now works for Godolphin. Once again, the term 'small but perfectly formed' springs to mind; we all knew that if it didn't work out, it wouldn't be because of the staff.

For the first few months it was touch and go as to whether we'd make it, and at one point we even had a meeting about what would happen if we didn't. It was a very emotional hour or so. Micky in particular had been really down, and must have thought that it was only a matter of time. By the time we headed to Ripon with a horse called Industrial Star, I was really worried about the boss, not least because Industrial Star was the most accident-prone horse I'd ever known, and his recent record was just awful. Last time out he'd actually injured himself on the way to the start line and hadn't been able to race. If that wasn't enough to make us all nervous, just a few days before the meeting at Ripon we'd had Industrial Star on the horse walker, which is a kind of circular treadmill for horses, and when he came off we saw a cut on his leg. One of his owners was with us at the time, and when we saw it we just looked at each other.

'How the hell did that happen?' Micky asked me.

'No idea,' I replied.

After a thorough inspection of the horse walker, we were still clueless, so instead of worrying about it we just called the vet and asked him to come and stitch it up.

Providing we could get him there in one piece, we thought Industrial Star stood a good chance at Ripon, but by the time we arrived at the course I was a nervous wreck. As the race started, I was watching Micky rather than the screen. He looked ill, and probably hadn't slept in a week.

'Are you all right, Micky?' I asked him as the race began.

He didn't say a word, lost in his own world.

Micky didn't move a muscle throughout the entire race,

nor did he change his facial expression. It was as if his entire future depended on the outcome.

The race itself, called the Ripon Farm Services Handicap, was horribly close. Industrial Star started well, but by the halfway stage he was fourth out of a field of six. I thought to myself, *he's not going to finish anywhere!* Oh ye of little faith. With about half a mile to go he'd got up into second, and about three furlongs from the end he was neck and neck with the leader. I was screaming my head off by this point, as were the owners. Micky, though, remained silent. With just a furlong to go, Industrial Star nudged into the lead, and by the time they passed the finish line he was a neck and a bit in front. I swear that I could actually see the colour coming back into Micky's face. There was no shouting or jumping up and down, just a lorry-load of relief. That was the turning point, I think. He'd been so quiet, but the following morning he was back to his old, or should I say new, self.

Incidentally, Industrial Star could sometimes be a bit difficult in a box, and so he always travelled with two people in the back with him. One day – I can't say where I was going or with whom – I opened the side door after arriving at the course to find his two minders shagging like bunnies! Industrial Star finished fifth that day and I'm sure it was because he'd been traumatized. I certainly was!

Shortly after that another horse, Mr Crystal, had a good win at Beverley, and that too galvanized the entire yard. That race was achingly close, and because I shouted so much I ended up losing my voice! Mr Crystal tracked the leaders all the way, but didn't take the lead until the last twenty yards; by the time he crossed the line I was speechless – literally! Although the pressure wasn't entirely off, we allowed ourselves a few cheers that day, and none of us wanted to leave the winner's enclosure. Saying that, a few weeks later at Wetherby, Mr Crystal was about two lengths clear in a listed race called the Wensleydale Juvenile Novice's Hurdle. It was about £10,000 for first place and, just when we thought that all our troubles were at an end, he tripped over. We thought that was Industrial Star's job.

As I said, the only way to restore the owners' faith was to come back even better than before, and creating what has gone on to become a brand-new success story has been very much a team effort. Once we were up and running again, things like days and weekends off went completely out of the window. If a job needed doing, you just did it. Because we were all riding the same horse, so to speak, we all just buckled down. But even after the winners started appearing again, there were yet more weeks when Micky thought he wouldn't have the money to pay us. This time he managed to keep it a secret and, apart from me and Karen, who's been Micky's accounts manager since 1996, nobody else knew. In the end he managed to find it somehow, but even if he hadn't we wouldn't have cared. As horse lovers and racing fanatics we weren't just living a particular dream; we were participating in something that had been built by passion and endeavour which was genuine, positive and honest. At the end of the day, a job's just a job, but when it turns into a way of life you either run with it or you don't. I ran all right. In fact, I haven't stopped since.

I remember picking up the telephone in the office one day. This would have been just after we'd had our win at Ripon. The person on the other line was the secretary of an owner we'd heard of but didn't know.

'We'd like to move two of our horses to you, if that's OK,' she said.

The feeling I experienced when she said that was indescribable.

'Of course,' I squeaked. 'Let me just go and get Micky.'

As important as things like networking obviously are, not to mention selling your services, these horses had been placed with us because of our reputation, and that was so gratifying. Like winning every race on a card.

A few weeks later some potential owners came to have a look around the yard. At the time we still only had about eighteen horses with us, and I don't mind admitting that we were worried this might work against us. Some people assume that unless you have a full yard you must be doing something wrong, but that's obviously not the case. Some yards could be at an early stage of development, like ours, but others that are jam-packed could be full of donkeys and bad payers, like we had been. We just had to pray that they could see what we were trying to achieve.

A day or two later the owner rang up in person and asked if he could place three horses with us immediately, and also asked Micky to buy one on his behalf at a forthcoming sale. That horse would also come to us. Yet again, I almost exploded with delight, but this was nothing to when we met the owner again.

'Do you mind if I ask why you chose us?' Micky enquired as we were chatting in the yard.

'The staff and the atmosphere,' the owner said. 'The staff are very friendly and the atmosphere's relaxed. That's what I want for my horses.'

To be honest, I was expecting him to say it was our current run of form, or perhaps the facilities. When he said the staff and the atmosphere, Micky and I turned slightly red. Not because we were embarrassed, but because we were just so incredibly proud.

I'd love to be able to claim this achievement as an exclusive to Micky Hammond Racing, but the fact is we're the rule in racing, not the exception, and I'd say that the vast majority of racing yards have something pretty similar going on. It's cultural, I suppose, but what makes it special is that it's very rarely forced. Idiots notwithstanding, racing yards are full of young people who've been standing on their own two feet from a very early age, and good behaviour, especially in front of the public and owners, isn't just preferable, it's essential. But because it's been drummed into them from such an early age, it's become the norm, and that's another reason why people tend to stay in the industry. I mean, who wouldn't want to work in a warm and friendly environment? OK, apart from Monday mornings and most of February.

Because we had so few staff at the stables, there was no actual career structure in place for anybody. Nobody had time for things like that, and so it was all done pretty much on the hoof, if you'll pardon the expression. More responsibility made possible by a bit more delegation was basically how it worked. Although, to be honest, I don't even think I was working towards anything in particular, at least not consciously. Micky must have had some idea about where my future lay, but since becoming assistant head lass and travelling head lass, I had been too busy to wonder about it myself.

Bearing in mind I'm now an assistant trainer (one of the youngest in the country, apparently), there's definitely an advantage in working for a trainer who's growing their business organically. You get involved in pretty much everything, including, obviously, training. Micky would ask me which track I thought suited a certain horse. Whether or not he agreed with me was a different matter, but the fact that he was consulting me made me think like a trainer, and from then on I started airing my opinions, no matter what. Some of them were welcome, I should imagine, and some not. But they were always well meant, and the thought process itself opened up a whole new world for me. Had I been assistant and travelling head lass in a different yard, I probably wouldn't have been as involved and couldn't say for sure if I'd have stayed in the industry.

When Ashley left for a different yard in 2003, I was really sorry he'd gone. Then, after evening stables one day, Micky called me into the racing office.

'Sit down, Gemma,' he said sternly. Very sternly, in fact.

I couldn't remember the last time I'd been in trouble with Micky, and after he spoke my brain immediately started running through a range of catastrophic scenarios. What on earth had I done wrong? Oh god! Oh my god! Micky now seemed to be writing something down, so without further ado I asked him what was up.

'Have I done something wrong?' I said, trying not to sound too petrified. I was, though.

As I asked the question Micky just looked at me – still very sternly. *I am so in the shit*, I thought. I was convinced I was on my way out. It was the worst feeling ever.

Eventually Micky put down his pen and sat back in his chair.

'Don't cry,' I said to myself. 'Find out what you've done. Then cry.'

'Ashley leaves tomorrow,' he said eventually.

This was a strange thing to say.

'Yes, I know,' I replied. 'I've organized his leaving do. You are coming, aren't you?'

'Of course I am,' said Micky. 'I'll bring the new stable lad along, if that's OK. Have you met him yet?'

'No,' I replied. 'Not yet.'

I was pretty sure I was in the clear by now, but still had absolutely no idea what he was getting at.

'He's only seventeen, this new lad,' said Micky. 'Not twenty-one like you.'

'Fresh out of college?' I asked.

'That's right.'

Suddenly it started dawning on me.

'So, who's taking over from Ashley then?' I asked.

'Finally!' said Micky, putting his head in his hands. 'Gemma, would you like to be head lass?'

Because of the torture he'd just put me through, I was half tempted to tell him to bugger off.

'Yes please,' I said, grinning. And crying. That was inevitable, I'm afraid.

'I can't believe you didn't twig,' said Micky. 'Who did you think was going to take over from Ashley?'

'It hadn't occurred to me. I've been too busy!'

Micky shook his head. He often did that when talking to me!

'You'll get more money, of course, and we'll go through the job itself with Ashley tomorrow morning. I know you know it inside out, but I just want to make sure, OK?'

'OK!'

After blowing my nose and drying my eyes, I raced off to find Tim. He was already head lad at George Moore's and had been present when Micky had promoted me the last time. I'm not sure if Micky had already told him, but Tim didn't seem at all surprised.

'You work your arse off, so why not?' he said. 'I reckon you deserve it.'

Tim is very straightforward.

One of the main practical differences between this position and the positions I held previously – apart from initially not going to the races quite as often, which was a bit of a bummer – was that I was now responsible for the medical side of things, which meant that as well as treating any superficial wounds, I was the vet's first point of contact. From a horse care point of view – and from the point of view of being stable staff – this was the final piece of the jigsaw, as it was the only part in which I was lacking experience and was the only job I hadn't done.

Funnily enough, a lot of stable staff wouldn't touch the role I'd just taken on with a barge pole, and for good reason. Because of the responsibility involved, you have to cut yourself off from the tack room and, as you're not really part of the training team either, you can often be left in limbo. A proper Billy no-mates! If our yard hadn't been so small and tightknit, and if Micky hadn't involved me a bit in the training side, I would have given it a wide berth.

The reason you have to maintain that degree of separation is simple: you're responsible for the standards in the yard and you can only do that if you're impartial. The only exceptions to the rule I've ever known (although I'm sure there are more) are my sister Becky, who is now our head lass, and the inimitable Crooky. As well as being a decent jockey, Becky's very hands-on in the yard and so leads by example. Better still, she also aspires to train, and because Micky's encouraging her, it makes the gap between the office and the yard almost seamless. Crooky was a different breed again, and is the only person I've ever known who has managed to succeed at being a head man while remaining one of the boys and never compromising his position in the tack room. He's a true one-off.

Not long after I became head lass, a new horse arrived in the yard that would have given even Polo Venture a run for his money in the kind and beautiful stakes. Her name was Charlotte Vale. She was the most gorgeous chestnut filly I had ever seen in my life, and from the moment she set hooves in the yard we became inseparable. I used to spend hours and hours cuddling her. She was an absolute doll.

Charlotte Vale was a two-year-old when she arrived, so in racing terms we had her almost from the word go. She was ever so slightly nervous at first, which was another reason I took to her, and watching her grow in confidence and finally come out of her shell is still one of the most amazing experiences I've ever had. All Charlotte Vale wanted to do was please, which was part of the reason she was nervous, and I had to try and teach her how to relax and be herself. All I had to do was appear relaxed and take things slowly, and she soon cottoned on.

Although we still didn't have a full yard, things were definitely going in the right direction at Micky Hammond Racing, and when Tim and I took a weekend break to

London in the autumn of 2003, life was pretty good. I was head lass in one of the most talked-about yards in the north and, as well as being madly in love with a chestnut filly, I was also rather keen on a certain blond head lad. If somebody had asked me then if there was anything they could do to improve my life, I'd have told them no: that it was absolutely fine as it was. Tim, though, had other ideas, and when we arrived in our hotel room, instead of unpacking, or at least seeing if there were any free biscuits, he ran off and locked himself in the bathroom.

'What are you doing in there?' I shouted after about fifteen minutes.

'Nothing,' he shouted back. 'Won't be long.'

When Tim eventually emerged, he strode over to me and said, 'Erm Gem, will you marry me?' He had been in the bathroom psyching himself up, bless him. I was glad he didn't get down on one knee, though, as the chances are I'd have started laughing.

'Yes, all right,' I said. 'Why not?'

This seemed to calm Tim somewhat, so I gave him a quick kiss, patted him on the bum, and took him for a pint. He looked as if he needed one. I certainly did!

The first thing we changed once we'd become engaged was our living arrangements. We definitely needed a bit more room. And, if possible, somewhere that had walls that weren't like sponges and windows that didn't have several different species of moss growing on the inside of them. At the time there was nothing suitable in Middleham, which forced our hand into moving further afield. In the end we finally settled on a little two-bedroomed cottage in Wensley, which is about two and a half miles from Middleham, and that became our home for the next five years.

Back in the thirteenth century, Wensley had been the largest town in the area, and is obviously how Wensleydale got its name. Funnily enough, almost every other dale in Yorkshire is named after its principal river, and even though the River Ure runs straight through the dale and through Wensley, they still chose to use the town name instead. 'Uredale' definitely doesn't have the same ring. By early 2004, though, when we moved in, Wensley was probably one of the smallest towns in the dale, with a population of just a hundred or so, but because it's on the main road from Leyburn through to Hawes, it had managed to maintain a pub called The Three Horseshoes. It wasn't exactly buzzing, but that wasn't what we wanted. It was quiet and unbelievably picturesque. That was good enough for us.

The cottage itself was on the edge of – and was owned by – the Bolton Estate, which belongs to Lord Bolton. He lives in Bolton Hall, a seventeenth-century country house, but his ancestors lived in the fourteenth-century castle that today is part ruined but still guards the dale. It is most famous for the fact that Mary Queen of Scots lived there for six months after she fled Scotland. The cottage had previously been used to house the estate gardener, and in addition to having twice as many bedrooms as we were used to having, it also had . . .

central heating! Tim, Benji and I were more than happy to take up residence here.

The only downside to the move, apart from a slight increase in rent, which was inevitable, was that we now had a commute. The five-mile round trip was hardly London to Edinburgh, though, and not being right in the throes of everything was actually a refreshing change. I'd been living in Middleham right from day one at the yard, and Tim had done so all his life. Not living there made me appreciate it more. We were so taken with Wensley, though, and not least because of the dog-walking opportunities: Benji was in seventh heaven.

Living outside Middleham also helped me to appreciate that there was life outside of racing. I obviously wasn't bored with the job – far from it – but I could see that some aspects of it were all getting a little bit too familiar. After moving to Wensley, I realized that we needed to break things up occasionally. Tim felt exactly the same way and so, from 2004 onwards, we started taking a few city breaks and foreign holidays. Nothing too drastic. Just a weekend in Paris or a couple of weeks in Portugal. It had the desired effect, though, and in no time at all I felt like a more rounded human being. There was more to me than just Middleham and horses.

One of these holidays was actually our wedding, which took place on the island of Rhodes in June 2004. Basically, it was a week-long party with a wedding stuck in the middle of it, and we managed to get about sixty of our nearest and dearest to travel over there. The ceremony itself took place on a beach, so it was about as far removed from the yard as you could possibly get. Not a bridle or a muck heap in sight! Tim scrubbed up well in his suit and even I didn't look too out of place with a wedding dress on.

Broadening my mind with travel – and having something other than horses to talk about – proved a big help now that I, as head lass, was coming more into contact with our owners. The relationship an owner has with his or her trainer, or the stable staff, is obviously down to them. Some like to be very hands-on and others less so. All we can do in the first instance is keep them updated and let them know that the door is always open. Then, if they want to get involved, they know they can.

Before syndicates were allowed, racing had been a very elitist sport, and only the very rich could afford to buy a horse and keep it in training. These days, you can enter the sport as an owner, or should I say a part-owner, for as little as a few hundred pounds a year, and this has changed racing immeasurably. In my own experience, racing syndicates are a joy to deal with. Why? Because nine times out of ten they're there for the craic and are just thrilled to be involved. Sometimes you'll get a syndicate made up of very wealthy individuals, and in those circumstances things can get very interesting. Their budget, when it comes to buying horses, is often vast, and although they're great fun to work with, obviously the whole operation is taken that bit more ser-iously.

We meet all kinds of people in racing, especially owners, and you have to be able to communicate with them on whatever level, so having a bit more life experience really helped. Micky once summed it up perfectly by saying that you have to be 'all things to all people', but you can only do this effectively if you enjoy it and have a genuine interest in those you are dealing with. Some of the owners become regular fixtures at the stables, and having them around feels right; it completes the set.

Occasionally we have a celebrity owner, and that can cause a real buzz, especially with some of the younger staff. Not long after we moved to Wensley, Micky took on a horse owned by Ray Parlour and a couple of his mates. To anybody who doesn't like football, or is under the age of forty, Ray Parlour was a footballer who played for Arsenal, mainly, and when word got out that he'd be visiting the yard, the lads started flapping around like demented penguins.

'Oh my god, Ray Parlour's coming. *Ray Parlour!*'

Micky, who is a big Arsenal fan, was a friend of Ray's, which is why we got the horse and, although I had absolutely no idea who he was, he was always very polite. Two of Micky's most high-profile owners since I've been with him are Paul and Clare Rooney, who are very successful business people. I shudder to think how many horses they have in training, but when they arrived at the yard it would be via helicopter. The helicopter would fly over the town to get to the helipad, which was two or three miles away, so once again this would always cause a real buzz of excitement.

The first owners I actually befriended at Micky's, apart from Peter, of course, were Mike and Eileen Newbold. They'd had horses with Micky back in the 1990s for a few years, and in 2004 they came back. After getting to know them, I discovered they knew my dad through his Leeds Rhinos connection, but what drew me to Mike and Eileen was that they were just two genuine, down-to-earth people who loved horses. Without even realizing it, they taught me how an owner thinks, or might think. Understanding an owner's concerns and being able to empathize was hugely important. First and foremost, the horses actually belong to the owners and, as much as we stable staff love them, we don't know what it means to own such expensive animals. They're not pets, after all, and are in training because the owners want them to win races. In that sense, they are a commodity, just as a football player is to a club. Even owners who do it just for fun want their horses to win races, so to all intents and purposes it's a business. Their business.

If Mike and Eileen Newbold hadn't been responsive to my enthusiasm, then the chances are that I might have gone into my shell a bit. They were completely happy to reciprocate, though, and partly thanks to them I gained confidence very quickly with owners, which did me the world of good.

A few years ago Eileen called me up one day and said that if there was ever anything I wanted – be it money, a place to live, or just a chat – I was to pick up the phone. I didn't really know what to say at the time, but I remember being very touched. I could tell that she really meant it, and I'm pleased to say that Eileen and Tony Newbold are still owners of ours. More importantly, though, they're still friends.

16

They're Under Starter's Orders . . .

The only attainable ambition I had left in racing when I became head lass was riding a winner on the flat. Hayley Turner I was not, but I could obviously ride, and now I had some good contacts. Just the thought of lining up in the stalls at the start of a race filled me with an intoxicating mixture of excitement and fear and, however much I tried ignoring it, it would not go away. There was only one thing for it: I was going to have to give it a go.

Of course, my original ambition had been to become a jockey, but that had fizzled out years ago. Like so many other lads and lasses before and since, I realized quite early on that I wasn't cut out for it, and the only saving grace was that nobody had to sit me down and tell me. To be honest, the ambition had always been quite ambiguous, in that I was never bothered about where I raced or on what horse. I just wanted to do it. I think I was as much in love with the thought of doing it as the act itself.

It's possible you could argue that by asking a stable lass or lad what their ambitions are, as Stee did with me, you're giving them false hope, but I don't agree. For a start, unlike me, a lot of stable staff are resolute about becoming jockeys, and so reeling off the statistics about how many people fail might be construed as being slightly unkind! What you do is let them have a fair try. You'll know within months whether they're cut out for it or not, and if necessary you can let them down gently. Some people can remain on the cusp of the profession for some time but never quite make it, and they're often the ones who suffer the most when the end eventually comes.

The best possible scenario – if you're not going to make it as a jockey – is to come to the realization yourself, preferably at your own pace, and to be offered the odd ride every so often. That's what happened with me. For those of you who aren't aware, having the odd ride is vastly different to being a full-time jockey. It's amateurs versus professionals, basically. That said, you do have to be up to a certain standard if you're going to get a ride, and unless you're a good team player you won't even be considered. This was good for my career as it motivated me to get involved in the yard, which my initial shyness might not have allowed, and gave me the impetus to want to improve as a rider. And improve I did. But there's no fixed schedule as to when these rides might come along. You just have to keep your fingers crossed.

By the time my first one came along in 2006, when I was coming up to twenty-three, I'd actually given up on the whole 'make do with an occasional ride' malarkey, and was happily getting on with my job. I was still going through the motions of trying to improve as a rider, but that was now second nature and, with everything going swimmingly in the yard, I'd just forgotten about it. I was also going to the races more often by this point, and not doing so had been my only gripe.

In January 2006, Charlotte Vale and I had been at Wetherby Races. She'd just finished second in a good hurdle race and, as I led her around afterwards, I couldn't have been prouder. When we got to the winner's enclosure I met up with Peter Davies, who was Charlotte Vale's owner. He's a lovely man and I got on just as well with him as I did with Charlotte Vale, just without the cuddles! After that Micky arrived, and once we'd all finished talking about the race, Micky came out with a rather surprising proposition.

'I'll tell you what, Peter,' he said. 'If Charlotte Vale wins over the hurdles, how about Gemma getting her licence and riding her over the flat?'

Before I had time to remonstrate, Peter came back with a counter-proposal.

'If Charlotte wins over hurdles, Micky,' said Peter, 'I'll pay for Gemma to apply for her licence myself. How about that?'

'Sounds good to me,' said Micky.

After that they both looked at me. They were obviously expecting a reaction of some kind, but I was dumbfounded.

'Erm, OK then,' I said eventually. Charlotte Vale was a

flat horse mainly, and although she'd shown promise over hurdles, there was no guarantee that she'd ever win. *It's a nice idea*, I thought. But the chances were that it would come to nothing.

Next time out Charlotte Vale won by a length, and it was over the hurdles.

The race was at Sedgefield, and Charlotte's jockey that day was Tony Dobbin. He'd won the Grand National on a horse called Lord Gyllene the year I'd surprised Conor O'Dwyer with a kiss, and was without doubt one of the nicest jockeys on the circuit.

'Jeeez, that's a good horse, Gemma,' he said after the race. 'In fact, I should be paying you to ride it, really.'

I didn't dare tell Tony that next time out it would be me on her back. He might have ruptured something!

By the time I saw Micky in the winner's enclosure, he was grinning from ear to ear. 'We'd better sit down and put a plan together, Gemma,' he said.

Now it felt real. Very real!

Incidentally, to get a jockey's licence, I had to go on a three-day course at the Northern Racing College which, after I'd learned about the rules of racing and had satisfied the examiners my technique was in order, culminated in a rigorous fitness test that I was absolutely dreading. I'd never been to a gym before, nor have I since, and as far as I was concerned things like treadmills and cross-trainers were nothing more than instruments of torture. We even had to do a bleep-test, which winkled out the heavy smokers, and believe it or not I ended up coming top for strength! That was in a class of eight; four men and four women.

When we sat down the following day, Micky made the suggestion of running Charlotte Vale in the Queen Mother Cup Handicap at York. This is only open to lady amateurs, and when Micky suggested it my reaction was immediate and unequivocal.

'*Yes!*' I yelled.

The reason for my enthusiasm was the fact that the winning jockey of the Queen Mother Cup always gets her weight in champagne, and although I didn't weigh very much, I knew there'd be enough for at least a few cases. There's a similar race at Ascot, which is known as the Diamond Race, and whoever wins that gets a diamond necklace. That would be wasted on me, I'm afraid. Give me the champers any day! All I had to do now was win.

Before the Queen Mother Cup took place, Micky suggested giving me a ride out at Wolverhampton on a horse called High Country. He was an easy and quite experienced horse and, because Wolverhampton is an all-weather track, Micky thought it would be the perfect combination for my maiden ride.

The meeting itself was quite low-key, which I was happy with, and because High Country wasn't fancied, there wasn't a great deal of pressure. This probably lulled me into a bit of a false sense of security, and when High Country and I made our way to the stalls from the parade ring I was feeling quite relaxed. My, was I in for a shock!

As much as I thought I knew about horse racing, and as addicted as I'd become to the sport and to the excitement of attending a meeting, nothing could have prepared me for the atmosphere in the stalls just before a race. The usual anticipation, enthusiasm and exhilaration of a race meeting are all heightened tenfold. What's more, the mood is generated not by a crowd of people but by the horses themselves.

I'd seen dozens of horses prior to a race – i.e. in the parade ring – but never just prior to a race, and the difference is frightening. This is when you see the true character of a racehorse, and, to a lesser extent, the jockey. Some horses, like High Country, take it all in their stride, and although they're excited they remain quite composed. Others cannot wait to get out of the stalls, and if a horse starts playing up, that can trigger a chain reaction. In situations like that, the start can't come soon enough.

On this particular occasion, all the horses behaved, but the electric atmosphere, not to mention the movement within the stalls from the more excitable animals, took me completely by surprise. It's quite tight in there and so you don't have to move very far to hit something. By the time the race started I must have had at least a gallon of adrenalin pumping through my body. The only thing I can really compare it to is being let loose on the gallops for the first time, but this was a lot more extreme.

As soon as the race started, I felt an enormous surge of relief. It seemed to be over in a flash. The thing I remember most was becoming tired after about a mile – me, not the horse. Bearing in mind the race was over a mile and five furlongs, that was obviously a problem, and my admiration of professional jockeys grew hugely. We were in a group of five for the majority of the race, and until we were two furlongs out we were doing OK. After that we gradually lost pace, though, and ended up finishing sixth out of eight. I was exhausted afterwards, and the next day I was in agony!

About a week and a half after the race, I led High Country out at Pontefract and, while we were in the parade ring, his jockey, Dale Gibson, pulled me to one side.

'I think this horse is going to be spot on,' he said. 'And do you know why?'

'No,' I replied, feeling a bit puzzled.

'I watched him have a quiet run out at Wolverhampton last week,' said Dale. 'And if it hadn't been for the jockey, he might have done OK. Whoever was riding him looked knackered.'

With that he gave me a wink, patted me on the head and gestured to me to give him a leg up. Because of where we were I couldn't say anything, but as he looked back on his way to the stalls I gave him a quick two-fingered salute. Micky and the owner were standing next to me so that was the best I could do. Cheeky bugger!

Three months later, in June 2006, I had a race at Haydock Park on a horse called Arctic Cover, and came last. As with High Country, he wasn't fancied at all and, despite the result, I managed not to tire before the horse. The following week I was supposed to ride Charlotte Vale in the Queen

Mother Cup, but the ground wasn't right and, in the end, we pulled her from the race. This was a huge disappointment, not only because of the champagne, which would have been nice, but because winning a race on Charlotte Vale represented the extent of my ambitions on the course.

As opposed to running her in a different race, we decided to bide our time and wait for the following year's Queen Mother's Cup, in 2007. Once again, I rode at Haydock the week before, this time on a horse called Terenzium. Seventh out of seventeen was our position at the end so, given the size of the field, it was my best result to date. Good to know I was managing to keep my expectations in check!

I'm not sure if this was a sign or not, but a few days before the next Queen Mother's Cup was due to take place, the heavens opened and didn't close again for about a week. Unfortunately, and for the first time ever, York Races' entire three-day July meeting had to be postponed, as did my ambition – again.

'We're not waiting another year,' said Micky after the news came through. 'There's a lady amateur handicap taking place at the night meeting at Hamilton next week. That'll do.'

That would indeed do. I love Hamilton Racecourse, and when Micky made the suggestion I was thrilled. By waiting for the Queen Mother's Cup I was putting all my eggs into one basket, and had I waited another year the pressure to win would have been ridiculous. Was it fate? I think so.

One of the many things I like about Hamilton Racecourse

is the shape of the track. It's a dewdrop shape, and because this race was going to be roughly the length of the track – one mile five furlongs – we'd start in front of the stands, go down the loop and then back up the straight towards the stands again. This meant we'd hear the roar of the crowd at the start of the race as well as the finish. I couldn't wait.

Micky had been at another meeting that day, so I'd gone up in the box by myself. I was actually getting used to the process by now and, although I didn't feel like a jockey, I was comfortable with most of it. Apart from the weighing room, that is. I'm not sure if it was a female thing, but I couldn't get out quick enough.

Despite being at another meeting, Micky had assured me he'd be there in time for the race. Even so, he'd asked a friend of ours to saddle up for me, just in case. He hadn't made it to Haydock a few weeks ago, and I'd been fine. Have horse in box, will race . . . This time it was different, though. I was third in the betting and knew I had a chance. Probably the best chance I'd ever have of winning a race, and on the only horse that really mattered. Destiny isn't a word I use much (I prefer fate), but winning a race on Charlotte Vale felt like my destiny. Our destiny. All of our destinies! Bearing in mind how I'd got this far, it was important that Micky was there. To me, anyway.

By the time I got to the stalls, Micky still hadn't arrived, and I'd already accepted the fact that he wasn't going to make it. Everybody had been very helpful and encouraging, but only he knew the significance of the ride. Well, him and

Peter Davies. Financially the race was worth very little and, even if I won, it would barely cover Peter's costs. He and Micky had been so good to me and – win or lose – I would always be very grateful.

As I sat in the stalls, the atmosphere was lost on me. It was like being the odd one out at a party. I desperately wanted to join in and appreciate what was going on, but something was stopping me. I think it was nerves mainly, but I also felt slightly isolated. There must have been a good few thousand people at the course – I felt surrounded by total strangers.

All of sudden I heard somebody calling my name. It sounded like Micky but I knew it couldn't be so I didn't turn my head. A few seconds later I heard it again. Louder this time.

'Gemma! For Christ's sake look to your right!'

'Oh my *god*,' I yelled. 'I thought I was imagining you!'

If I hadn't been hemmed in, I honestly think I'd have fallen off.

'Well, you weren't. I'm here. Right. One piece of advice. Don't be slow out of the stalls. OK? Have fun!'

I can't begin to tell you how relieved I was to see my generous but cantankerous boss, and for the first time since arriving at the course I felt alive. And, dare I say it, confident.

Fortunately for me I was anything but slow out of the stalls. In fact, I got an absolute flyer. Heading anti-clockwise, the other thirteen horses and jockeys all tracked slightly towards the stand side for some reason, whereas I went slightly to the left. I'd walked the course twice earlier in the day and had worked out what I considered to be the racing line. The fact that it was different to everyone else's unnerved me slightly, but I decided to stick to my guns. Charlotte Vale always travelled nicely so I didn't need to be in the pack.

For the first five furlongs or so, another horse led by about four lengths. Micky told me afterwards that he was shouting for me to go around her, but I didn't. I just sat back and bided my time. By now the rest of the pack had moved over and were just behind me. *Patience, Gem*, I thought to myself. *Don't let them force you into making a move.* My plan was that the moment the girl in front started to slow, I'd go around her, but after a mile they were still going strong. The pack were closing in on me now. I could feel them. Something was going to have to give. Suddenly, at about a mile and one, the horse in front slowed quite dramatically, and the moment I noticed it slowing I gave Charlotte a quick squeeze, tensed the rein, and off we went. Racehorses are taught that the shorter the rein, the faster they have to go. That's why jockeys change their hands at a finish. They have to keep the bit up in the horse's mouth so the horse knows to keep going forward, and it can be a struggle sometimes.

I was surprised at the rate Charlotte accelerated after I gave her a squeeze, but also relieved. She obviously had a bit left in the tank, and with five furlongs to go it was looking good. Charlotte Vale was such a genuine girl. Some horses either have to have cover when they're going for a race, or they have to make it, which means they hate having anything in front. Charlotte Vale just didn't care either way.

I knew full well that when I'd gone around the pacemaker, the pack had followed. The question was, how far behind were they? It felt like about a length and a half and so, as we went into the dip that lies just before the run-in, I decided to pull Charlotte back slightly and give her a bit of a rest. The run-in at Hamilton is only about three furlongs, but it feels more like seven or eight. If I gave her a furlong or so now, she should be good for the final push.

The feeling I had going into the run-in was terrifying, but it was nothing to how I felt about halfway up. I remember shouting 'Come on,' with about a furlong and a half to go, and for some reason it seemed to turn up the volume on everything that was going on behind me. This was truly horrific; a ceaseless and chaotic soundscape that translated into five simple words: 'We're coming to get you!'

What made it worse was that it was getting louder. Hooves pounding and shredding the turf, bits clicking against horses' teeth, whips being slapped against their hindquarters and a dozen or so rabid women all screaming for my downfall. My response to this was to give Charlotte a quick smack behind the saddle, but in doing so I almost fell off. *Sod that*, I thought. *If I fall off now, I'm dead!*

Once I'd managed to compose myself as far as I could

under the circumstances, I tried smacking her on the shoulder instead, and from the second the whip made contact she just flew. That was it for the whip, though. From here on in my chosen method of persuasion would be good old-fashioned bellowing!

As we went into the final furlong, the horse running closest to me was Compton Dragon, the 4/1 favourite. He was being ridden by a woman called Sarah Bosley who, in terms of experience and success, was the antithesis of me. Since 1993 she'd ridden in over six hundred races and had won almost fifty of them. She'd also been the Great Britain Lady Amateur Flat Jockey Champion in 2000 and 2004, and had once won the Diamond Race at Ascot. This race was actually Sarah's swansong, and because she was riding the favourite everybody assumed, and probably hoped, to be fair, that she'd come in the winner.

Sorry, Sarah. You've already had fifty winners. I just want one!

With less than half a furlong to go, she was about a head behind me, and as we went over the line I honestly couldn't tell you who'd won. This was partly because I didn't know exactly where the finish line was, but also because for a few seconds at the end I had my eyes closed. I just couldn't look.

The thirty seconds or so it took to confirm the winner seemed like an age. It was like waiting for the result of your driving test.

Charlotte's owner, Peter Davies, had been watching from

London, and when he spoke to me on the phone afterwards, he wanted to know why I'd looked so pensive.

'Because I didn't know I'd won, Peter,' I explained.

'But you won by at least a head,' he told me.

'I know that now, but at the time I had my eyes closed,' I replied.

'*What?*'

As soon as our win was confirmed I leant forward, wrapped my arms around Charlotte, and began peppering her with kisses. Whenever I tell people I've ridden a winner, I always follow it up by saying that I had very little to do with it. That's not false modesty, by the way. It's fact. My beautiful girl just ran away with me.

The first person to come up and congratulate me after the race was Sarah Bosley. Bearing in mind what I'd done to her retirement party, I thought that was lovely. She did get a big bunch of flowers, though, and because she'd had such a long and illustrious career I don't think she lost much sleep. The young pretender I was not.

Night meetings at Hamilton are always really well supported, and usually by genuine racing enthusiasts, rather than groups of friends there for a special occasion. The cheer I got as I entered the winner's enclosure was huge, and that's when it hit me. I tried telling them all I had nothing to do with it, but because they were cheering for both of us, I decided to ignore the modest me and soak it all up. What a feeling!

Micky's reaction to the win was typically understated.

'Well done, Gem,' he said calmly as we were led into the winner's enclosure. 'How about a ride over the hurdles before you retire?'

'Ooh, do you mind if I pass on that one,' I said sarcastically. 'Let's just get back to normal.'

'Fair enough,' he said. 'You did well, though. It was a good ride.'

With over two hundred winners to his name as a jockey, that was a huge compliment.

As with every other winner, Charlotte Vale had to be tested after the race, and, just my luck, she was about as willing to part with her pee as I would be a case of Bollinger. This meant that we didn't leave the course until half past eight, and by the time I kicked the bottom latch on Charlotte's box door, it was almost midnight. What a day it had been, though. Whatever happened here on in, I would always be able to say that I'd ridden a winner. Nobody could ever take that away from me, and I had every intention of dining out on the achievement for at least a week. Maybe two.

Before I closed the top of Charlotte's box door, I paused for a few seconds and just stared at her. I'd adored this horse from the moment she arrived, but from now on things would be different. As daft as it sounds, I never thought I'd love another horse as much as I loved Polo Venture, but I was wrong. In fact, I've loved two: Charlotte Vale and Fair Spin. Charlotte Vale was something special, and the bond we shared, especially after that race, was unbreakable.

I know it's not the first time I've spun a romantic theory, but it genuinely felt as if she knew exactly what had happened – and what it had meant to me. That's the thing with horses; they scream perception. Dogs may be known for being trustworthy and obedient, and cats for being aloof and independent. Horses, though, are all-seeing and all-knowing. They observe, they digest, and, most importantly, they understand. They don't always tolerate what they see, but the fact is they take a view. Ask anyone who works with horses and I'm pretty sure they'll agree with me.

Although stationary – statuesque, even – Charlotte Vale remained on her feet and, as I continued admiring her, I was once again reminded of how incredibly beautiful horses are. And how incredibly lucky I was to work with them. I knew that the moment I bolted her door Charlotte would be making herself comfortable, ready for a long sleep. She must have been exhausted, bless her. As I said, it was she who'd done all the running. I was just grateful to be part of it: part of the race, part of the job, part of the life. It was all good.

After saying goodnight, I blew Charlotte a kiss, pulled the door around as softly as I could and then bolted it shut. After that I had a last look around the yard, switched off the lights and then made my way to the large wooden gates.

As I dragged my exhausted but triumphant body up the road into Middleham, I saw a couple of drunken stragglers pile onto the road; the final two hurdles in what had probably been the landlord of the Black Bull's long race to bed. I bet they're going to Castle House, I thought. It was still the place to go if the pubs weren't having a lock-in. I stopped and thought for a second. It was Thursday. Start of the weekend. Something had to be going on. Hopefully without any slapped policemen.

Just then the bells of St Alkelda's Church informed me that it was now the day after what had officially been the best day of my life. 'What a shame,' I said out loud. I was in the square now, but nobody heard me. I was the final straggler. Conscious of the silence, I carried on the conversation in my head. The best day of my life had only lasted five hours, and most of that had been on the A66. Five more, and I'd have to be up again.

It's human nature to want good things to last, but by the time I passed Castle House on the way to Tim's dad's house (where I had left my car), I'd realized, thank heavens, that experiences like this could never be measured by days. They were just part and parcel of life itself. It would all be there in the morning. Me too, god willing. Then we'd start again.

Acknowledgements

I would like to thank the following people, without whom there would definitely be no book: Ingrid Connell, for her constant help and guidance; Stee Hogg, for having such an astonishing memory and for going above and beyond; Philippa McEwan, for making lots of things happen; Charlotte Wright, for words, pictures and social media; Tim Hogg, for the stories which had to be repeated several times; Andy Crook, for putting me right about Ubedizzy; my sister Becky, for always being there; Micky Hammond, for being incredibly patient; and Jamie Hogg, for the original idea and for helping me write it. I'm indebted to all of you.

I would also like to say a big thank-you to Equine Productions and to Middleham Trainers Association for allowing us to use the footage of the gallops.

extracts reading groups
competitions books new events
discounts extracts extracts discounts
competitions extracts
books reading groups

new extracts

events books

books extracts new title reading groups

interviews

extracts events extracts extracts books

discounts events interviews new books extracts

events new events reading groups

discounts extracts discounts books

www.panmacmillan.com

extracts events reading groups
competitions books extracts new books